Running From The Demons

Deborah Anne Kimberley

Dedication

I dedicate this book to my "representatives," who, for all of my adult life, have been trying to lead me out of darkness and into the light.

This is my story. *REMEMBER, "I AM NOT MY STORY."*

Page Blank Intentionally

Introduction

I was born in Victoria, British Columbia, Canada. At the age of one, my Mom, brother, and I took the train and moved to Barry, Ontario, because my Dad was in the army and was stationed there in Camp Borden. He was supposed to go to Germany, but he found out he was allergic to wool, so we couldn't go there as the uniforms were made out of wool. My mother told me she was really disappointed because she had always wanted to travel, and she would have loved to go to Germany. Mom had been married before, but her husband was crushed by some logs when her son was only three months old. There was little welfare in those days, so she was forced to move back home with her folks, who ran a boarding house, and they also had some acreage on the prairie they tried to run too. My mother met my father when her son, my half-brother, was around six years old. They married and had me when he was about seven and a half. I am the only child of my mother and my father. My mother was brought up a strict Catholic until she was sixteen and left the little town of Horizon, Saskatchewan, where she was born, to come to Victoria. My father claimed to be Protestant and was brought up near Niagara Falls, Ontario. To the best of my knowledge, he was born in Niagara Falls. He joined the army at seventeen, even though you were supposed to be eighteen to join. He fought in two wars, World War II and the Korean War. I brought myself up to believe in God, but there was a time I lost my faith. My faith was always there. I just stopped thinking about it for a while. We spent six years in Ontario until my Dad decided it would be best for all of us if he left the army. It was a bad influence on him. He tried looking for a job in Ontario, but all the jobs were going to the Italians. He was told to go back into the army when he was looking for work, but we moved back to Victoria, where my mother's family were all living

1

instead. I still live in Victoria. You might as well say I was brought up here. My Dad called it God's country. I suppose because the scenery is so beautiful.

My father had been married before, and he had two children from his first marriage, for whom he had custody. Still, because my father was in the army, he could not look after them, so he gave his daughter to his first wife, who was Catholic, to care for, and he gave his son to his mother to care for. My father's mother was Catholic, and my father's Dad was Protestant. My Dad's father died when he was only three years old. He had two other siblings at the time: Toby, who was younger, and Bill, who was older. Dad only had a grade four education because he was forced to work the fields to help care for his family. His mother remarried and had a large family, comprising around thirteen children in total. I think this is where the religious rivalry began.

I always remember my Dad telling me that there are three things in life that you don't talk about: religion, politics, and finances. So, like the good kid I always tried to be, I never spoke about them to anyone, and I still don't. It wasn't until I was dying at thirty-eight that I really found my faith again. Eventually, I found myself in this religious, political, and financial mess that I never wanted anything to do with, but like it or not, that is my life, and I was stuck with it. I soon realized I had to be involved to survive. I was dying of bladder Carcinoma In situ, and I was also having a severe episode of PID, Pelvic Inflammatory Disease, unknown to me at the time. No one would give me the medical treatment I needed or I deserved, so after many times going to the emergency room seeking treatment, a nurse finally took pity on me and told me to go to Eric Martin Pavilion, a Mental Institution in Victoria. She said, "They will help you there." Help me, all right. They tried to kill me off, hoping they could make it look like my death was because of the kind of life I was living, or it was suicide, or just a plain old accident. And believe me, the so-called authorities tried everything in their power to snuff me out, and I think they still are aiming for my deathbed. I hate the word mental. I am a Professional Counsellor, although I haven't counselled anyone professionally. But I know all about the (DSM 4), the "Diagnostic and Statistical Manual of Mental Disorders" Fourth Edition, and hopefully the last. I am going to tell you it is all a bunch of crap. I believe it was designed for one reason and one reason only, and that is to hide all the crime created by Catholics and the likes of them, which exists in our corrupt world. Who would think this kind of corruption would exist in a country my Dad always called "God's country," but it does. Everyone who is flying their Canadian flags can damn well take them down while they read my book because it's not the free country so many think it is. Religious rivalry exists in this country like any other country. And you can stop the fireworks on July 1st

About my family

 My mother's parents were Hungarian Germans. My grandfather immigrated to Canada at a very young age. My grandmother was born here. When they married, they settled in a little town on the flat prairies called Horizon, in the Province of Saskatchewan. When my mother started school, she could hardly speak any English because they always spoke Hungarian German at home. Mom told me her parents had a store, and that there were only two stores in the whole town, all of which were really close. Both stores were beside each other, and a Chinese family owned the other one. Some of the kids would come into the Chinese store and steal peanuts, and the owners would run after them, but they never caught them. The school was just down the hill, and so was the church, as well as a hall; that was about all the town consisted of, besides three grain elevators. My grandmother would bake bread and goodies all the time, such as cinnamon buns, to sell in the store. She used to churn butter and make homemade preserves, and she also made soap, all of which she sold in the store. Mom said the store had a crepe floor, and Grandma always had her and her older sister, Mary, clothed in dresses she made, along with white stockings that would get dirty from the floor, but they were always spotless. Grandma would have to heat up the water and boil the clothes to get them clean. To her deathbed, my grandmother made her own clothes. When they had a bath, Grandma would heat the water on the wood stove and fill the big tub, which was kept in the middle of the floor. My mother would always have to bathe in her older sister's bathwater. In the winter, my grandparents took turns at night feeding the potbelly stove in the cellar with coal so they could keep warm. Even though it was the depression, they always managed to have good food on the table, unlike some kids my Mom grew up with, who would bring a pancake to school for lunch with nothing on it, and sometimes it was all they had to eat all day. One of my mother's friends only had corn on the cob to eat for every meal. No butter, no salt, nothing on it. Mom would rush home after school, knowing her mother would have hot bread coming out of the oven. She would bring her friend Mary Dean, who was dirt poor, and they would both think they were in heaven, feasting on the hot bread with melted butter and strawberry jam on it. They could smell it when they left the schoolhouse. Mom kept in touch with her to the day she died. You would have to order some items from the catalogue, which could not be purchased from stores, if you were lucky enough to have the money to do so. Mom got her shoes from the catalogue, and even though they wouldn't always fit, she'd say that they did, because she was afraid that if she sent them back, she wouldn't get another pair, and the money would go for something else. That's why she had corns on her feet. The catalogue came in handy because they used to have to use it for toilet paper. If they were lucky enough to get Japanese oranges, they would use the paper they would be wrapped in. They didn't have bathrooms; they had outhouses, and at Halloween, the kids would knock them all over. Because they couldn't afford toys, Mom sometimes cut out the models from the catalogue and used them to play with. She said the school was just a one-room schoolhouse, and everyone, of all ages, was taught their lessons there. The teacher favoured my mother, and when it was her birthday, he would give her empty pill bottles of all sizes, which he had collected for her, along with other small trinkets. My mother would make furniture out of the pill bottles for her paper dolls. He would also occasionally flip her a nickel or a dime, and back in those days, you could buy a big bag of candy for just a nickel. And I mean a big bag. One day, Mom got the only toy she ever had, a doll with a porcelain face, hands, and feet. She still had that doll, but Dad had to tidy her up. Someone made a doll carriage out of an empty orange crate, and it had jam jar lids for wheels. She didn't have the carriage very long because some brat got hold of it and threw it down the hill, and it shattered into pieces. Mom was heartbroken. Every Sunday, my mother and her sister, Mary, were forced by their father to attend the only church in town, where they had to confess their sins, although their parents never attended. My mother said she would have to make things up because she couldn't think of anything she had done wrong. Even back then, my grandfather was considered lazy, and I know firsthand that he was an evil son of a bitch. When he was around, he would get mad at them for any little thing, and he would throw things at them, whatever he could get his hands on at the time. If they had their elbows on the table, he would grab their elbows and slam them down on the table. He had the big job of bartering for things to sell in the store, like apples and fresh produce. He also ran the tractor and cut the grain field on some acreage they had just outside of Horizon, and then he would take it to various towns to sell. There were only three grain elevators in the area where they lived: the Ogilvie, the Federal (which my grandfather owned), and the Pool. He had a brother, George, who worked alongside him on the acreage. They also had pigs, chickens, turkeys, and ducks, which my grandmother had to tend to, sort of a mini farm. As if it weren't enough for her already to be managing the store and raising kids. My mother said she can still see my grandmother cutting the head off the turkey for Thanksgiving, and it running around with its head cut off before it croaked. The ducks would run after the kids and peck them on the rear all the time. At harvest, they would have a big dance and feast in the hall, and people from all the neighbouring towns would come with their wares, and they would have a big shin-dig. Some Romanian kids would come from out of town to the festival. One time, my mother was dancing with one of them, and my grandfather yanked her off the dance floor by the hair in front of everyone. I guess eventually my mother got fed up with this kind of treatment, so she got a job for a dollar a day, which was big money in those days, so that she could get the hell out of there. She worked for a school teacher, slaving her ass off cleaning her house and polishing her silverware. Mom also made her dinner, and everything she made for her had to have a cream sauce. She saved every penny she made, and at sixteen, her cousin Betty Nagy, Betty's sister Mary, left the flat barren prairies by train for the Province of British Columbia, Canada. She said they were like three country hicks who were looking around in amazement at the huge mountains and the thick coating of massive trees that they had never even dreamed of ever seeing. Mom had a friend, Kathleen Clements, who moved to Victoria on Vancouver Island, and she kept in touch with her. One day, she said that if she came out this way, a job would be waiting for her at the girls' school on the Island, over the Malahat, in Lake Cowichan. My mother jumped at the chance, and she said some of her best memories were of working in the kitchen and serving all the rich young girls who came from all over the world to attend that girls' school. They lived in the school, and my mother stayed there for a while as well. She said there was a beautiful May tree just outside her bedroom window. Every spring, it was just loaded with pink blossoms. By the time my mother left home, there were two more siblings, ten or more years her junior, that her overworked mother had to take care of. A sister, Carol, and a brother, Max. It was like a separate family all over again. My mother met her first husband, Eddie Erickson, who was a logger in the district of Lake Cowichan, at a popular cafe in what was then a quaint little town. Their marriage was short-lived as a cable broke on a crane, which was transporting a load of logs, and my mother's husband was under them when it broke and was crushed to death. They had a son, Brian Eddie Erickson, who was only an infant at the time. Her husband was Protestant, and my mother refused to relate any of this to religion. I gave up a long time ago trying to convince her it does. I can see it as plain as day now. Mom never heard from her first husband's family again. Her dead husband's sister, Blanch, came and cleaned Mom out of everything she and her husband had accumulated together, which wasn't much. I suppose it was because my mother had no other choice but to move back home with her parents, who now ran a boarding house in Victoria on Empress Avenue. Blanch thought my Mom wouldn't be needing any of her possessions again anyway, given the old Catholic ways. Mother suspects that she may have even taken a check from the government, which had been mailed to her. I feel that was evil, considering Mom had a baby to care for with no income from anywhere. God only knows what was going through her mind.

At that time, my grandparents still owned the acreage on the prairie, too, and my grandfather's brother, George, would look after it in the winter. However, come springtime, my grandparents would go there to plant the crops and help with the work until after harvest. My mother was left to man the boarding house on her own. She was also left to look after her younger brother, Maxi, who was still at home and attending a Catholic school, although he rarely attended. However, her parents would take Brian with them whenever they left for the prairies. Mom would have to deal with the school phoning all the time because Maxi wouldn't be there.

Mom said she never kept a penny from the money that was made at the boarding room house because her parents were mortgaged for it and needed every dime made to pay for it. She worked like a dog for her parents, cooking, baking, doing the laundry, shopping, and cleaning. She also harvested and preserved the vegetables from my grandmother's huge garden. When Mom's parents were home, and my mother would go shopping for them, she sometimes had to take Brian with her. She said he would always take off on her and hide among the clothes racks in the stores. When mom got hold of him, she would take his hand and squeeze it in her anger as she would be so beside herself with fear for him. He was a handful. One minute he was on the sidewalk riding his bike, and the next thing you know, he was gone. One time when the fair was a few blocks away, he took off, and that was where they eventually found him. There was no disciplining him because if she tried, her father would say, "Come to grandpa." One time, Brian ran away from home and walked along bustling streets all the way to her older sister Mary's house on Quadra. Mom's sister, Mary, and her husband, Sid, had two children, Raymond and Gail Bradford. Raymond was a couple of years younger than Brian, and when they were little, they used to play cops and robbers together. I suppose that childhood game, along with his upbringing, is how he later became the bad guy in life. Raymond became a crooked cop. Mom said that the two of them didn't get along that well. Never did. Gail was a few years younger than Raymond, and Mom said that it was pretty evident at a very early age that there was something wrong with her. When her sister Mary would feed her in her high chair, she would throw fits. I believe their religion thought she had the devil in her, but really, she was an epileptic. In the winter, Mom would work at Royal Roads Military College in the kitchen. She would have to leave at five o'clock in the morning to take the bus to work. For six years, she worked for her parents and at Royal Roads until she met my Dad, Len Thomas Kimberley, who was penniless. My mother's insurance money from her first husband's death bought them the things they needed when they first got married. Not to mention, my mother bought my grandparents a sofa with the money she received, and they had that sofa until they both passed away at the age of seventy-nine.

My Dad was a proud and very private man. He never spoke much. It seemed like he was always preoccupied with something on his mind. Mom did all the talking. He told me very little about what it was like for him growing up, because I think he never liked to complain or compare himself to anyone; he was always thankful for everything he had. And that is how I was brought up. He never asked for anything. Mom would have to go out and buy him new clothes; otherwise, he'd wear the same ones year after year. He was brought up near Niagara Falls on a farm, too, but he was forced to work the farm at a very young age to help provide for his family. His father, who I know was English, died very young of a phenomenon, they said, and my Dad was only three years old. Like my brother, he never knew his Dad at all. At the time his father passed away, his mother, who was also English, was a young mother of three children. Dad had an older brother, Bill, and a younger sister, Toby. He said he taught himself how to swim in the Falls, and they were so dirt poor that all he ever had was a bike that he got out of the trash, and it had no tires. One day, he found a garden hose, which he tried to use as tires for the beat-up old thing. By the sounds of it, he rode it like that. They used to heat their house with wood, and his stepfather would wake him up in the middle of the night to go and steal it for the stove, the righteous Catholics that they were. I suppose Dad didn't have much of a childhood, having to work on the farm all the time to help support the numerous children his mother kept having. He also missed out on schooling, but that doesn't mean he wasn't a wise man. He was the most innovative and most talented person I ever knew, and he never flaunted it. And I see a lot of people, as up till now I have been trying to make friends with everyone I meet, with no luck. All the so-called friends I did have would always use me, hurt me, and then take off on me. I couldn't understand why, but now I know. Thank God for that. When Dad got older, he found himself a job for a few extra pennies working at the local race track, exercising the horses and working in the concession. He never said, but knowing my father, I bet that money went to his mother's family. I suppose that when Dad turned seventeen, he wanted something better for himself, but there wasn't anything out there for him, and it was the depression, so he enlisted in the army. Somewhere along the way, he met his first wife, and they had two children together around two years apart. Lenny and Sharon. His first wife slept around, so he got custody of them both, but gave his daughter to his first wife to look after, and his son to his mother to look after, so they would have some kind of a stable life, seeing he was in the army and never knew where he was going to be posted next.

Mom and Dad's relationship started at a dance in Victoria at the CCF Hall, which was a politically based hall at the time. I guess they met while my Dad was stationed here in Victoria. Dad used to walk from the barracks by the University of Victoria to my grandparents' house on Empress Ave., to date my mother because, of course, not many people had cars in those days. Mom said that when they met, all Dad had on was the uniform. They spent most of their time together at dances in the city of Victoria's dance halls, where Mom said Dad could dance up a storm. I saw them dance many times, and they were always the light of the evening. Mom had a few dates before my Dad, who all cared for her, but she never cared for them in the way they did for her. One time, she told me about two military guys her friend and she met at a dance, and they brought them back to my mother's parents' place. These guys got so drunk they passed out on the sofa, and while their lights were out, Mom and her friend looked inside their jackets for their identification because they were suspicious about them. When they found out they were both married, they gave both drunks a swift kick to wake them up, then threw the two of them right out the door.

Mom and Dad eventually got married, and about a year later, they had me. When they first got married, they purchased a small two-bedroom house on Stoba Lane, located off Quadra Street. They used most of the $500.00 in insurance money my mother received from the death of her first husband to buy that house. It was really run down, and they didn't have much money, so my Dad got some green army paint and painted the whole inside of the house with it. There was an oil stove to cook on that was always breaking down. They were also able to buy an old Stud-a-Baker car. No sooner did we get settled in that house than we ended up moving to Ontario because my dad got stationed there again when I was one year old. My brother, my mother, and I took the train to Ontario after my Dad left. She remembers my brother was sick with the croup the whole time, and I was just starting to walk, so she had her hands full with the two of us, and she was ever so worried about my brother. The only good memories I have of my life are from when I was little and living in Ontario, but even then, life wasn't at all rosy.

CHAPTER ONE

I was kneeling on a chair in the dining room, my face pressed against the window, looking out at my brother Brian, who was playing ice hockey under the streetlights with all the neighbourhood kids. The snow was piled as high as the telephone poles, and the thick icicles around the house were almost touching the ground. We couldn't even get out of our home until my Dad dug us out. I couldn't understand why I was not allowed to go outside and play. "Mom, please, can I go outside and play too?" I kept begging and begging, but my mother was firm and said, "It is too late and cold out for little girls." I remember it all like it was yesterday. Thinking about how I hated to be called "little." Just then, my Dad came in the door that led into the kitchen, and I excitedly asked him, "Is the rink ready yet, Dad?" "Not yet," he replied. "Not for a couple more days." I knew if the rink were ready, he would let me go outside and play too. Dad was a big softy when it came to little kids. I was just learning how to skate, and there were trees in our backyard. My Dad had to cut some of them down to make this rink for me. Every night, when he came home from work, he would faithfully go outside and hose the yard down so that it would freeze overnight and form another layer of ice. Dad was always doing things like that for us. He took my brother to his hockey practice early in the morning, and he would take us bowling on the weekends. I remember wanting to know who won, but Dad would ask, "Did you have fun?" Of course, I'd laugh and say, "YES," and he would say, "Well, that is all that matters." It is amusing how one can recall wise words from childhood when they put their mind to it. In the summertime, we would go to the beach, Oswego Beach, and I remember the sand being so fine, almost like the dust in an egg timer, and ever so white. The beach was as far out as the eye could see. My Dad taught me to swim. Yes, I took swimming lessons, but it wasn't until I swam with my Dad as a teenager that I got brave enough to go out to the wharf and to dive.

There was a time I always felt safe with my Dad. I would watch POPIE on our black and white TV and think that was my Dad. He can do anything, and he doesn't even have to eat spinach, and then there came a time when all that was taken away from me, from us, and I was still very young. I never felt safe again after that.

In the summer, in Ontario, sometimes there would be violent rainstorms, and the ditches would fill up with water, and my friend Gerald and I would wade in them. We would pretend we were swimming because, of course, we were too young to know how then. He was my best friend, and his father was in the army as well. We did everything together. There were other kids we used to play with, like Debbie Pellen, and she had an older brother whose name, if my memory serves me right, was Timmy. They had a barn in their backyard, and we would play in the hay loft and get all itchy. I don't remember having many toys; just a big panda bear that I got on one of my birthdays. At the time, it was bigger than I was. Once, Dad bought root beer from A&W for a birthday party I was having. I felt so special when he did that. But feeling special was short-lived because no one came to my party. Anyway, who had time for parties and toys? Besides, Mom and Dad could never afford them. They were too busy just trying to survive.

I don't remember all of my brother's friends, but I do remember a kid named Murray Nut, who used to play records on the photograph my brother had in his bedroom. They would sing the songs at the top of their lungs, too. What a name, Murray Nut. No doubt I made fun of it back then. I always wanted to go into my brother's bedroom when Murray was over, but my brother always chased me out. Well, he was a teenager and I was just a little kid.

I don't remember Lenny, my half-brother from my father's side, being in my life at that time. Mom told me they wanted Lenny to come and live with us, but he was so used to living with my grandmother, Dad's Mom, who had one of her daughters living with her, who also had a lot of kids, that Lenny didn't want to come and live with us. Besides, Lenny and Brian didn't get along. One time, my half-brother Lenny shut the door on my fingers when he was over and just about took them off. I don't remember that incident, probably because it was so traumatizing. Looking back now, I don't believe he was brought up with any kind of discipline, as he himself told me that almost all of the kids he grew up with were in some kind of trouble with the law. Nevertheless, Lenny continued to live with his grandmother, while my half-sister, Sharon, remained with her mother. I suppose my Dad didn't have the heart to tear either one of them away from a life, by this time, they were both accustomed to. That was what my Dad was like: all heart. I know for a fact, though, that he never got over the loss of his first two children in his life.

While living in Ontario, my mother had to rely heavily on her neighbour, Mrs. Zinger, because my Dad was always helping people. I think he felt guilty for the war, which he shouldn't have, and was always trying to make up for it by helping out different people. Mom said he put a new roof on a church once. She also said he would be away on weekends doing odd jobs for guys he had served with in the army. They would pay him with booze, I guess, to drown out all those bad memories they all must have had of the war. Mom said, one time, he fell asleep on the couch with a cigarette and put a big hole in it. Another time, he must have come home drunk because my mother was in my bedroom, and she was going, "Shh shh be quiet," as I woke up to her presence in my room. I groggily asked, "What's wrong, Mom?" and she said, "Nothing. It's Okay." "Just go back to sleep," but I could tell by her voice that something was scary to her. There was an opening in the wall of my bedroom that led into the utility room, and from this opening, you could see the door that led into the kitchen from the outside. I saw my Dad stagger in, and then that was when I felt scared, too. Mom told me years later she got so fed up with the way my Dad was carrying on all the time, she found out one weekend where he was and phoned up the authorities at the army base, and told them about how she thought he was drinking with army buddies, and she wanted their car home. A little while later, Dad arrived home.

 Dad never talked much about the war; he always avoided the subject, but what he used to tell me was that he picked up the dead, and he was on the medical team. After that, I never asked many questions about the war. Dad left the army a year before he was entitled to a pension because of his drinking. He gave up his firearms at the same time. Mom said it was a good job he did. Eventually, just before he died on February 8th of 1998, he told me he had made bombs and designated them, too. My poor father was always too ashamed of himself to tell me before or to tell anyone, for that matter. Once, he told me he used to draw pictures on his army buddies' leather coats. That was when I discovered, one day, what a talented artist he was. He could even draw people. In my eyes, there was nothing that my Dad couldn't do.

 Mrs. Zinger, who lived right beside us in Barry, Ontario, was an older lady with grown children. She was a hairdresser. She permed my hair once for a job my Dad did for them, and I can still see myself sitting on the sofa with my arms crossed, mad as hell at my mother for making me go through such an ordeal. I couldn't sit still, and Mrs. Zinger was giving me treats to try to keep me occupied. Bananas. After it was all over, my mother kept telling me, "Oh, you look just like Shirley Temple," but it didn't make me feel any better. I never forgave her for doing that to me, and it wasn't till midlife that I got a hair perm again. My mother had me dressed up to the hilt in little dresses all the time, just like her mother did to her. In Ontario, she would take me to Sunday School dressed in white gloves, a white hat with a flower on it, and I had my very own white purse. I did have the hat and the purse tucked away in a box with a few of my children's keepsakes, but as I got older, they all disappeared. It was the only thing I had left from my childhood. All the terrorists, who have been after me all these years, got the rest of what little I had. Mom never drove, so when she had to go to the store, she would take me with her on a little wagon and put the groceries in there with me. And in the wintertime, it was a ride on the toboggan. She started learning how to drive as a kid on the prairies, but after that, she became too scared to drive, for reasons she never elaborated on. My mother hired a professional photographer to take some pictures of me, I remember. In those days, the pictures were only black and white. He had me sitting on an end table in various poses, trying to coax me into smiling. I have the end table now. I recall telling this photographer, "I can't smile." "I don't know how." I find myself thinking the very same thing to this day. My parents adored me as they have always adored all their children.

My entire family was animal lovers, but we never had much luck, so to speak, with animals. We had two beagle pups when I was small, but they got into the garbage and choked on some chicken bones. Or maybe someone fed it to them? After that, we had a beautiful white Samoyed. I was feeding him from the table one day, and he couldn't see what I was giving him. I asked my dad, "What's wrong with him?" and he said, "He has distemper and is going blind, and we have to put him to sleep." When my parents bought him, they were told he had all his shots. Perhaps someone was trying to convey a message in a twisted, distorted way. I also had a white Persian cat, but he would never come to me. I suppose I was too rough for him because I was only small then. I wanted the cat in the pictures the photographer was taking of me, and the fellow got a shot just as the cat was jumping off my lap. My eyes were bugging out of my head in surprise.

 I recall going to Victoria for a holiday just before we moved there. We stayed at my grandparents' boarding house, and my Dad worked for them the whole time. He installed new shelves in their pantry and repaired the slanted floor in their kitchen. My grandmother allowed us to pitch the tent out in their backyard by her goldfish pond so I could play in it, but my grandfather got mad. He said the grass was going to die. He was a sinister old man when it came to my poor cousin Gail and me. While we were staying there, I woke up in the middle of the night, and I don't know if I had a bad dream, but I remember being really scared about something, and I couldn't call for anyone. Finally, I got up, stood by the door, and called out, but no one answered me. So, I went back to bed and stayed there, frozen, until I fell asleep again. I never stayed the night at my grandparents again.

CHAPTER TWO

I hated the thought of leaving the only home I had ever really known and all my friends in Ontario, but my brother Brian took it harder than I did. He said, "When I'm old enough, I will come back here, and you won't be able to stop me." As we left, I looked out of the rear window at all my friends standing in the street waving goodbye to us, and I remember asking my parents, "I won't ever see them again, will I?" "Who knows," my mother said. "You just might." It was a long way to Victoria. We travelled across Canada for over a week to get here, and we camped most of the way. We pulled over for pizza, my favourite food at the time, and after we crossed over this long bridge, I told my Dad, "Stop the car. I am going to get sick." For years, I couldn't stomach pizza. And to this day, if I'm not driving, I'll get car sick.

We rented a house on Selkirk Street in the municipality of Esquimalt, in Victoria, when we first arrived, and lived there for a little over a year while my Dad built us a house in the municipality of Saanich. My brother, who was fifteen at the time, helped Dad build the house when he wasn't at school. My Dad worked on and off for a guy who had his own company building houses. My parents' property only cost $1,200.00, but I suppose back then it was a lot of money. Dad had the plans for the house drawn up for him by a woman, and my uncle Gordie, my mother's younger sister's husband, helped him with the electrical. My aunt Carol and uncle Gordie had two girls, Laurie and Valerie. They were about six or more years younger than I am. Most of the time, though, my uncle Gordie was drinking his beer with my other uncle, Sid. Both of my uncles were in the Navy. I suppose that is why they are both alcoholics.

It was hard to make new friends. It seemed like everyone who lived around us was older than I was and younger than my brother. There was a house just up the street from us that had some kids, and one time, loud music was playing over there, with the front door open. I took it as an invitation and went over. The kid who came to the door told me, "Go away and don't come back again." Right across the street were some other kids, and one time they allowed me to hang out with them, but I didn't like what they were up to. They were groping and mugging each other the whole time I was there, and I felt out of place and uncomfortable, so I left not long after I got there. They were only around ten or twelve years old, and even though I was younger than they were, I had a feeling that they shouldn't be doing what they were doing. I ended up walking to Victoria West School by myself all the time, and after school, I would ride my bike looking for someone to play with, but I always ended up playing by myself. One time, I was riding my bike, and I saw my grandfather coming up the road. I was so excited to see him. I was coming down the steep hill right by where we lived, and when I saw him, I sped up, and just as I did, the crazy old man pretended he was going to run into me. When I turned my bike to avoid him, he turned the wheel of his car. Well, I fell off my bike, and I hit my mouth on the curb, and the screwed up old man just went into our house. I couldn't believe what had just happened, and I also couldn't believe the amount of blood that was coming from my mouth. I had chipped my front tooth, and for years after that, my parents spent a small fortune on it, and I suffered teasing and the agony of it all. I ran into the house crying my eyes out, and right away I told my mother what Gramps, which is what we all called him, did. I remember her saying," Oh no, he didn't do that." "OH YES, he did," I demanded, but my mother refused to believe me. I think eventually she had me believing it was just an accident.

There was a nice old man who lived in a house on the Gorge waterway, and he would allow me to come on his wharf. I would spend a lot of my time alone poking the jellyfish with a stick and watching them curl up. The man who owned the wharf told me not to touch them because they would sting me. The house beside ours had a giant weeping willow tree, and one day, when I was eight, almost nine, I found myself under it more alone than ever before. My parents were out that day, doing business for the house, no doubt, and my brother was looking after me. I lost all trust in my brother that day.

It was just before Christmas when we moved into the house, which Dad, with my brother's help, had built us. By this time, Dad got a job at the mill in town called British Columbia, Forest Products. He worked in the sawmill. A year after that, my grandparents decided to sell their boarding room house and the acreage they had on the prairies and buy the property a few doors down the road from us. Of all the properties they could have bought at the time, they had to buy close to us. One of their agendas was to have my Dad build them a house. My mother didn't like the idea too much because her home wasn't even finished yet, but my Dad, who always helped everyone, felt he couldn't refuse. By this time, my father had a lot of practice building houses, and so he even drew up the plans for my grandparents' house. Mom said, My grandmother was always phoning for Dad to come over and do something for them. They weren't the only ones, as over the years, many people did. My grandfather would come over all the time, just when he saw Dad coming home from work, and harass the hell out of us. Dad would want a shower when he came home from work, but the old man would be there, so Dad was polite and stayed there with him until he decided to leave. Sometimes, we would be eating supper, and the old crazy ass would still be there. While Dad was building their house, his tools would go missing. My grandfather would ask all the other workers if they wanted something to drink, but not my Dad. I don't know how my Dad put up with all of that crap, but he did. If Dad wasn't working for BC, Forest, Products, he was working on my grandparents' house, and I was beginning to miss all the times we used to spend together back east in Ontario; so was the rest of my family.

I was in grade four when we moved into our house, and the trauma I had in my life, so far, was starting to take its toll. I found myself unable to concentrate in school, and when I read, I would skip lines. However, I was so ashamed of myself that I never told anyone about it either. I just thought it was happening because I was naive, and there was nothing anyone could do for me, even if I had told someone. So, I decided to avoid the embarrassment. I also began getting very severe pains in my knees. When the pains in my knees first started, the evil family doctor told my parents it was growing pains. In my early adulthood, I asked the same jerk again what it was, and that is when he told me it was arthritis, but he did nothing for me. Much later, I was told that it was Somatization Disorder. That is the psychological term I was diagnosed with when I was taking my Counselling Program in my early forties. The cause was severe trauma. But because I believe the DSM-4 is a load of crap, I tend to lean towards thinking that all along it was what they call now, juvenile arthritis, and I say that because I am plagued with osteo -arthritis in my back, and at times the same pain is all over my body. I was officially diagnosed with that when I was thirty; however, again, nothing was done for me till I was finally able to find a doctor who actually cared about me and wasn't trying to kill me off. It would hurt me so much when I was little, I'd cry and cry, and my mother would rub absorbing junior on my knees, and she would put a hot water bottle on them, too. I'd take aspirin to try and help get rid of the pain, but I couldn't swallow it, so my Mom would crush it up so I could take it with strawberry jam. I'd eventually fall asleep crying, and when I woke up, the pain would be gone. I would have breaks away from all the pain over the years. However, it has basically been an ongoing misery I have had all my life.

   I don't remember making any friends when I first moved into the house my Dad built. There was a girl, a couple of years older than I was, Penny, who lived across the street, who was always bragging about the horse she had at some stable. Once, she let me join in skipping, but other than that, she was always off riding, and when she was home, she never wanted to play with me. I guess she thought she was too good for me or something. Both her parents gave me the creeps because they had real red faces like alcoholics, which I later found out that they both were. The first year in our new home was one of my many nightmares in my life. By this time, I had a gold cap on my front tooth. All the white temporary caps I had to go to the dentist for many times kept coming off when I bit into something hard, like an apple. The dentist said that he couldn't put anything permanent in because my mouth was still growing, so that is what I had to put up with for quite a few years. After I got the gold cap, kids kept calling me names because it looked so ugly. With problems concentrating, life was not getting any easier for me. I would watch the teacher's mouth moving, but I just couldn't hear what they were talking about. At the same time, I would hear the bus going by, the kids having their Physical Education class outside, and the birds. I would hear everything else but what I was supposed to be listening to, and not for lack of trying, either. I became afraid of the dark. I wouldn't shut my light off at night, and I couldn't seem to go to sleep with it on either. I would call out to my mother, "Mom, come and shut my light off," and for a while, she would. Then she stopped doing it for me. I would cry for what seemed to be hours for her to come and turn it off, but she wouldn't give in. Eventually, I fell asleep with the light on. I started having nightmares, too. I don't remember what, but I would wake up all the time, either crying or scared. I failed that year. Some boys were riding bikes and tried to run me over with them. They were teasing me because I had failed. They must have found out from Mary and Pam, who didn't pass either, because they were the only ones who knew. They never got teased about failing, though. My parents put it down to me being the new kid on the block, not dreaming it was much more than just that. Mrs. Mary was our teacher that year, and the following year we had her again. She never did like me much. She was always on my case for something or other, like wanting me to hold my pen like everyone else. I just could not do it. The following year that I had her, she sent a note home to my mother about it, and my mother sent her a note back asking her if my writing was untidy. She told her that if it was, she could see the point, but seeing that it wasn't, my mother told her to let me be. I still hold my pen the same way as I did back then.

  Mary, Pam, and I were always in competition with each other for grades. They were popular and were more developed than I was. They had bras that were considered cool, and in PE class, they would undress in front of everyone and show off their bodies. But I was ashamed of myself, dressing in the toilet room. One day, Mary invited me over to her house to sleep outside in their tent. She must have been desperate for a friend that day or something. We didn't sleep much because crows were sitting on the telephone lines crowing, and they just wouldn't shut up. We'd throw rocks at them to go away, but they would come back and crow at us again. I bet the crows had a message they were trying to tell me and warn me about all the evil that was in my life. There was a Catholic Elementary School, St. Joseph's, and a Roman Catholic Church next to the school, both located beside Marigold Elementary, where I attended. One time, Mary and Pam, who had become best friends, invited me to go into the field of tall grass that lay between the two schools. The Catholic boys would run after them and feel them up. Thank God, they left me alone. When I found out what they were up to, I didn't go back there again. Anyway, on the last day of school, when all the kids were running after me, calling me names because I had failed, and when I got home, I had to listen to my brother call me names too. My mother scolded him for doing so, but from that time on, whenever he got the chance, he would tease me behind her back. He also kicked me under the table, and this would piss me off so much I'd yell at him to STOP kicking me. As soon as I opened my mouth to defend myself, I would get in trouble, and it would piss me off even more. But it seemed like it would please my mentally abused brother, and that infuriated me. My brother's favourite name to call me was spaghetti, and so after telling him to SHUT UP, I'd come back with meatball, which I thought was really funny sometimes. However, really, I was so distraught over all of this, I swore to myself I would never fail again, and I never did. I suppose my brother was living in his own Hell, and that was why he was acting the way he was towards me. You would think a kid his age should know better, though.

 Because I felt so utterly alone, I turned to God. I hadn't gone to church or Sunday School since leaving Ontario, but I felt I didn't have anyone else. I used to pray for myself to do "good somehow," because I thought I was bad. One of the reasons I thought I was bad was because when my evil grandfather caught me alone, he used to tell me that I was the Devil's child, and if I weren't good, I would end up in the orphanage. That is where my parents would put me. He would deliberately stop by the orphanage on our way to his house for a visit when my grandparents were still living on Empress Avenue, in their boarding house. He'd point it out and say, "See, this is where you will go if you are bad." I was terrified of this, so I did my best to be good, but nothing ever seemed to work out for me. My grandfather was such a lunatic. My cousin Gail and I thought he was being funny when he would drive like a madman, and we always wanted to go in his car with him. One day, my cousin Gail, my mother's older sister Mary's daughter, was in Gramps' car with me, going somewhere with him and the back door wasn't shut. It came open, and I was being sucked right out of the bastard's back seat. He never stopped the car when my cousin Gail asked him to. In fact, he sped up. Gail pulled me in, shut the door, and saved my life that day. When we went to my grandparents' boarding house for special occasions, my grandfather would play the accordion, and all the grandchildren would gather around him. I would be left out. I would try to squeeze in, but the other kids wouldn't allow it. My cousin Gail was around four years older than I was. They said that she had the mind of an eight-year-old. She, too, was not accepted, and our younger cousins would also try to exclude her from the circle, but my grandmother would step in when they did. No one ever seemed to notice how rejected I was. Gail was the only friend I had, and we used to play house together until one day she asked me to pull my pants down and pretend I was going to the bathroom. She was the mother, and I was the baby. I did it even though I felt it was the wrong thing to do. I told my mother about what she got me to do, and my mother said, "Stay away from her, she's crazy." My parents could see that I was lonely, so I told them, and my Dad came home with a dog one day. I called her Toby. I couldn't think of a name for her, so I asked my Dad what I should call her, and he suggested Toby. I had never heard of that name before, so I asked him, "How did you come up with that name?" That is when he told me he had a real sister named Toby. He said she lived in the United States, in Reno, Nevada, and had twin girls around my age. When I was three, we went there to visit them. "You looked like triplets," my Dad told me. Toby was a border Collie, and I remember her being the most intelligent dog I ever had growing up. She also became my best and only friend. I taught her many tricks, and she quickly caught on to them. She had ten puppies, and two of them died when they were born, so my Dad buried them in our backyard. It wasn't hard for us to find homes for the rest of them, because they were so adorable, plus we just gave them away. Toby used to wait for me to come home from school. Mom said she would cry to be let out around the time she knew I was coming home. She usually waited on the front steps. As soon as she saw me coming around the bend, she would run like hell to meet me. One day, my mother let her out and didn't watch her, and she got onto Burnside Road behind our backyard somehow, and some hard ass mowed her down. I didn't talk to my mother for months after that. The last thing I said to her before I stopped talking to her was, "Toby was the only friend I had, and you killed her."

I had a couple of so-called accidents when I was growing up. Around this time, my parents went to a New Year's Eve party. My Dad was an active member of the Social Club for British Columbia's Forest Products, and they were always hosting events. They brought home a New Year's Eve blower for me. Back then, the ends of them were made out of metal. I was blowing out and in with it when the metal end came off and got stuck in my throat. My Dad turned me upside down and was patting my back, but the thing wouldn't come out. They hadn't invented the Holmic maneuver yet. My parents were so upset about what was happening to me that they got the Norths, our neighbours, to drive me to the hospital. My Dad came with us, and we waited for six hours before they finally did an operation on me, as I waited, coughing up blood. A little while after that, I was playing with some tractor tire inner tubes with Cindy, who was about two years younger than I was. We stacked them one on top of the other, and then I got on first and started jumping up and down. The middle one slipped out from under the top one, and I fell to the ground on my arm. I ran all the way home, crying my head off. My Dad took me to the hospital then, to see if I had broken it, as it sure felt like I did; it hurt so much. I had chipped my elbow, and all that evil quack of ours did was put it in a sling and send me home, nothing for pain. My whole arm went black and blue. I wanted to play with

Cindy again, but every time I went over there after that, she wasn't
allowed to play with me. I could never understand, because it was
little Cindy who arranged for us to play on these inner tubes made
from tractor tires. After all, I was the new kid on the block and
didn't know anyone.

In grade five, I met someone with whom I became friends for a
while. Her name was Sylvia. She was half the size of me, and my
mother used to call us Mutt and Jeff, which I didn't like, but never
said anything about. I was just happy I finally had a friend. We
were in the same grade, and we developed a secret code so we
could talk to each other in class by sending each other notes. She
would go Pis…it and that would get my attention, and then she
would pass me a note. We never did get caught doing that. Her Dad
was in the Navy, too, and she had a younger brother, Tommy.
Funny, now that I think of it, she always came over to my house. I
only remember one time going to her house and her introducing
me to her mother. Her mother never really acknowledged me. She
just looked at me after I said hello to her, and that was all, which I
thought was weird at the time. Her mother and her house gave me
this creepy feeling. Sylvia never introduced me to her father. I
guess, because he wasn't home at the time. She wanted to show me
all the toys that she had, so we went up to her room. She had her
own phonograph and posters all over her walls. We listened to
"Hair" and sang to the music, which I thought was a lot of fun. She
had a ton of books and magazines, too. She also had a lot of
different Barbie Dolls, clothes, and furniture for them. She even
had a car for her Barbie dolls. Most of the time, she came over to
my house with her Ken doll and some clothes on hangers in their
very own case. At the time, I was friends with Sylvia. I only had
one Barbie doll and a Debbie Doll, which I had won at a BC Forest
picnic, and a few clothes for them. I never thought anything about
it then, but Sylvia would show me all kinds of sexual acts with the
dolls. Once we were down in my brother's room, where we

weren't supposed to be. I think I was just showing her his bedroom because she wanted to see it. I was about to go upstairs to the bathroom when Sylvia said she knew of a way that would make me stop having to go. She instructed me to lie down on the bed on my belly and cross my legs. She said, "See, it makes you feel good too." The next thing I knew, she started to invade my privacy. Before it could happen again, our dog Duke, a Pekingese, bit her, and shortly after that, she disappeared from my life. I don't even remember her going to Marigold Elementary anymore, either, so I thought she moved. I suppose her parents pulled her out of there to try to cover their tracks from what they got their daughter to do to me.

We had Duke, our dog, only for a short while. He came from a family that had little kids who used to terrorize him all the time. The kids used to dress him up in clothes and give him rides in a doll carriage, and finally, he got mean because of it, so they said. They thought that if they gave him to a family with older children, he would outgrow his meanness. I think they did more than just that to Duke, because he never liked anyone except my Mom and me, and eventually, we started to get leery of him. We used to put him on the close line for a run, and I would play with him there, running back and forth with him. Once, he went to bite me, but Mom and I loved him so much that I never told, for fear they would want to get rid of him. Then, one night, my brother came home late, and he bit him right on the nose, and it was all swollen and red. I remember thinking it served my brother right to get bitten, even though by this time he had stopped teasing me. In fact, he did an about-face and was overly friendly to me. My parents wanted to get rid of Duke then, but my brother convinced them not to. So, Mom and Dad decided to give the dog another chance, I guess for my sake too, because once again, he was the only friend I had. The last straw was when my grandmother came over and he bit her as she went to pet him from the chair she was sitting at around our kitchen table. That is when Mom and Dad got rid of him. They put him to sleep because it was obvious Duke was never going to stop biting people. He was the last animal we ever had, as I was growing up, because my mother said it was too heartbreaking when they died, or we would have to get rid of them for some reason. After that, a seagull became our family pet. He came just at the right time, as if he knew I needed someone or something in my life again. Every day at supper time, he would come and sit on the clothes line pole and patiently wait until we finished dinner. Sometimes he would squawk at us to hurry up and finish, though. I would feed him scraps from the table, and I looked forward to seeing him come. Then one day, he just disappeared like every other friend I had in my life.

After Sylvia, I felt angry with my life, but I was lucky to have found an outlet for that anger. Sports are something I became very good at. There was a girl in my grade six class named Allison, who wasn't very good at sports but was really smart, and boy, did she like to flaunt it, making big announcements about her good marks all the time to everyone who would listen. She was always going around bragging about how she would go snow skiing with her parents and taunting me with the fact. I suppose that is what kids do when they want to make others jealous. She wanted what I had, and I wanted what she had. I can't remember what happened between us one day, but I got distraught with her and pulled her fiery, red hair. She told everyone she was afraid of me, and she wished that she could be my friend. I didn't want anyone to be fearful of me, so I made an effort to befriend her. I thought we had worked out our differences, but it turned out to be all just another hoax on me, so to speak. Allison told me she would like it if I came with her and her family skiing one day, and she was sure her parents would allow it. Of course, I was really excited about that. I had never been skiing, my family couldn't afford such a luxury, and I thought I had made a real friend. She lived right across from

Marigold Park, not too far from my house, and one day she invited me to come over to play after school. Allison's younger sister, Penny, came to the door when I arrived and said that Allison was out somewhere, and she didn't know where she was, but she would play with me until Allison came back. Penny suggested we go across the dirt road to Marigold Park to explore in the bush. I thought maybe Allison was in there, but all of a sudden, Penny came running out of the bush, screaming, "There's a garbage bag of body parts in the bush." I wanted to go and see it, like all kids would, but she told me not to, and that she was going inside to phone the police, and she ran right past me. As soon as she got in the house, the Saanich police came up the road. As a kid, I never thought they had arrived a little too fast. I got so freaked out; I ran all the way home without stopping and told my mother about it. There was never any report on the news or in the paper about this incident, and later, when I questioned Allison about it, she told me there was some guy who lived on Grange Road who had committed suicide, and it was his body parts that were in the garbage bag. That was the end of that. However, I now wonder how those body parts got into that garbage bag.

Around this time, my parents began to give me a bit of freedom, and they allowed me to walk to my aunt Carol's place to visit them. They lived on Baker St., about a half-hour walk from our house. I was around twelve years old at the time, and I was getting old enough to start babysitting. I had lots of practice being around all my little cousins. My auntie Carol had a big basement, and I used to play hide and seek with her two girls, Laurie and Valerie. I'd play lots of other games with them, too, like ping pong, because they had a ping pong table. Come to think of it now, they were little brats. They broke my only other doll, my Chatty Kathy doll. They pulled the string that made her talk right out of the back of her. My mother gave them my big panda bear, the only teddy bear I ever had, shortly after we moved into our new house when I was still young. My mother's younger brother, Max, had a family of three children: Mary-Anne, Pam, and Darren, all of whom were significantly younger than I was. They lived in Vancouver. He was the British Columbia Manager of Helen Curtis, and I would sometimes go over to Vancouver to babysit for them. My Dad would drive me to the Ferry, and then my uncle Maxi would come and pick me up at the other side. He would never pay me any money for babysitting or for all the help I was giving them. He always had something to give me out of the shed in his backyard in Langley, Vancouver. Most of the time, it was cosmetics that I was too young to wear. This shed he had was full of Helen Curtis products, enough to last their family a couple of years or more. One day, he gave me a telephone. That is when my mother stopped me from going over there. He was then the manager of all the Burger King Restaurants in British Columbia. Later on, he became the Canadian Manager of Hershey Chocolate Bars. Every year at Christmas time, he would give us a great big Hershey Kiss, and that would piss my mother off. My auntie Dot had some kind of condition with her hands; they would get all red, and she'd develop a rash, a very bad case of eczema, I believe it was, so I would help with the housework when I was over there, too, always doing the dishes. They used to have wine at supper time, and we would say Thanks to God for our food before we started eating. I asked my mother, "Why do they have wine every time they have supper?" and she told me it was a Catholic tradition. I have always really liked kids, and when my uncle Maxi and his family came over for a visit, they would stay at my grandparents' place. I would rush over there and make up stories to tell his kids before they went to sleep. Even though I did that for them, the youngest, Darren, wouldn't go to sleep at night unless his mother lay down with him. I never had any books, so I couldn't bring any over to read them. As I mentioned, my parents couldn't afford much, but by this time, I had given up reading because I would often skip lines. I would have to use a bookmark to read something for school, and I would only read the front, the middle, and the back of a book because reading every page of a whole book was an impossible task for me. Then, I would ask smart ass Allison what the book was about before making my book report. I can only recall reading one book from front to back growing up, and it was for my own so-called enjoyment, Peppy Long Stockings. I took it out from the library one day. I must have really been bored. I was determined to finish it, though, and I did, because I think I related to her. To this day, I still don't read books unless I want to know about something.

There was this family who lived at the end of the road on the same side of the street as us. They had a little girl, around seven years old, at the time, named Dena. I found out through the grapevine that they needed a babysitter from time to time, so I went up to their house to tell them I was available. I would tell stories that I would make up, too, and they gave me the job. I babysat Dena for a couple of years, and she always looked forward to my visits. I started looking after another couple's kids, who lived behind my parents on Burnside Road, after a couple of years, also a navy dude. My Dad said that the house they lived in, along with the other house beside it, was built with matchsticks and a good gust of wind would blow the two of them right down. They had two babies, a boy and a girl, an infant, and the other not much older. I was getting a good reputation with kids, and that just couldn't happen, so they all got together to help ruin it for me. When I first started to look after their kids, I had to phone my mother to come over because I couldn't get the infant to stop crying. My mother had the touch because she was able to get the baby to stop crying right away. My mother said that she thought their children were too young to leave with a babysitter. It was New Year's Eve, and I had promised I would sit for these people. All of a sudden, Allison came onto the scene again and invited me to go to a New Year's Eve party. She said everyone I knew would be at the party, and she would meet me there. I told her I had already committed myself to babysit and I couldn't go, but she wouldn't take no for an answer. She said, "I know someone who has been looking for a job babysitting on New Year's Eve, and he is really responsible and has done a lot of babysitting before." She convinced me that Gordon would come over and take my place babysitting after the people left so that I could go to the party, and they would never know I was gone, because I would be back before them. It was also Allison and Gordon's idea to take the phone off the hook in case they tried to call. Allison had me meet Gordon beforehand, and he was known as the good guy, so I agreed, which turned out to be a big mistake. I went to where this party was supposed to be, but I couldn't find it, and when I got back, they were home pretending to be as mad as hornets. They said they came home because they couldn't reach me by phone; the phone was always busy. I was only gone for about half an hour. Needless to say, I lost all my babysitting jobs after that.

When I wasn't playing sports or doing something with my cousins, I'd catch the bus for a quarter, and go downtown to the movies by myself—watching a movie cost only fifty cents then. I used to save all my money so that I could go to the English Sweet Shop as well. I would buy myself some cheese corn to eat on the bus on the way home because I liked it better than the popcorn you got from the theatre. I'd buy a big hunk of toffee as well. The allowance I got was two dollars every other week for keeping my room clean and helping my Mom by drying the supper dishes at night. In the summertime, there was the good old Marigold Park, just five minutes away from my house, and every summer, they offered free programs in the park that I would participate in. I did plaster work in Piraeus, copper work, braiding, and many other art activities. I was always trying to make a friend, but I never did. On Thursdays, a bus would arrive, and most of the kids from the park would take it to the Crystal Gardens for swimming lessons. We had to pay for the bus ride and the admission to get into the pool. I was a good swimmer, but eventually I could never put my head down and dive into the pool, because I was too chicken. On Fridays, it was dress-up day, and I would dress up in the beautiful Korean pyjamas my uncle Sid bought for my mother when he was in Korea. My mother had to alter them because they were too big. She would also style my hair and apply makeup for the contest. They would give out prizes for the best dressed, but I never won. I also remember going to the railway tracks not far from where I lived, because sometimes there were kids there sliding down the sandy slopes beside the tracks with cardboard. I kept praying to God for a way to do good, because I thought maybe that was why I never had any friends. Because I was bad, and that is also why I had the pains in my knees, too, because I was bad, just like my grandfather always led me to believe. I asked God, maybe I could do well in sports… or run anything, please. I was desperate to do something good, so perhaps then I would have at least a friend. I participated fully in all sports, including baseball, ice hockey, and basketball, both in and outside of school, for years. And the one thing I excelled at in school competitions was long-distance running. I could run for a very long time without getting tired. I'd be miles ahead of everyone. By the time I was in grade seven, I was the fastest female long-distance runner in the city. That too petered out, but not by choice. I was also good at Fastpitch Softball and played it outside of school. By the time I reached Senior Women's, our team, "Esquimalt High Grade Radio," was the best in British Columbia, and we came fourth in Canada.

Around twelve, my family was going through some hardships. Dad got laid off from the saw mill at Point Alice because he hadn't been employed very long for BC Forest, and he was looking for another job. Dad once told me he applied at a place on the outskirts of Victoria in Langford, and they wanted him to do a psychological test for the job. He told them to shove it. I suppose they wanted him to take their test because he claimed to have served in the army for twelve years and fought in two wars. My Dad was still drinking at the time, but not as much, and I remember my mother always having his meal warming in the oven for him when he came home. One time, Dad came home drunk and he fell asleep in his food. That's because he always worked so damn hard. He felt guilty when he drank because he would come in and ask my mother, "What's wrong with you?" And my mother wouldn't say a word. It did not matter what my father did; I was always proud of him, and I always will be. Once, my mother went through the glove compartment of my Dad's car while he was passed out. That's when she found out Dad was still sending money back East to his mother, when he no longer needed to.

Dad ended up working on Vancouver Island in a dissolute logging community. You had to fly in there by helicopter; it was the only way into that logging camp. Dad never did like flying, especially in a dinky helicopter. But he had to have a job. He was only employed there for three weeks because he said there were young guys working for this logging company that he had to bunk up with, and they kept smoking pot all the time, and he just couldn't stand the smell of it. He was strongly opposed to such things. After the logging camp, he managed to get a job in the mill about half an hour away from Victoria. He drove up and down the Island every day to work until one day, he got sick. Really sick. That evil family doctor of ours said he didn't know what was wrong with him. I remember going with my parents to a lab to find out the results of some tests that the bastard ordered, and Dad coming out of that room in tears of relief, saying it wasn't cancer. Little did that poor man know the torture all these terrorists had planned for him. My Mom, Dad, and I stood right there in the lab, crying while hugging each other. They had the nerve to tell my father that it may have something to do with the stress of him driving up and down the Island all the time. I guess they had to come up with some kind of answer. So my Dad stayed in a trailer at a campsite, coming home only on the weekends. The doctor also told Dad he couldn't drink alcohol anymore, or this would kill him, so immediately, Dad quit drinking and never drank a drop again. Eventually, our righteous country of Canada, the home of so-called free opportunities, put a label on this illness., Crohn's Disease. When Dad was first diagnosed with this, he was the only one in British Columbia who had it, and there were only a few others in all of Canada. Now, there are thousands and thousands needlessly suffering from this disease. Who would have ever thought that it is an untreated sexually transmitted disease? My father's righteous Catholic ex-wife is responsible for giving this to him. Apparently, my father's own mother didn't want him cured either. I say, who the hell was she to make such a decision? All because of religion.

CHAPTER THREE

With my Dad sick and away from home all the time, he thought he should find some other job, so he decided to apply at BC Forest again. Only the saw mill was closed down at this time. He managed to get hired back on. My brother had finished school and was working at BC Forest Products as well. Brian used to buy me really nice gifts at Christmas time, to make up for all he had done to me growing up. He bought me a bed and a dresser for my Barbie Doll. I couldn't believe my eyes when I opened it up that year. All the years after that, he would buy me really nice outfits to wear. Once, he bought me a lime-green leather jumper and a nice, frilly white blouse to wear under it. I wore it with my white Go-Go Boots, and boy, did I ever think I was cool then. Sometimes he would play catch with me because I never had anyone else to play with. Mrs. North, our next-door neighbour, used to give me hand-me-down clothes because her girls were older than I was. They were of English descent. Mrs North would give me beautiful, bright, plaid, wool kilts with big pins in them, all in excellent condition, and I thought this was just great. Across the street from us, there used to be three big, green houses, but a little while after we moved into our house, they tore them down and built three large houses with basements. Not too long after the houses were built, a Victoria City Police officer moved into the middle one. His name was Dale. They had a little boy who was only two at the time they moved in. Dale would come over to our house and borrow beer. Even though my Dad never drank anymore, he would buy it and have it in the house just for the likes of him. In my early teens, Dale started to really befriend me. He gave me some black-light posters and a black-light to put in my room once. Of course, I thought this was really neat. He told us that when there is a robbery, the police give the victims a certain amount of time to claim their goods. If they don't pick it up within that time, the police officers who made the bust retain the goods. Little did I know what the cop had up his sleeve for me.

My grandparents, my mother's two sisters' family, and our family started going on picnics in the summer at Elk Lake, one of the lakes just off the Pat Bay Highway, which takes you to the Ferries. My brother, Brian, and my cousin, Raymond, wouldn't be there because they were both in their late teens to early twenties at this time and were interested in other things. My Dad would do all the cooking at the picnics, and my useless relatives would sit there sucking on booze. They had all the time to harass my Dad by asking him, "So, how's your guts?" I recall not liking their comments they would make to my Dad, so that I would drag him to the lake, and we would go swimming together. It was at this time that he got me to get the courage up to swim to the wharf, which seemed a long way away. I would try to impress my Dad by diving off the wharf, but because of my fear of going in headfirst, I did belly flops. All the other kids would be in the shallow end, and although Gail was a few years older than I was, no one ever paid any attention to her except for my Mom and Dad. After Dad and I came back from the wharf, we had water fights with Gail. Every chance my mother's family got, they were harassing the shit out of my father, and I am going to repeat it. I can't see how my Dad put up with all of it. He never showed any anger towards them, ever. On special occasions, we would visit my grandparents' house, and my grandmother would prepare a feast for us all. My mother and I would be the only ones asking her if she wanted any help with it. All my mother's siblings would be sitting on their asses, seeing what derogatory remarks they could come up with for our family.

My brother was interested in hot cars and motorbikes. Because he was working at the mill, making good money, and living at home for next to nothing, that was where all his money would go. Sometimes at supper time, the whole house would start shaking because his friends would all come over on their motorbikes. They all looked like the guy on Happy Days, with their short black pants, white Bobbie socks, white T-shirts, and slicked-back hair. He got caught for drinking and driving once when he was living at home. He put his motorcycle in the ditch at the end of the street. He decided to give up his bike after that. That is when he got into hot cars and bought a fully loaded green Dodge Dart; it even came with a fire extinguisher. He would pay me a dollar a day sometimes to iron his shirts because my mother refused to do it. He was constantly changing his shirts, three times a day, and throwing them on the spare single bed in his room. In those days, there were no permanent-press items; everything had to be ironed. Brian also paid me to clean up his room whenever my mother would scold him for leaving it a mess. Because his bedroom was down in the basement, when he would go out drinking and when he woke up the next morning, he'd be hungover, so he'd go to the fruit cellar to get a big can of juice to drink. I guess he was dehydrated. I would find these empty cans of juice all under his bed, along with the dust.

My Dad was ill, and they said that they didn't know what was wrong with him, so my mother decided she should look for a job. I suppose deep down, she was worried about being left without any money again. She was hired by a department store called Woodwards, which was later renamed The Bay, now closed, located in the Mayfair Mall on Douglas Street, where she worked in the jewelry department during the Christmas season. They would phone her at the last minute, wanting her to rush into work, and sometimes this was right at supper time. Dad liked his food on the table when he came home from a hard day of working at the mill, so he got fed up with it. He used to say, "You have enough work to do at home." He was steadfast about it, and my mother was worried about him, so she decided that maybe it would be to his benefit if she were there at home for him. Dad had a special diet to follow. Mom was just like her mother because she always planted a vegetable garden, and she had strawberry plants and raspberry canes. We also had a large pear tree and an apple tree in our backyard, and Mom would preserve the fruit from both. My Dad made a goldfish pond with a little fountain in it, like my grandmother had at the boarding house, but he eventually jackhammered the cement out and then made a flower bed there. It was too much to keep up. My mother had rose bushes and flowers all over the yard. When Dad was digging one day, he did something to the cartilage in his knee, and had to have an operation to take the cartilage out. That laid him up for a long while. He walked with crutches, and then with a cane. I believe he only hurt the one knee, but they removed both cartilages from both knees? Another time, they did an operation on the wrong arm. I can't remember what they said they had to do to him then, but they were always performing some kind of operation to torture that poor man. I remember going to the hospital once when he had one of his many attacks, and they put tubes through his nose down into his stomach to pump out all this black shit. They didn't give him any painkillers, and my brother was yelling at the nurses to give Dad some painkillers. They told him he couldn't have any because none was ordered. When that no-good doctor was asked, he made up some piss poor excuse why Dad couldn't have any. He was always sucking us into believing he was this righteous doctor so concerned for our well-being, but really, he's an animal with no conscience. Needless to say, Mom was left to do all the yard work because Dad would be so tired when he came home from work. No doubt in pain some of the time, too, but he used to hide it all so well.

 Dad joined the Social Club at work again, and it was the only time my parents would socialize other than at the screwed up family gatherings. They were always hosting functions, and Dad was fully involved in this. He was part of the executive, so he would have to attend meetings as well, some of which we held at our house. In the summer, they would put on a picnic at the Ranger's Station in Metchosin, and Dad would run around doing all the work. All the food was free: hamburgers, hot dogs, and corn on the cob with all the trimmings, Chips, Revels, Fudgicicles, Freezes, and different kinds of pop and coffee. They would have all kinds of races for kids and adults, and you could win prizes if you came in first, second, or third. I did pretty well in those events. Especially the sack race and the egg-and-spoon race. That is how I got my Debbie Doll in one of those two races. My Dad would enter the races sometimes, too, and despite having knee problems, he'd also win a race or two. They had a hammer and nail contest that I used to participate in, but it was pretty tough. I kept missing the damn nail. And there were a lot of butch like women who could really pound those nails in that plank. They also had horseshoes, darts, and a pie-eating contest. There was a small wading pool for all the little kids, and a playground, too. At the end of the day, a train would arrive with clowns on it, and the clowns would run around throwing candies out to all the kids, and we would run after them, laughing as we scrambled to find them. Sometimes you would come across quarters, too. While this was going on, they would have a draw and give out loads of prizes if they picked your numbers from the barrel from which they pulled the ticket. My Dad deserved to win every draw because of all the hard work he did at these functions. Mom and Dad were lucky to win a prize in the draws a few times. Everyone in the Social Club soon found out what a pushover Dad was, and it seemed like no sooner had Dad finished building my grandparents' house than he was asked to do work for some guys who were also in the Social Club. He rebuilt some cupboards for a couple from the Social Club, of course, at no charge. My mother said that one day, a lady called their home to see if Dad had left yet, because we had all eaten our supper. This woman, whose name was Betty, snapped at my mother, saying,

"He's not finished yet." They would always want to come over and socialize, but after that, Mom would make excuses. Another time when Dad was on holiday from the Mill, his buddy, with whom he worked all the time, Russ, and he went over to Salt Spring Island to frame a house for a guy named Slim, who was also a member of the Social Club. For a whole year, Dad went over there in his spare time, working on this house for next to nothing, basically, for what it cost him to go over there. Eventually, Dad built some cupboards for that evil doctor Turd, and yes, for NOTHING. I suppose Turd thought he would let my Dad live long enough so he too could suck him dry before he kicked him off. Mom was so worried about all this because Dad was so ill, and she told him, "You are going to drive yourself into the ground." I think Dad kept himself busy because he wouldn't have to feel the pain he must have been in at times, along with trying to make up for the wars, which I know he felt guilty about.

Another one of our neighbours, on the other side of us, was very friendly, although you could hardly understand them because of their heavy accent. They were from Finland. They had two boys who, I know, were further apart in age than my brother and I are. My mother once mentioned that the old lady told her their older son had commented that they should be ashamed of themselves for having another child so late in life. Their younger boy, who was a couple of years younger than I was, committed suicide (an overdose on drugs, apparently) when he was around sixteen, but I wonder about that now. His older brother was a doctor, and I believe he had something to do with it; I know I am not alone in that assumption. Before they moved into the house beside my parents' place, and just before the cop, Dale, moved in across the street, a cop had lived in their home. My Dad was so artistically crafty that he made Christmas figurines to put out in the yard at Christmas time. One year, our big Santa went missing. I remember my parents saying they thought it was the cop who lived beside them who took it because this cop was always coming over, walking into our basement, and helping himself to whatever he wanted, without telling us about it until he got caught once. Then our blue flood lights for the figurines went missing, so my Dad stopped putting anything out. Just before I left the father of my two children, my Dad made Santa in his sleigh with presents, and all the reindeer, but the Nut Case I was married to never made time to come and get it all, and put it up for the kids, so I told my Dad just to sell it all. It cost him over $300 to make, and he sold it for $200. I was heartbroken about it, and I am sure so was Dad.

When my Dad got hired back at BC Forest, he told me he worked with this man, who had a daughter named Wendy, and they lived just a couple of streets away on Jasmine. Wendy and I were in the sixth grade together. Wendy had failed a couple of grades. She and I became the teacher's pet. We were often asked to do things for the teacher after school, such as hanging pictures on the wall, and this made me feel exceptional for the time being. Wendy was always asking me to go horseback riding with her, and one day I went. I had told her I had ridden before, but really, I had never even seen a horse before. I guess this is the kind of thing kids do when they don't have any friends and are desperate to make one. Anyway, I went with her and I got on this great, big horse. Her horse was big too, and it took off right away, and of course, mine followed hers. They were both running to beat the band, and I was beside myself with fear. I was holding onto the neck of my horse as I rode, trying to stay on, but my body kept bouncing all over the place. I was sure I was going to fall off, and it was only by luck that I didn't. Finally, Wendy's horse stopped at the end of this field, and then so did mine. I thought she just found out I had been lying about knowing how to ride, but really, now I believe she knew that already. We ended up going back to the stables and getting a pony for me to ride, and I was so embarrassed about the whole episode. After that, Wendy invited me over to her house to sleep in their family's camper. I thought this would be a fun thing to do, but I sure found out differently. Wendy had a bad case of acne, and she put some stuff all over her face before she went to bed that night, and it stunk like hell. I thought I was going to throw up, but I didn't. That night, she too invaded my privacy. Our friendship was short-lived because I never saw her again after that. I don't remember her going to Marigold Elementary for grade seven either.

Our next-door neighbour, Mr. North, offered to take me to their Anglican Church on Burnside Rd., St. Columbus (now closed), where they went on Sundays. I asked my Mom to ask the Norths if I could go along with them. I knew Mary attended that church, and she had once been nice to me, so I decided I wanted to go there. I was also curious about God. Mary and I sang together in the choir, and we were always competing to see who could sing the loudest. Around Christmas time, the choir kids would visit the Old Folks Homes and sing Christmas Carols for the residents. That gave me great gratification. However, attending church was short-lived because I couldn't understand what God was all about.

Mary talked me into joining ice hockey with her. You couldn't have any physical contact with each other in women's hockey. I only played ice hockey for a couple of years because I didn't like the physical contact, and I kept getting penalties for it. At school, Mary and I would often be on opposing teams for floor hockey, and we would always slash at each other with our sticks and ram each other into the boards. Then, instead of going to the show with my allowance, I ended up going to Friday night skating at the Arena because I heard it was where everyone hung out. It was the end of grade six when I met Theresa. She was the same age as I was, but she was in grade seven, and going to High School the following year, because, of course, I had failed a grade. She used to go to Friday Night Skating all the time, but we never really started hanging out with each other until Junior High School. I was involved in sports and struggled to stay on top of my schoolwork. I didn't have much time for friends, even though I was still trying to make some. I was on a basketball team outside of school in the fall. By the time I started Junior High School, I began to lose my faith in God. I remember asking my Dad if he believed in God, and he said, "If there was a God, why would he allow all this destruction in this world?" I thought, and still think, that's a good question. I worshiped the ground my Dad walked on, so I started to believe him for a while. After all, I still didn't have a friend, and life wasn't being very nice to me.

My auntie Mary was over visiting one day when I asked my mother if I could join a baseball team outside of school. My auntie Mary said that she used to play ball on a team right up until she was a woman, and she inspired me even more. They were living near the Pearks Arena, not far from Hampton Park, and she suggested I go there to check it out because she thought they had girls' teams that I could join. Hampton Park always had a good team, and some seasons we would win the City Finals, and other times it would be Esquimalt who would win the Cities. The first coach I had was Alvin. He was really tough with us girls. Alvin would line us up against the backstop and fire the ball at us as fast as he could, and you either caught it or got hit with it. And boy, if you got hit with the ball, it hurt, and it would leave a whopper of a bruise. Some of the girls quit as a result. I was one of the pitchers, just like my auntie Mary said she was when she played. I pitched for the first couple of years, and then I transitioned to a back catcher.

After a couple of years of coaching us girls, Alvin disappeared. Someone told me he was charged with rape and wasn't allowed to coach anymore. I questioned Alvin's cousin, who I knew from

Junior High School, and Sam said it was a lie. Alvin was never charged with rape. By this time, I had buried my memories from my earlier childhood. Alvin helped with that, and it was part of his job in this terrorist plot, this outrageously insane government had against me. After they had me notified of this so-called rape, they decided that they had to get rid of Alvin to make it all look legitimate. I never got an explanation for why Alvin quit coaching us girls, something he seemed to enjoy so much. The first crush I ever had on a boy was while I was playing ball, and Alvin was coaching. Denise was his name, our Junior High School jock. He would watch us practice in the school field. He had a crush on me, too, because he invited me to come to his house one day to meet his parents. I thought we were going out. He lived just up the street from the school, and when he came to watch our practices, he would invite me to attend his hockey games at the Pearks Arena, and I would. I was starting to hang out with Theresa at that time. I would coax her to come and watch his games with me, and she did a couple of times, but now I believe she had another agenda in her mind. She was the righteous Catholic who used to have fish and chips every Friday. Nice, they could afford that. I told my mother she would have fish every Friday, thinking maybe we could have it one night, and that is when I found out it was a Catholic tradition.

One day, out of the blue, I got the hint that it was over between Denise and me because, for some unknown reason, he stopped talking to me and was constantly avoiding me. I never understood why then, and I never asked why he dumped me, but I have a good understanding of it all now.

My mother's family, except for my uncle Max, who lived in Vancouver, all had the same doctor, Dr. Turd, who was also a Roman Catholic. His fee was prolonged agony for everyone's greed. My mother would take me to see him while I was growing up because of all the pain I was in. My knees were a constant cause of pain for me, and that was when the absorbing junior and aspirin, which I would have to take with strawberry jam, along with the hot water bottle, would come out. He told my mother the pain in my knees was growing pains, and the stomach pain and headaches I had from time to time were probably due to the stomach flu. When I started my menstrual cycle, I went to him because I would be in such excruciating pain with stomach cramps and headaches. He told me a lot of women go through that and to take Midol for it, and eventually the pain will subside or go away. But it never did. Then, after pestering him all the time about my pain, he gave me the pill and said that the pain would go away with it, but it never did. I would be so sick with cramps that I would want to throw up. I'd come home from school because of it, barely able to walk. My crazy grandfather would pick me up from Junior High School because my Mom could not drive, and I would be in the back seat, doubled over in agony, and he would be laughing at me, that crazy jerk. The Midol would come out, and so would the hot water bottle again. I'd finally cry myself to sleep. In adulthood, Dr Turd told me the pain in my knees was arthritis. I know now he has been the leading cause for all my pain and suffering all my life, both physically and emotionally, and he could have prevented it all. He should have kept his big mouth shut, done his job, and treated my condition of Pelvic Inflammatory Disease (PID).

In Junior High School, I kept myself pretty busy playing every sport I could inside and outside of school. At lunch time during school hours, all the stoners would be at the Colquitz Creek across the street from the school, smoking dope. I rarely smoked the stuff then, but someone always seemed to be offering it to me. A couple of East Indian boys seemed to have a bag of pot all the time. One of them was in my home room. And his brother, who was always after my ass but never got it, took me for a ride on his motorcycle once, did a wheelie as he took off, and my long hair almost got caught under his back tire. Sure, I got off in a hurry and avoided him. Everyone would talk about how soon pot was going to be legalized because it was organic. There was even a teacher at this school who everyone said smoked it, and he used to carry a Snoopy lunch box, which they said he stored his pot in. We'd all laugh about that. The media are also used to advertise different brands of cigarettes on television. There wasn't the knowledge available to the public that there is today around smoking. They are only now trying to stop killing people off with this kind of thing because the government has finally come to realize there just may not be any health care left, even for them, the dignitaries, if they don't try to do something about all this abuse in our health care system. Anyway, Mother Theresa and I hung out for a year or two. She was the one who taught me how to smoke, and she got me into drinking. We would walk the half hour to school together because she just lived on Grange Road, behind the dead-end street where I lived. On Friday nights, we would hang out at what used to be called the Tasty Freeze, a malt shop at the small strip mall on Burnside Road. Everyone used to hang out and get their booze and smokes or whatever else they happened to be into from there. You could get anything you wanted. We would go into the field by the Pearks arena and drink the booze we got at the Taste Freeze before we went skating. Sometimes we'd watch the movie through the holes in the fence of the outdoor theatre, which was also in this field, now the site of the Tillicum Mall. One time, I was drinking Vodka in this field with the gang before we all went skating. I once went around the skating rink at the arena, and everything started spinning. I ran into the bathroom and got sick all over the place.

That was my first and last experience with Vodka. Management kicked me out and told me they were going to call the police on me. I never drank much hard stuff again after that. The girls Theresa hung around with were mostly into stealing clothes, and they would often go to the Hudson's Bay Company downtown to do it. I went with them a couple of times, but I was ever so scared.

One day, Theresa came knocking at my door to let me know that one of her friends had gotten caught, and it was a good thing I hadn't come with them this time. That was the only time she ever came over to my house. My auntie Mary had managed to get me a job at Christmas time working in the toy department of the Hudson Bay Company downtown. My auntie Mary worked in the housewares department, and I didn't want to ruin the job she got me by getting caught stealing, so I was trying to straighten myself out. After that, I secured a position at the Memorial Arena, now known as the "Save on Foods Memorial Arena," which the vets had to fight for to retain the name "Memorial" in the arena's title. I worked in the concession stand at the arena, and I thought it was a great job to have because I was able to attend all the concerts for free and get paid for it, too. I remember Theresa once suggesting that I tell my parents I was staying the night at her house, and she would tell her parents I was staying the night at her house, and we would go camping. So, that's what we did. I bet her parents knew about this little trip, or she used someone else's name for where she was staying. At the campsite, there was a plastic container of fuel. It had been raining out, and Theresa was trying to get a fire going. I came onto the scene just as the container burst into flames while Theresa was holding it. The plastic container stuck to her hand. She was screaming, trying to get the blazing thing off of her hand by shaking it all over the place, and then it started her pants on fire too. Finally, someone pushed her to the ground and started throwing dirt on her to put out the fire. It was a good thing her pants were wet; otherwise, it could have been a lot worse than it was. Many times, I got fed up with the drinking, smoking, and all the drugs this crowd was starting to get into. I wanted to take playing ball seriously. But the government never let up on trying to destroy my life.

I had been playing ball already for a couple of years when another girl by the name of Gail came on the scene to do her damage to me. Funny enough, Gail's father was in the Navy, too. Her mother used to call me a scrag, and I used to think it was because I was such a baseball freak, but I know differently now. Gail started playing on the same team as I for Hampton Park. I thought she was my friend, but now I realize I never truly had one, except for my dogs and the seagull I befriended. Gail mentioned that she enjoyed hanging out at the Tasty Freeze in the Burnside Plaza, but I had never seen her there before we met at Hampton Park. She and I started playing catch in the Tasty Freeze parking lot, in the little mall, where we impressed all the boys who hung out there. We'd fire the ball back and forth like two mad women. I suppose she was trying to freak me out, too, but she never did. Gail lived a couple of blocks away from Mount View Senior Secondary, which was located on Carry Road at the time, not far from Hampton Park. She was as wild on the field as she acted off the field. She played second base, and I played first base for most of the years we played ball together. There was no escaping the drinking, smoking, or drugs. Even our coaches at the time, Lenny and Randy, would come to our games with a briefcase carrying booze. A mini bar was set up, and they would tell us, "If you win, we will all go to the Esquimalt Lagoon and have a big bash on us." And that is just what we did. Gail was a smoker, or when she was around me anyway, so of course, I took up the habit again. When I think about it now, it was off the wall what we would do after the games. At the Lagoon, there were these massive dunes, and I mean they were big. We would get all pissed up and climb them and then slide down them on some cardboard. These huge dunes could have collapsed and buried us alive. But I suppose when you have been so corrupted, you don't think about that or even care about it, for that matter. At least I thought Gail was drunk too, but I tend to think now it was all just part of an act. When we won the Cities, we would head to Nanaimo to play for the Island Championship. Teams from all over the Island would come, and some of them would stay in the Number Seven Hotel. The entire hotel would be full of Fast Ball Teams of drunken, young girls and their coaches. Gail was no innocent kid, so she led me to believe. One time, I went over to her house, and she had the idea to steal her parents' old coin collection and take it to the corner gas station to get the cash for it all. I told her, "Don't do it," but she said her parents never look at their coin collection and will never notice the coins have gone missing. Well, her mother did see, and she phoned my mother about it. Gail was surprised I never got in trouble for doing that. I suppose it was because their little plan wasn't as effective as they had wanted. She explained, "I got grounded for two weeks," and I wonder now if it was before or after she asked for forgiveness. Once and only once did she stay the night at my house, the only kid who ever did, and it was because she wanted to talk me into sneaking out with her and raiding gardens. It was the middle of the night, and I didn't think we would get caught, so I agreed. We went to the next block, Snowdrop, and I thought Gail was with me, but I soon found out she wasn't anywhere to be found. The people whose yard I ended up in were out, but they arrived home just as I got into their backyard. Right away, they turned on their outside lights while I was in their yard. I wasn't making any noise, and now that I think about it, I don't believe they saw me either, so that is why I wonder about that night. I recall hiding behind a tree and the people asking, "Who's there?" I was so frightened I couldn't move, but finally I thought if I didn't want to get caught, I'd better make a run for it. I got away and ran home, shitting myself. Gail came back to my house shortly after I did, and I told her, "I'm never doing anything like that again." And I never did.

Sometimes, after our games or practices, which we had at Hampton Park, Gail, and I would go to the Chinese store on Burnside Road, not far from the Park, to get some freezes. It's now closed, but it still exists as a herbal outlet. The owners of this store lived in the back of it. The Chinese man would come and shut the freezer door on our heads if we were looking in there too long. We would laugh about that. One day, the door that led to their house from what was the front of the store was open, and Gail pointed out, "Look, they have a big Hookah Pipe." I wondered what they used it for, and so Gail told me, "To smoke a drug called opium." She knew all about this pipe, telling me there was water in it so the drug wouldn't be so harsh on their throats. I wonder if she got her education from her ex-boyfriend's two brothers, both cops. Gail had an older brother, Barry, who would sometimes come with his friends to watch our games. Once her parents invited me to go on holiday with them, and we stayed at a cabin in Parksville, but her brother Barry never came. We stayed in a cabin across from the ocean. Gail and I did some acid while we were up there. I have never done anything like that before. We got so high that we walked to Qualicum Beach and back again. Her parents were so worried about us because we were gone all day and half the night, too. I wonder why they didn't call their friends or the authorities on us, given we were only around fourteen at the time? While we were walking on the beach, we saw some mongoloids all carrying a large boat, and I remember getting really freaked out and saying to Gail, "I don't want my children to turn out like that." Gail seemed to know a lot of people who smoked pot and did drugs. No doubt given her connections. Once she and I smoked a whole bag of real potent pot with a guy she introduced me to by the name of Steve. Steve was a junkie. He used heroin most of the time, but I think he poked a needle in his arm with anything he could get his hands on. We even saved all the roaches and rolled them up into what you called, "a bone of goosy." We were so stoned that we were walking down the road afterwards in an aggressive slant. It was a super-hot day, and we were both walking to Gail's house from the Creek and laughing our heads off about it. It seemed like the sun was pushing us over, and it was why we were leaning so much.

I now know her relationship with me, along with all the other friends and acquaintances I had in my life, was all part of a vicious, calculated plot by the Government of Canada and the British Columbia Government to try to kill me off. Getting so-called adults to use innocent children to commit acts of deception, acts of violence, and acts of crimes against other innocent children, and by the looks of things, back then, they were particularly after me. You see, I was the first in Canada born with a sexually transmitted disease, which a filthy Catholic caused, and they just didn't want me to find out because of all of the Catholic's greed for money and power. This corruption continues to this day, which has shocked me to no end.

CHAPTER FOUR

Gail and I continued going to the Tasty Freeze to play catch in the parking lot. One day, we caught the attention of two good-looking and popular guys. Their names were Steve and Bob, and they appeared to be pals. Gail was attracted to Bob, and he seemed to be attracted to her. They started groping each other almost immediately. Steve and Bob would come and watch our games all the time and hang out with us afterwards. Steve, who looked like my brother, used to live in Victoria with his family, but his family had recently moved to North Vancouver. Steve said he hated living in Vancouver because he missed all his friends, so he moved back to Victoria and lived in this tiny, run-down, one-bedroom house with Bob on Jasmine, a few blocks away from my house. Steve was two years older than I was. I was around fifteen when we started going out. His friends used to call him Cookie. That was his nickname. It was not love at first sight by any means. Once, Gail, Bob, and I went to where they were living, and there was a big drug party going on, which I didn't like one bit.

As a matter of fact, for a while, there was always a party going on, so I didn't go there much. Everyone called it their home, "the party house." Steve the junkie was sitting on the floor in the living room with his back up against the wall and head between his knees, blasted out of his mind, and I went over to him one time and said, "Steve, you shouldn't do this to yourself." I knew he had been poking shit into his body again. There were all kinds of people stoned out of their minds, smoking dope and shooting up in the bathroom. I asked Gail and Bob, "Where's Steve?" and they told me, "He is in the bathroom," so I questioned them. "Well, what is he doing in there?" They told me that Steve was doing speed. I asked them, "You're not doing it, are you?" They said, "No."

When Steve came out, I asked him what he was doing, and he didn't answer. I said, "Never mind." I could tell he was bombed out of his skull. I broke up with him, and I told him I didn't want anything to do with that stuff or YOU ever again, and stormed out of the house.

I said it right in front of everyone there and loud enough for them all to hear. There was a girl sitting at the kitchen table whose name was Ronda, and I was standing beside her when I said it. As the rumour went, her boyfriend, the father of her child, whom she was carrying at the time, died of an overdose of Methadone, trying to get off of Heroin. I remember her looking at me, and I looked at her as I left. Even though I broke up with Steve, Bob and Steve continued to come to our baseball games and practices. Steve approached me after a game at Hampton Park one day and promised he wouldn't do anything like that again. Being the trusting type, I took his word for it, and we started a relationship again. Steve continued to live in the same house with Bob, so it was hard not to go over there to see him from time to time. One day, the four of us were in their shared bedroom, and Steve started to make a move on me. It looked like Gail and Bob were making out, but I didn't want to do what I thought they were doing. Thinking back now, it was all an act. Steve ended up forcing himself on me and taking advantage of me. I didn't want to make out with him or anyone, let alone do it in front of people. I was not into that at all. And I told him that. I kept saying "No", "NO", but he never took "NO" for an answer. That day, he raped me. On the way home, Gail made me think it was just regular girlfriend and boyfriend stuff, so I just accepted what he did to me. Besides, I believe I was ashamed of myself at the time.

Steve would often come over to my house late at night, even on school nights, and my parents didn't like it one bit. So, of course, they wouldn't let him come in. They never liked him right from the start. One night, my mother's cousin Betty was over, and Steve came to the door just as she was leaving. Since the door was open, he scared them. My mother and Betty both told me he gave them the creeps. By this time, in my mind, I was obligated to him because of what he did to me. The house Steve lived in stopped being a big party house. It was a place where Steve's friends still came to hang out. I got to know some of his friends, and they were nothing but hoodlums, always up to no good. Steve and I once went to the home of Bruce, one of his best friends, to have a drink and a toke. Bruce was a real shit disturber, and he reminded me of a gangster, and that was just the way he wanted people to look at him. You could tell by the way he acted all the time. That day, Bruce and his girlfriend Vickie talked us into going up the Island to pick magic mushrooms in Duncan. They convinced me, "They are organic and they won't hurt you." We went to a field outside of Duncan and picked some mushrooms. I recall someone we met there telling me that you have to look for them under cow dung. This person was supposed to be the expert on them. He had a book and showed me what the magic mushrooms that got you high looked like. I couldn't believe how many different kinds there were, hundreds and hundreds, some very poisonous. So much so that they could kill you, I found out later. We went to this person's cabin. I ended up going blind a little while after I took them, and I was so freaked out when it happened. I was lying on the bed in this guy's cabin, telling Steve over and over again, "I can't see." "I CAN'T SEE.' I don't remember how long I was without vision, but it was a while. I never touched magic mushrooms again after that, and I didn't want anything to do with Bruce and Vickie, either, or any of his gangster friends, for that matter. I put losing my vision down to the magic mushrooms for most of my life, but now, because the same thing happened to my daughter at the same age that I was, I wonder about that. Not that I am condoning doing magic mushrooms by any means. However, I believe it has something to do with the condition of Pelvic Inflammatory

Disease, which I am now convinced my son and my daughter have inherited.

Things at home started to get heated because I was never around. Dad was very strict with me, and I had a curfew of ten o'clock on school nights and eleven o'clock on the weekends. All my other friends had to be in at eleven o'clock on a school night and twelve o'clock on the weekends, but not me. If I were ten minutes late, Dad would have a fit with me, telling me that I must be up to no good if I wanted to be out late. And my mother dared not stick up for me in front of him, so she said. Shortly after Steve and I started going out, I went to Dr. Turd because I was feeling nauseated all the time. Everything seemed to make me sick. He told me I was pregnant, and because I was only fifteen, he had to tell my parents about it. That must have thrilled Turd to no end to share that news with my parents. I remember being in Burger King, and my parents both scolding me about being pregnant. What was going through your head my father asked me. My father made me feel so ashamed of myself. He must have had his dirty ex-wife on his mind when he was doing so. He told me that if I had the baby, it would ruin my life. Abortions were just introduced to society, unknown to me at the time, but it was a real issue. However, this was the only way out of the mess, according to my parents, and it seemed I didn't have a choice at the time. I suppose I didn't. I was beside myself crying, and every time I cried, my mother would tell me not to, that I was going to make myself sick. That is what she always said to me when I cried. I think it is good to cry and express your feelings, but my parents were brought up to think children should be seen and not heard. That is what I heard too often when I was growing up. Well, I had the abortion, which made everything for me much worse. The relationship I had with my parents changed after that. And from time to time, when my father got upset with me, he would throw it all back in my face.

Even as a grown adult, he had to stop himself from doing that to me. And all along, I had been raped.

Steve and I were always fighting and making up, and most of the time it was because of his friends, so I thought. Once we had a big fight when we were at Marigold Park, and he tried to run me over with his Volkswagen, just like my grandfather tried to do. I was running through the park, and the madman was after me in his yellow Volkswagen through the large, closely knit trees. I had broken up with him again, and he wouldn't accept it. He just wouldn't. He ended up raping me in his car that day, too. Whenever we fought, he always said he was sorry, and he'd be crying. Then he would promise he would never hurt me again. That is more than anyone else ever said to me. I suppose I thought my Dad had changed, and my mother had given him another chance, too, so I should give Steve the opportunity to change.

Cookie, the nickname given to Steve, always had a big bag of pot on him, and when I was attending Mount View Senior Secondary, he would pick me up at lunch time and after school to get stoned. There was no getting away from the dope, and eventually it became an escape for me from this utterly frightening world I was living in. It seemed like everyone did dope, and the ones who never did didn't want anything to do with me. And I couldn't turn to my parents, not only because of what they were going through with my father's illness, but also, when they did find out I was in trouble, it was automatically my fault. Always. Perhaps I was just tired of being blamed for things that weren't my fault. That, and the fact that I forgot my childhood, is the only explanation I can come up with for putting up with my troubled life. And as it turns out, I couldn't win for losing anyway, no matter what I did or did not do, as the authorities were all in on destroying my life, which I found out many, many years later.

I hated the house Steve was living in, and I wanted him out of that place on Jasmine and away from all the hard ass drug scenes. Hence, he moved into his brother Bill's suite, who was living in a big, old house off Cook St. At this point, I believe Bob had left Victoria for a job well done, and I heard he got a manager's position up North. Steve couldn't afford to live in that house on Jasmine anymore anyway. His brother Bill was going to university to be a teacher at the time. Near the end of grade ten, I started skipping school to hang out with Steve in Bill's suite. It was the day before my sixteenth birthday that my cousin Gail died, and on my birthday, my auntie Mary decided to call my mother and tell her about it. Now that I know what my life was all about, I realize it was a little too well planned. Gail had been in and out of the Mental Institution for the Less Fortunate, Eric Martin, most of her life. Her parents couldn't be bothered with her; they were too busy making their small fortune. In the Institution, they were filling her head with all kinds of drugs. Apparently, she died of a brain clot on the way to the hospital. I suppose the explanation was that Gail was having another epileptic seizure; I'm not sure, because I never asked. I now know the medication which our evil family doctor prescribed was meant to kill her with her loving family's blessing. Gail had just gotten married and was living in an apartment with her husband, Robert, when this happened. Before Gail married Robert, my aunt Mary got her sterilized so she couldn't have any kids. She started talking about wanting some. I guess that is what sent the bastards off. My mother said Grandma was upset about her sister Mary doing that. Gail and Robert would often come over to my parents' house by cab. They would visit grandma, too. They knew who really cared for them. I can still hear my cousin saying, "Oh, Auntie Anne, you're so funny," and her laughing. Anyway, by the time I reached grade ten at Mt View, my school work was becoming very difficult for me to do. I was in the academic program, but it was obvious to me that I would never make anything of myself, which was exactly what the government wanted to achieve. Besides, I thought my parents didn't have the money to send me to college even if I did have the brains. During my school years, I tried to get help from my parents, but my mother said she only went to grade ten and she couldn't understand the math I needed help with, and my Dad was busy getting schooled by my brother so he could become a millwright, so he never had time to help me either. Out of two hundred people who took the Millwright exam, most of whom were university students, only three passed, and my Dad was one of them. The other two were a university student and a retired mill worker. Dad was already a carpenter and a carpenter millwright by trade. My mother and I would often get into heated arguments with each other, because, again, I was never home, and I suppose she started worrying about who I was with and what I was up to as well. One time, she threw a frying pan in my direction. She always threatened she was going to tell my Dad on me when I mouthed her back, but it wasn't working anymore, so my mother was getting frustrated with my behaviour. Dad had such a short fuse, so she always told me, or she would say, "I don't want to go to your Dad because you know what he is like." I remember feeling like no one gave a shit about me. One time when I called my mother a nasty name, she threw the damn iron in my direction. She was ironing when I said it. That is when I made up my mind that I was going to leave as soon as I turned of age. So just after I turned seventeen, I moved to North Vancouver to live with Steve and his parents. I knew the legal age was seventeen because my Dad used to tell me when I threatened to leave that if I did leave, he would call the cops to bring me back again because I wasn't of age to leave home. I found out what the legal age was, and days after I turned seventeen, I left.

Steve's Dad was a city bus driver, and his mother worked in a laundry mat on Lonsdale in North Vancouver. His Dad was Catholic, and his mother was Protestant. Steve's mother got me a job at the laundry mat where she worked, stamping dirty laundry and putting it in nets to be washed. Sometimes, if I wasn't busy, I got to press the shirts, which is what Steve's mother did. Steve's brother, Bill, was still living in Victoria but was married by this time to Lenore, who was also going to university to be a teacher. They were putting themselves through school. Cookie also had a younger brother, Teddy, who was still living at home when Steve and I moved in. Steve was collecting unemployment as usual. He was never too keen on working. I saved up all my money and bought a three-room grouping. His parents let us live with them for free so we could get on our feet. While we were living there, Steve bought another car, a Javelin from American Motors in North Vancouver, which was a real lemon. Steve's father and he went to the dealership to confront them about the car because the engine went out in it just days after Steve bought it. They did not want to do anything for him. That evening, someone threw a rock into the showroom window, and they accused Steve of doing it. Who knows, maybe he did because he always liked to create disturbances. He eventually got another Volkswagen. A brand new one this time. At night, we used to go across the Lion's Gate Bridge to downtown Vancouver stoned on pot or hash and drive around for entertainment because I was too young to get into any pubs or nightclubs. We became friends with one couple while living in North Vancouver. The girl lived at the bottom of Grouse Mountain with her parents, and sometimes we'd go there and get high on dope with her and her boyfriend. That's who we got our dope from. Her parents didn't mind us smoking up and getting high in their house. The girl, whose name I can't remember now, as our friendship was short-lived, was always busy attending school to become a teacher, like both her parents. That's why we didn't see them very often. I tried to encourage Steve to get a trade or go back to school, but he didn't know what he wanted to be was his excuse. We went snow skiing a couple of times at Mount Seamore, while living in Vancouver, as it was a good place for beginners to learn how to ski. Eventually, we got our own apartment in North Van, but we only lived in it for about a month.

After ten months of living in Vancouver, we decided to return to Victoria and make it our home. I was beginning to miss my parents, and whenever I phoned them, they offered for me to come back home, but at that point, I still had hard feelings towards them. When they offered, if I took them up on it, I thought I would be a failure again. When we left Vancouver, we left our belongings that were in the storage unit. It was everything from my childhood, lmy Barbie doll, bed, and dresser, which my brother had bought for me, and my Chatty Kathy doll. Steve had forgotten some tires and some other junk of his in there. We went to retrieve our belongings the following weekend, but one of the tenants informed us that everything was gone. No one seemed to know what happened to it, and we didn't have time to confront the manager about it because I had to get back to work, so we went back to Victoria empty-handed.

Steve and I got married on his mother's birthday in March. On the 16th of 1974, we had the wedding in Victoria at the little Anglican church on Burnside Road, St. Columbus, where I used to go when I was a kid. I was seventeen going on eighteen. There were about eighty people invited to the wedding, and I knew the day I got married that it was the wrong thing to do. I was doing it to save face, not just for me but mostly for my parents. Steve and I had gone to my cousin Raymond's wedding, who was now an Esquimalt police officer. At the wedding, while we were sitting in a dark corner by ourselves, my Dad came up to us with tears in his eyes and asked us not to live in sin. Steve and I had just moved in together at the time. I knew I was hurting my Dad once again, and it was the last thing I ever wanted to do because, despite the trouble I had with my parents, I never stopped loving or caring for them. Gail, my old baseball buddy, was one of my bride's maids, and when we left Victoria for Vancouver out of the blue, she became engaged to a guy by the name of Clay, whom she had been going out with before Bob. At the time, I thought that was a quick decision, but given the circumstances behind all this, I suppose it wasn't really. Clay, like I said, had two older brothers. They were both Saanich cops, moving up on the ladder quickly for reasons I now understand. My other bridesmaid was Valerie, whom I had known from High School, and she was going out with a guy named Ted. Valerie taught me how to drive in her little Volkswagen. Steve started hanging around with Ted before we moved to North Vancouver. We used to get together at Ted's parents' house on Harriet Road and smoke up. I thought he was lucky because he had his own suite above his parents' house. Ted was the best man at our wedding, and Steve's sister-in-law, Lenore, was my Maid of Honor. I suppose because I didn't have anyone else to ask. The day of the wedding, Steve came up to the altar with a black eye, a fat lip, and a sinister smile on his face. I was pretty embarrassed. He had been to his stag the night before and had gotten into a fight at a nightclub in town called the Purple Onion at the time. At the reception, all his mobster friends showed up despite the fact that none of them were invited; there ended up being a big fight. I had told my brother that if they came, I wanted them to leave, and so my brother confronted them with that when they all arrived, which started a big brawl. My uncle Gordie and the cop across the street, Dale, were sitting together with the rest of my screwed up relatives, and they were actually the ones who started the fists flying. I remember my brother telling me later, when the dancing started and the hoodlums were gone, that if I ever needed anything, I was to come to him. I suppose then he started to realize what I was going through and just what I had gone through in my life so far. Later on, I took Brian up on the offer, but it was always work-related. I just continued to hope my problems would just go away one day and kept them all hidden from myself.

Steve and I settled in an apartment on Fifth Street after we moved back from Vancouver, and I got a job right away at Victoria Laundry on Fisgard Street (now gone) across from what used to be the Hudson Bay downtown. I walked to and from work every day for a couple of years. Steve continued to be a lazy son of a bitch and sat on his ass most of the time we were married until, eventually, after hounding him, he got an apprenticeship in a cabinet-making shop. He hardly ever went, though; he would stay home from work at every and any chance he got, once because of a mild sunburn. I joined Fast Ball again, Senior Women's, and when I wasn't slaving my ass off in the hot laundry mat for peanuts, I was practicing or playing a Fast Ball game. Gail and I got picked up to play for Esquimalt High Grade Radio that year. They won the Island Championship. We were working out, running around the field, doing sit-ups and push-ups, to prepare for the British Columbia Championship in Vancouver. The girls at this stage were all wearing spikes, and some of the girls weren't being very nice to me, stomping on my feet as they went past me when I played first base before I got picked up for Esquimalt High Grade Radio. Nevertheless, I took their offer and started working out with them. They put me at shortstop, and although I had never played the position before, I was pretty good at it. At this stage of the game, though, all the girls could play any position. No one got to play full-time because the coach didn't want us to get tired, which I wasn't used to. I began to feel I was just wasting my time. Besides, I found it hard living on my own, going to work, fundraising, working out, along with everything else I had to put up with, being married to an abusive man. Believe me, we always had good workouts playing ball. Besides, my glove conveniently went missing from Steve's Volkswagen. He got into an accident one day while driving his new Volkswagen, all juiced up. My glove was in it. There was no way I would be able to break in a new glove before the Championships, so I took it as a cue to quit playing ball. It was the biggest mistake of my life. That year, Esquimalt High

Grade Radio won the Fast-Ball Championships and came forth in
Canada. The Canadian Championships for Fast-Ball were in New
Brunswick that year. Some of the girls from Esquimalt were
selected to represent Canada in the Commonwealth Games. They
had just introduced Women's Fastball to the games. I was once
again heartbroken when I found this out.

Steve was in the bars most of the time while I was off working
my bloody butt off in the Chinese-owned and operated laundry mat
pressing shirts. In the summertime, it would be over 110 degrees in
there behind the presses, and there was no air conditioning. The
girl I worked with would get nosebleeds all the time because of the
heat. She was the only other white person working there besides
me; all the rest were Chinese. The Chinese people who worked
there would often talk in Chinese, point, and laugh at me. Once,
they gave me a pig's ear to eat, and they wouldn't tell me what it
was until after I ate it. They all laughed aloud after they told me
what it was and saw my reaction to it. Now I wonder what it was
they heard about me that made everyone so mean. I managed to
get into the bars with Steve a few times, and he would kick me
under the table just like my brother did to me growing up. If I
talked to any of his friends, you could count on a huge fight when
we got home. He was so jealous of me, so he let on. I now know it
was all one big performance. I recall that it was around this time
that my half-brother, Lenny, first appeared in our lives. Dad was so
excited to see him. My brother Brian wasn't excited to meet him,
though. He saw through Lenny right from the start. I went to the
airport with my father to pick Lenny up, and \Dad started crying
because he hadn't seen him since Lenny was a kid. I suppose some
Catholic prick or the like phoned him up to tell him about Dad's
illness, and he should come out and get acquainted with us if he
wanted to get in on the Will. Looking back, Lenny always seemed
to show up in Dad's darkest moments, in his illness. I could see it
in all the pictures we took of the two of them when he came over.

They are now in the garbage. Anyway, most of the time, I couldn't get into the bars even though I was of age. I didn't have a driver's license as I didn't know how to drive yet. Even with the British Columbia Identification Card, they wouldn't allow me in, and I couldn't understand it. I started to get fed up with Steve's mistreatment of me and his constant attendance at the bars and whatever else he was up to with his gangster friends, so I told him one day I was going to leave him. We got into a big fight, and he punched me in the eye as I was going out of the back door of the apartment building we lived in. It didn't go away for three weeks or more. Finally, I couldn't stay away from my parents any longer, and I went over there when my eye was yellowing and told my parents I wanted to leave Steve. Right away, they told me to come home. They asked me what happened to my eye, and I told them I hit it when I fell into the coffee table, a famous old line. I knew if my Dad found out Steve hit me, he would go ballistic, and there was no telling what he would do to him.

I was twenty when I left Steve and moved back home. I got the chance of a lifetime, packed a suitcase, and ran out the door. I wanted to leave him many times before, but I was afraid because he would always threaten me when I said I wanted to leave him. By this time, Steve always wanted us to have kids, and sometimes he would take advantage of situations I got myself into, not caring if I got pregnant or not. In other words, he'd rape me. Not even a couple of years after our marriage, Steve discovered that the girl he had always had a crush on, Wendy, had left her husband, George, and they started dating. I knew then it was my chance to go, and I had better hurry up and take it.

By this time, I had become friends with one of Steve's druggy friends ' ex-girlfriend, who mysteriously appeared in my life out of nowhere, only months before I was about to leave Steve. Her name was Lynn. I knew Steve's friend, whose name was also

Steve, whom Lynn went out with, was up to no good all the time (he was heavily into drugs), and I told Lynn that. She said she had the same idea about him, too. She broke off with him around the same time I left my husband, Steve. She slid into my life by introducing me to ceramics, and we went to classes together for a while. Then we started to hang out in nightclubs, which I liked better than bars, because at least instead of getting pie-eyed, you could dance the alcohol off. Lynn always got pissed to the gills, but looking back at that now, it was all a sick performance. Lynn had a brother, David, who was going out with a girl named Vicki. They would come to the nightclubs with us from time to time. We liked going out to Esquimalt to a place called the Bacchanalia because they would always have live bands playing there. Besides, neither Steve nor any of his friends hung out there. At first, Lynn tried to hook me up with her cousin's ex-boyfriend, Laird. He looked like my brother, too. We started seeing each other for a very short time, but I quickly realized he was just too wild for me. He was into drinking lots and lots and taking downers, and Lynn got into taking downers too when she brought him with her. At least it was what she led me to believe. I suppose it was an attempt to get me hooked. One time, they came over to my parents' house, stoned on them and pissed to the gills, and Laird's van was all dented up. He had gone into a ditch with it. They were making such a scene, and I didn't want my parents to see them, so I immediately chased them away. After that incident, I didn't want to see Laird again. Luckily, he took off to live in Vancouver to do the lights for some rock band. I should have dumped Lynn, too, but I didn't because of all my insecurities and this one twisted government that was continually trying to mess with my mind, which I didn't realize at the time.

When I left Steve, I took the receipts for all the furniture I bought while living in Vancouver with him. I told the cop across the street, Dale, I wanted to get my furniture and the rest of my clothes, and I would appreciate it if he could escort me to the apartment. I was afraid of a conflict, and rightly so. Dale said, it was a good job I took the receipts with me when I left Steve, otherwise the police wouldn't be able to help me. Lynn told me she would ask her brother David if he would help get my stuff,, but he was too busy, so she said, doing something else. She told me Vickie's brother, Robin, would come and help. I got my brother to come with his truck to load it all on. Dad came too. Dale and another cop escorted me to the apartment building where I had been living with Steve, on Fifth Street. Robin never showed up to help. I suppose he was told he shouldn't be around because of what they had planned to come down that day. Before my brother and my Dad came to move all my stuff, Dale rang the buzzer at the front entrance of the apartment to get Steve to let us in. There were only two cops and I at the door at this time. The apartment was located on the ground floor of the apartment building, facing the parking lot, which was situated at the rear of the building. Dale said over the intercom, "Steve? … this is the Victoria City Police, and your wife is here to pick up some stuff." Steve yelled at them, "Well, you're not coming in, and if you try, **I Will Blow Your Fucking Heads Off.**" Dale asked me if Steve had any guns, and I said he used to go hunting, which I thought he did. The next thing you know, the whole apartment building was surrounded by cop cars. With that, Steve let us in. It wasn't until I was inside the apartment that my brother and my Dad showed up. The cops waited while we moved all my furniture and clothes out. However, the so-called authorities succeeded with their plan to traumatize me.

When I left, after the Laird ordeal, I was interested in finding a better job or a career for myself; I had no interest whatsoever in meeting a guy; it was the furthest thing from my mind. I had applied to all the places I knew you could make good money, like Safeway and all the hospitals, just before I left Steve. I was going to apply at BC Tel (now Telus) and BC Hydro because I knew one could make a good income there, too, but you needed a grade twelve education to get hired, which I did not have. I was still working in the laundry, and my Mom and Dad didn't want me to quit until I found another job, but I thought to myself, that's probably why I wasn't getting a job, because I already had one, and I was putting it down on my job applications. I quit the laundry despite what my parents were telling me to the contrary. I was tired of working like a slave for next to nothing. By this time, I was saving my money to buy a car. Valerie was teaching me how to drive in her little Volkswagen. I didn't see Valerie after she taught me to drive because she and her boyfriend, Ted, were still good friends with Steve, so she ended up drifting out of my life like everyone else always did. Soon after, I bought a little, white Toyota Corolla from someone my Dad knew from work. I went to the unemployment office to see if I could take a hair-dressing course because I was always doing my mother's hair for her, and I liked doing that. My righteous aunt Carol was coming over to cry on my mother's shoulder all the time about her husband Gordie's drinking, and one time she was there while I was doing my mother's hair, and she said to me I should be a model. Priming me up for what they all had going on in the works. Every chance my auntie Carol got, she would say that to me and how pretty I was. Back then, models were still considered by some to be promiscuous, which I had no idea of at the time. A little while after I applied at the unemployment office for hairdressing sponsorship, they called me offering one at Malaspeno College over the Malahat in Nanaimo. At the same time, I was trying to organize things, I received a phone call from Jubilee Hospital, and my parents informed me that it would be a secure job working there. I would have benefits, a pension, etc. I would also earn more money than I ever would as a hairdresser, so I listened to them this time and accepted the job offer from the hospital. It was in the Food Service Department of the Jubilee Hospital, and what a big mistake that turned out to be. Big mistake.

When I first started at the hospital, I worked in the Veterans Hospital, also known as Memorial Pavilion. I was on call at first and bounced around all over the place. Later on, I got a permanent part-time job there. The evil government was right on top of things, as I found out that the Dietitian at Memorial and my evil family doctor, Dr. Turd, were responsible for the real abusive relationship I ended up having next. It was with Robin, the guy Lynn, my good old friend, introduced me to. They had him stalking me while I was in a battle and being stalked by my first husband, Steve, for a divorce. Steve would come by my parents' house all the time and call me filthy names, and it was in the middle of the summer when all our neighbours were out in their yards. It was obvious the cops weren't going to do anything about this guy because Dale, a Victoria City Police officer, still lived across the road from my parents' home, and he knew everything that was going on. I eventually got a Peace Bond out on Steve, and this I found out about through a lawyer, not a cop, like I should have. To my knowledge, nothing was done about Steve and all the rage he got in and took out on me, which I believe all the authorities were aware of.

Lynn wanted to go to the Red Lion Bar before the nightclubs because the booze is cheaper at a bar, and she said that it won't cost as much when we are in the nightclub. That's where she introduced me to Robin, her brother David's girlfriend's brother, at the Red Lion Hotel. Steve would come in there instead of the Colony Inn, where he usually went, so Lynn and I would leave as soon as we saw him come in the door and go downstairs to the nightclub there, as it started to be a popular hangout for people Lynn knew. They played Disco music in this bar, which made a nice change away from the regular Rock and Roll I was always listening to. This girl, Dawn-Lee, was one of Robin's acquaintances, and out of the blue, she started going out with Steve. I told her he was crazy, but she went out with him anyway. I guess she had something to hide. One night, Dawn-Lee came out of the nightclub, which was downstairs in the Red Lion Inn, and said to me, "You're right, he is CRAZY." Steve had just attacked me in the Red Lion Parking lot and dragged me off to his Volkswagen by the hair, then floored it right in the parking lot, purposely hitting two parked cars before flying over the railway tracks and coming to a sudden halt on them. My face hit the window shield, and my knee hit the tape deck, bending it into a V shape. He was mad about me taking everything. I was leaving the nightclub because I didn't want to get into an argument about it, and he followed me. Lynn saw the whole thing because she was coming with me when I left. Dawn- Lee came out of the nightclub after the fact. Lynn wanted me to go to the hospital, but I said that the cops would be involved, and that would just make him angrier. So Lynn and I went to her parents' house to pick the glass out of my face. Her parents were not home. Luckily, I didn't need stitches, but my knee sure as hell hurt, and it went black and blue almost immediately. For years, a piece of glass was embedded in my eyebrow. While I was going out with Robin, he told me once that I should get it taken out because I might go blind because of it. I wonder now what he really was referring to because I was told that wasn't true. Turd said, the glass would dissolve, which it did after about ten years or more.

Yes, Robin, he looked like my brother, too. He kept calling and calling me at my parents' house, asking me to go out with him, and he turned out to be a persistent stalker. Finally, I gave in. In my mind, I thought the guy wasn't very good looking; he had these black, horned rimmed glasses, and the lenses were as thick as airplane glass. I thought he wouldn't hurt me. He acted like such a gentleman at first. Robin would always come over to our table when I was out with Lynn, and there was a time when he even pulled the chair out for me. One night, I was out with him at the pub in the Red Lion, and all his friends were sitting with us.

Dawn-Lee was going out with one of Robin's bar acquaintances, Wayne, and they were both there when Steve came up to our table, asking me to pay for a divorce. There were probably around twenty of us sitting together. Anyway, that's why Steve was always stocking me. He wanted me to pay for a divorce. Again, I told him I didn't have the money for a divorce, and I wanted to wait for three years and write my own divorce. He said he wanted to marry Wendy. I said, "Well, you're going to have to wait for three years." That is when he pulled the chair out from under me, and I fell to the floor. Just as that happened, Wendy jumped on top of me and started to punch me in the face. Then she grabbed a beer glass from our table and crushed it into my face. As that was going on, some of the guys from our table were getting into it with their fists. Robin played the hero and jumped on Steve right away. Dawn- Lee managed to pull Wendy off of me, and we went into the bathroom together to assess the damage Wendy did to me while they were all still going at it. I had some cuts on my face just below my eye. I was lucky I didn't lose an eye like one girl who I went to school with did, only her boyfriend was the one who threw a beer glass in her face. Funny as it may seem, her boyfriend, who did this, was one of the kids who tried to run me over with his bike when I failed grade four. Needless to say, Steve got barred from the Red Lion for life, and because he kept coming to my parents' house yelling obscenities, I gave in and paid for a divorce. I suppose that's one of the reasons, too, why I started having a relationship with Robin. I looked at him as being my hero, along with being terrified because the law wasn't protecting me. I didn't want my Dad to know everything that was going on for fear of what he might do; besides that, he was ill, and this was the last thing he needed. Robin and I started a relationship when Lynn mysteriously disappeared from my life. No notice, nothing. I found out from her brother that she got a job in a group home somewhere out of town and had to leave for it right away. I guess that was her payment for a job she thought was well done, just like everyone else, and she got away with it.

  Robin was living with a bunch of guys in this house when we first got together, but I didn't like what was going on in this house; it was another one of those party houses, and I really wanted to get away from that sort of thing. Because he, too, had an agenda and wanted to keep me happy at any cost, he moved back into his parents' place. Right after he moved back home, Robin took me out to the High Steak House (a first-class restaurant) with his whole Catholic family and one of his friends who was getting married soon, Dale, and his fiancée, just to put the finishing touch on our fucked up budding relationship.

CHAPTER FIVE

Robin was a boiler maker working on and off for various companies, but it seemed like it was more off than on. He lived on Walnut Street with his parents almost the whole time we were going out. One of Robin's friends, Cameron, was living with his parents beside Robin's house. He was a cab driver. John, who was Robin's best friend, was a sheet metal worker working steadily at a shop in town somewhere, and he lived with his parents, a street or two away from Robin, off of Fernwood. Keith was another one of Robin's close friends, and he lived not too far away from them all, most likely with his parents, and I can't remember what he did for a living because he wasn't on the scene very long. Ron, Robin's cousin, was a diver for the Coast Guard, living with his parents somewhere in the city. Robin had three brothers: two older ones who were no longer living at home, and one younger brother who was still at home. His second-oldest brother was engaged to a girl whom Robin had gone out with, and she had gotten pregnant. She had his child but gave it up for adoption, being the righteous Catholics that they all were. His sister, Vickie, who was living at home and engaged to David, was also working in the Food Service Department for the Jubilee Hospital, but at Eric Martin, and was looking for another job as a secretary. I suppose they didn't want her to have any connection with me, so they suggested she find another job. They all attended Victoria High School, and I believe Robin and his friends graduated together. I remember Robin's father just having open heart surgery when we first started going out, so he wasn't working, and I can't seem to remember what he did or what his mother did for a living. I took Robin over to meet my parents, and right off the bat, my parents told me that they didn't like him. I should have listened to them and given Robin the heave-ho. There were other friends and acquaintances of Robin's,

too many to mention, but we all hung out at the Red Lion pub
before going to various nightclubs in the city. Robin seemed to be
into heavy metal music and rock and roll, and there was a place
called the Surf Side Cabaret on Wharf St on the Inner Harbour that
we frequented. The Surf Side Cabaret catered mainly to rock and
roll music. It wasn't live; there was a disc jockey. The place was
too small for a live band. Robin never worked much, so after we
had been going out for a while, we would go Dutch. That is, we
would each pay our own way. I really liked dancing to any kind of
music; it seemed to be another escape for me, and I felt somehow I
had missed out on socializing because Steve was my first
boyfriend, and I was never allowed to talk to any of his friends. I
eventually didn't want to anyway. All of Robin's friends were only
into smoking dope when I first met them, and drinking, of course. I
never bought any drugs in my entire life. I always had them given
to me, and hanging out with Robin and his friends and
acquaintances was no exception. Besides, I wouldn't waste my
money on the stuff. To me, money has always been too hard to
come by. Robin bought me a pair of white elephant pants with red
pin stripes down the leg and a matching white top for my birthday
when we were going out. He seemed to care for me deeply at first,
but I realize now it was all just a put-on. One weekend, a bunch of
us went over to Salt Spring Island for a camping trip. Dawn-Lee
was still going out with Wayne, and they went with us, along with
some of Robin's other friends. We were all drunk, and I should
have known the kind of person he really was on this trip because
he mooned everyone, but I just put it down to us all being so
intoxicated. Before I knew it, I was drinking more and getting into
heavier drugs like MDA. I soon found out that everyone who hung
out at the Red Lion was into doing MDA and cocaine regularly,
just like Robin and all of his friends were. I wasn't too keen on
MDA. It didn't do a thing for me the couple of times I did it, and
like I said, I never wasted any money on drugs ever. So it was no
skin off my nose, luckily.

Again, I was left without a friend. Dawn-Lee and I only hung out for a while when we were with our boyfriends, and the timing was right. Soon, she and Wayne had broken up, and she disappeared from my life, too. I managed to make a friend while working in one of the kitchens at the hospital in the main building. Her name was Diane. We worked together in her kitchen, Four Royal in the main building, for three weeks before I got transferred to the Veterans Hospital, Memorial Pavilion again. It was a very busy kitchen, with hard work and intense heat, and I was glad they moved me out of the main building. One time when Diane and I were working together in her kitchen, they had some disabled people training with us, and one of them threw the toast at Diane after it was toasted. That is how we started the conversation at the Surf Side one night when we bumped into each other. From that time on, everywhere I went with Robin, I seemed to bump into her and her friend Darlene, who always had a big bag full of pot she would always want to share with me. They were both overly friendly, coming to my table or asking me to come and sit with them, and soon we hung out on a regular basis.

Darlene's husband was a Chinese fellow named Dave, who never spoke to me the whole time I hung out with Darlene. They had a big grow op in their house, which they lived in together. I never saw anything like it before. The plants weren't in any soil, and they had these grow lights all over the place. I suppose Darlene was the main seller of it all, and that is why she had so much of it on her all the time. Darlene and Dave had two little kids, Cindy, the oldest, and Blaine, who was a few years younger, but every Friday and Saturday night, and sometimes during the week, Darlene would go out and party, and the kids would be shipped off somewhere. When Robin wanted to go out with the boys, I would go out with Darlene. And most of the time, Diane would go out with her boyfriend Doug. Doug was up Island at Shawangan Lake partying one night when he got into an accident with his truck and killed a family of three generations, a grandmother, a mother, and her daughter who were travelling in a van. From my understanding, he crossed over the center line, and he hit them head-on. Diane was supposed to go with him, but didn't, luckily for her, or she could have ended up dead too. Doug's defence was that he was allergic to cats, and where he was visiting that night, they had a cat, and he got a reaction, and that was why he crossed the center line. Because Doug was hurt so badly and unconscious, they couldn't do a breathalyzer or take any blood from him, which was the law then, so he got off the charges. Shortly after Doug had recuperated, Diane broke off with him. Things with Darlene and her husband, Dave, were always rocky, and Darlene ended up committing adultery with one of Robin's dopey friends, Cameron. She eventually left Dave for yet another guy whose name was Ralph.

One day, I went for my annual check-up like I always had every year, and Dr Turd told me that I had the Human Papilloma Virus (HPV), but he never called it that; he called it vaginal warts. I had no idea it was a sexually transmitted disease. I had never heard of sexually transmitted diseases before because, unlike nowadays, no one ever talked about sexually transmitted diseases, not in school or out of school. When I asked Turd what it was that the prick told me, it was NO BIG DEAL, but I would have to have an operation to get them BURNT OFF, is what he said, but he also said it was NO BIG DEAL. With that, I just thought they were like the warts a person gets on any other part of their body, but I was kind of embarrassed about the whole thing. I then asked him if it would hurt, and I remember him shaking his head **NO** and saying he would be giving me laser treatment for it. Laser treatment, my ass. I was never in so much pain in all my life. I thought I was on fire down there. I remember waking up after the operation in the Old Victoria General Hospital in Fairfield and screaming for the nurses to give me something for the pain; it was so UNREAL. To top matters off, the guy who gave this FUCKING VIRUS to me,

Robin, came to pick me up after the operation. He thought I was getting a cyst removed, of all things, because that was what I told him. Don't ask me why I didn't confront him then with what he did to me or report this; I guess this operation did such a number on me, traumatizing me to no end, I was terrified to say anything about what had just happened, along with being yet again ashamed of myself. I believe the nuns owned this hospital then, and the government took it away from them and eventually closed it down for a while for reasons along the lines of this operation, which I had, or worse, I would imagine. Also, the rumour is that the old Catholic school, which has been boarded up for years and was adjacent to the Old Victoria General Hospital, now called Fairfield Hospital, was haunted. That wouldn't surprise me for all the innocent lives that I believe have been taken by the likes of this man, Doctor Turd and all the evil Shrinks from the "Nut House." Nut means most everyone who works there, not the patients. Anyway, man, I was laid up for over a month, taking Demerol for the pain. Bloody hell fire, what an evil son of a bitch this man was. He was truly out to crucify me. I began dating Robin's friends. I wanted Robin to admit to what he had done to me, and I thought that by dating them, I would make him jealous, and he would then admit and apologize to me. That was bloody wishful thinking. I was always interested in John, his friend. I suppose because he was continually flirting with me and complimenting me, saying things like "You look good tonight," and "You have beautiful hair, it's gold." John made the move on me one night, taking me over to his parents' place and necking with me. But we never did anything else but that, and I wondered why we never had a relationship with the way he would come onto me all the time. Now I know it was all part of the plan. They wanted to make me look like I was the cheap tramp when, really, it was they who were, and I was a cover-up for their promiscuous behaviour. I think I lost my mind, though, for a while over what Robin and that evil Turd did to me, because after our ten-month relationship had diminished, I didn't want to let up trying to get Robin to admit to what he had done to me. And that just caused me more grief. I went out with a couple of Robin's friends. However, I soon realized that I was nothing but a garbage dump for these filthy Catholic animals.

I started to drink lots, smoke more, and do cocaine to drown out my sorrow and my pain. I'd go to parties after the Surf Side was closed with Darlene and sometimes Diane. But mostly with Robin's cousin, Ron, and his friend, Dave. The crowd from the Red Lion and the Surf Side were always at the same parties as us. I should have known Ron was up to something because he was always trying to befriend me, no matter where I went, and I wasn't interested in him beyond being friends at the time. I hung out with him and his friend Dave, acting as a kind of shield to keep all the other animals away from me. Ron and I were leaving a party one night at the same time, and when we came out the door of the party, I was shocked to see that someone had thrown an axe through the driver's side of the front door of my white Toyota Corolla. Little did I know it was my good old cop cousin Raymond. I was kind of scared to go to any parties after that happened, so I suppose it is why I always went to them with Ron and Dave. What a plan, hey? It was Ron who actually got me doing cocaine, and he'd have wicked smoke on him all the time, too. And I was into all that now. My Dad started to get on my case again, telling me that "You will never find your mate at a bar," as if he was telling me something I didn't already know. I was still traumatized from that bloody operation I had, and was out drowning my sorrows about it. I guess about everything else that had gone on in my miserable life, which I eventually blocked out. And it was like I lost all control for a while, just like the evil government had planned all along. I was heading down a path of no return, and the wicked demons were succeeding in destroying me.

One time, I was leaving a party, and Robin and some of his rang-a-tang friends climbed into my white Toyota. They insisted I give them a ride home, and once they pushed their way into my car, there wasn't too much I could do but give them a ride home. Actually, I shouldn't have driven at all. It was very early in the morning, and they were all carrying on in the back seat like a bunch of animals, and I was getting confused as to where I was supposed to go. Besides, I hadn't been driving that long and didn't know my way around the city. Someone yelled out, "Turn here." "Turn here," so I did. Then, the rest of them loudly chirped, "You're going down a one-way street," and they all started laughing. I quickly turned off of Quadra St., which was the road I was travelling on, after I turned off Pandora, and who was coming the other way but a Victoria City cop. He could see what I just did, so of course, he pulled me over, thinking he might have a catch. When he came to my driver's door and asked me for my credentials, I could tell that he was angry about what I had just done. Robin and all of his friends were making obscene comments to the guy and to me as this cop was trying to talk to me, and I thought This is it, I'm done now. He went back to his cruiser, and a little while after, he came to my door and said something like "Just watch what you are doing next time." And gave me my insurance and registration back. Everyone in the car pretended they couldn't believe I had gotten off, and I figured maybe Dale, who at the time I thought was a friend of the family, was working that night and had something to do with this cop letting me off the hook. No doubt he did. I suppose they didn't want it on record because then there would be proof of some of this shit. Another time, after Robin and I had broken up, I was so drunk I ended up sleeping with Robin again at one of his friends' houses, which he had just moved into. He wanted to show me where he lived. I remember telling him I thought his bed was dirty and pushing him away, but he assured me it wasn't dirty. When I woke up the next morning, hungover, Robin was nowhere to be found, and neither was anyone else. Some ass had stolen my Toyota right out of the driveway. I had to catch a cab home and tell my parents that someone had stolen my car from Darlene's place, where I said I had stayed the night. Little did I know or ever dream it was my cousin Raymond, the honest Catholic and Esquimalt Police officer, who stole my car. He took it to Esquimalt Pulp Mill, where the so-called cops found it weeks later, rolled and lying over on its roof, the tires off and the engine blown. But they didn't know who did it. Good law enforcement strategies. That's good old Victoria for you. My brother Brian fixed the car by buying a rebuilt engine for it. It cost $500.00. He put it in, and I kept it for a little while longer, but it was never the same after that.

I wanted to get rid of the crowd I was hanging out with, but I found it an impossible task. Darlene, Diane, and I started going to different pubs and nightclubs where they had disco music playing, in an attempt to find someone decent, at least that was my idea. That is when I met this guy, who I would see sometimes at the Red Lion Pub, and he was into disco music, so he would go to those kinds of places all the time, like the Sting in the Strathcona Hotel on Douglas Street, right downtown Victoria, being one of them. We didn't get together there. We got together at a Disco joint on the corner of Government and Fisgard, which had just opened up. His name was Larry, and he was considered a ladies' man, always surrounded by lots of young women. He was very good-looking, and he was also a very good dancer. I decided I would take him to meet my parents one night before we went out on the town. When I introduced him to my mother, she asked, "Is your mother's name Louise?" And he said it was. That is when I found out he was my third cousin, also Catholic. His mother and my mother were cousins, but my mother never knew her that well and hadn't seen her for years and years. His mother was Betty's sister, and even Betty never had anything to do with her sister Louise, Larry's mother, for some reason. While Larry was over, I questioned if we were to have kids, they could be deformed, and my mother said that it would be a good possibility, so we ended the relationship pretty quickly because we both agreed we wouldn't want that to happen.

Dale, another one of Robin's friends, was never out parting with us. His family owned a construction company, and they had just fixed up a big old house and made a few suites in it. I bumped into him somewhere, and he said to me that it was too bad Robin and I broke up because he thought I was nice and I was good for him. Dale and his family did a nice job on this house, and Dale offered me a little bachelor suite on the first floor to live in. I liked the fact that it had a brick surrounding this bar-type structure, which enclosed the little kitchen. It wasn't too far from the hospital where I was working, either. It was on Wark St, just off of Bay, a few blocks away. I really liked it, and with my Dad on my case again, I thought I should make the move. I took him up on the offer, but my new home didn't last long. Robin kept jimmying the window open and crawling into my suite in the middle of the night and raping me, so I decided I would move into a house with a girl by the name of Patty, the town's cocaine dealer from the States, after only living on my own for a few months. That way, maybe Robin would leave me alone.

I was still hanging around with Darlene and Diane at the time I bumped into Dale, but Darlene was spending most of her time now with this guy named Ralph. And Diane had found herself a new guy, too, Leaf, and she was hardly in the scene at all anymore. I was familiar with Patty, a girl from the Red Lion, and she was quite popular, but I never really knew why at first. I soon found out. She started to befriend me because she was into Disco Music too, and she knew Larry pretty well. I believe they had a fling at one time. One day, when I showed up at the Red Lion again, she came over to my table to chat with everyone like she did sometimes in the past. She told me her roommate, whom she said she had lived with for years and years, was moving out on her. All the furniture they had in this house they'd been renting belonged to this girl who was moving out on her, apparently. She heard I was not happy where I was living right now, and maybe I'd like to move in with her. I liked the idea of living in a house, and I knew she had a little girl who was around seven at the time, so I thought it just might work out. She also made me feel sorry for her because she didn't know what she was going to do or how she was going to get the money to buy furniture, and she didn't want to upset her daughter. I went over there to check it out the day her roommate was moving out, and that poor little girl only had a mattress on the floor, but Patty's room was nice and furnished. Beautiful clothes, fancy high-heeled shoes, and leather boots, too. She was always dressed to the hilt. It was quite the act when I think about it now, and at a little girl's expense. Anyway, my brother and my Dad once again moved me. This house was by Tillicum off of Craigflower. When my Dad and my brother moved me, they said it wouldn't last long, and they were both right. I suppose now that the evil government got me started on cocaine, they were out for the gusto and wanted me to get good and hooked on the stuff, so they found me a real nose blower. But lucky for me, I never got hooked on anything but pot for a while. This woman was wired on cocaine all the time. It was no wonder she never had any furniture; she never held down a job, and she would snort all of her profits from selling the damn stuff. The three months that I lived with her were nothing but a snorting affair. This guy Randy, with whom she started to go out while I was living with her, I also knew from going to parties, mostly. He would come over with his friend Mike all the time, and we would all get stoned on cocaine and dope, and then go out to the Red Lion so Patty could get rid of some of her cocaine to pay for what we all did. Randy and Mike were both a lot younger than Patty, but I never knew how much younger because I never even thought to ask. I was so screwed up at the time. All I knew was that Patty was about ten or more years older than I was.

 Randy broke off with Patty around the same time that I moved out. However, just before that, he told me about a party I should go to, and there I would meet real people who would treat me the way I should be treated. The house was off Craigflower, just past Admirals and under the trestle on the Old Island Highway. A girl by the name of Karen was renting this house and having the party. She was going through a heavy divorce, and she had a little girl around three that she was bringing up on her own, and apparently, she was having a hard time coping with it all. Her doctor prescribed her some Valium to take because of stress, apparently. At this party, she and I got into a conversation about where I was working. When she found out that I worked in the Veterans hospital, Memorial Pavilion, she told me she had a good friend who worked in housekeeping in the same building as I did. One day, this girl approached me at work because I was conveniently working on the same floor on the same day she was. She asked me if I knew Karen, and I said I did sort of. She invited me over to her house after work that day, and I went. She was married at the time and had two little boys. She said her husband didn't work; he had a gambling problem. She avoided me and ignored me after that day. Karen continued to have parties, and she had a different crowd of people at her parties, so I would go to them sometimes. Karen then invited me to go to a pub with her on Esquimalt Road, which was then called the Halfway House, and I took her up on her offer a couple of times. One night, as we were going into the Halfway House, she said to me, "I have a lot of friends with the Esquimalt Police Force that come into the bars out here." She was wired, and I could see she shouldn't be driving, and I told her that. It didn't dawn on me that maybe she knew my cousin Raymond. Another night, she just got up and left one of her parties she was having at her house because she decided it would be the only way the people would leave. She wanted the party to break up because it was getting out of hand. We decided to go to the Strathcona Hotel to a quiet place there called Little John's Bar. She talked me into taking some Velium with her. She said, I drink and take them all the time, and nothing ever happens to me. Go ahead, it will just mellow you out. I was so stupid to do it. I guess by this time, I had forgotten all about what happened with Lynn and Laird that night when they came to my parents, all doped up on downers and pissed to the gills. Anyway, I was driving her car, and we were on our way down Craigflower when I bumped right into the rear end of a car that was stopped at the stoplight right on Craigflower and Admirals. I staggered out to see if I had done any damage to either car, but I hadn't. After that, I don't remember all we did except for falling off the stool at Little John's bar in the Strathcona Hotel a few times. When I saw Karen next, I told her I was never going to do that again, and I never did. But I continued going to her parties for a while longer until I opened my eyes and saw how screwed up she was over a man popping pills all the time and drinking, so I said to her, "All the men in this town are a bunch of assholes." That is when she said to me she knew someone who would treat me like a real lady, and I'll introduce you to him if you want, but he lives in Vancouver. I thought to myself, what the hell, what do I have to lose? Maybe he'll take me away from this hellhole of a town, so I agreed to meet him. I was at her house one day, and this guy showed up. She introduced me to him, telling me that his name was John. "You know the guy who knows how to treat a lady." We went into her house, and at this time, she was living in Victoria West off of Lampson Street. Karen went into her kitchen cupboard to get the bottle of Valium and offered me some again. I don't know who she was trying to impress this time. That is when I told her, "You shouldn't do that stuff, it's dangerous, it could kill you if you drink with it." I think at this point I was starting to realize how crazy my life was, but I just didn't know why or what to do about it. Well, John asked me if I like to water ski and snow ski. I told him that I'd never been water skiing before, and I had been snow skiing only a couple of times when I was married to my first husband, and I loved it. He said he would take me sometime. He told me he owned a ski boat and his own house on Whistler Mountain, a ski resort located in Vancouver. Of course, that impressed me. I asked him what he did for a living, and he said he skied in the winter and skied in the summer. He never told me his last name, and I never pushed it because I thought once he got to know me, he would tell me his last name. I didn't really think he would call me because he never did for a long time. Anyway, I told him I would love to go skiing with him sometime, and I gave him my phone number. I never saw Karen after that day because she was a really messed-up lady. But one night, John, with no last name, called me, and he met me at the Surf Side, where Kathy, who suddenly came onto the scene, Darlene, Diane, and I all started to go again.

I would bump into Ron from time to time when I started going out with Darlene and Diane more often after I decided not to associate with Karen anymore. Diane broke off with the guy she had been seeing, Leaf, so she was single, and Darlene said she needed to have time away from Ralph because they were spending too much time together and were getting on each other's nerves. Ron and his bosom buddy Dave were still up to their old tricks, snorting cocaine, basically getting blasted all the time, and it didn't take long for me to get back into the swing of things. But the rest of the gang were all out of the scene now, going steady with girls, I guess, trying to straighten themselves out, if that is at all possible. I thought Ron really had feelings for me. I had known him for two years by this time. He never had any feelings for me. I realize that now. No one ever really had feelings for me. Well, one night when Ron and I were out on a date and coming home from a party at about one o'clock in the morning, we got pulled over by the Saanich cops. We were in his car and he was driving me home when it happened. There were other people in the car in the back seat getting a ride home, too. Ron said we were getting pulled over because of a broken taillight, but really, the Saanich cops had set him up with drugs to frame me with. When we got pulled over, Ron begged me to take it all and put it down my boot, and of course, I didn't want to, and we were arguing about that until finally I just shoved it down my boot as the officer approached Ron's driver's door. This officer made it sound like he knew a person who was sitting in the back seat, and after flashing his flashlight back there, he told us all to get out. While I was getting out, I managed to get one of the baggies out of my boot, and I threw it under Ron's car. I think it was a pot. I don't know about the rest of the baggies, but I was dragged into the Saanich Police Station, and I was stripped searched, and that is when the rest of the drugs fell out of my boot and onto the interrogation room floor. The female officer asked me, "What's this?" I said, "I don't know." Then she asked, "Well, how did it get in your boot?" I said, "We were at a party, and I guess someone put it in my boot at the party." Ron had told me, "I will lose my job with the Coast Guard if I get caught with drugs," when we were arguing back and forth about me taking the crap. I thought after I got caught with his drugs, whatever it was, if I told the cops who it really was, who knows what Ron and all his crazy friends would do to me then. They ended up fingerprinting me and taking my picture. Before I left, they told me I had to do eighty hours of community work for the so-called offence, which the Saanich pigs set up especially for me.

I was at the Surf Side one night when a guy named Gary came up to my table and said, "I heard you are looking for a car." I remembered meeting Gary at a big pig roast on a farm past my parents' house on Burnside Road, just after Steve, my ex-husband, and I split up. This guy who put it on was a rare acquaintance of Steve's, and it was his grandmother's farm. Although Gary himself was not a biker as far as I know, it was a biker party, but I didn't realize it then. I just thought it was a bunch of guys on motorcycles, no big deal. At the time I met Gary, I remember him saying he was married and had a little boy, and I thought to myself Too bad, because you are really good looking. " Anyway, when I asked Gary how he heard I was looking for a car, I believe the conversation after that went something like this: I said, "How do you know that?" and he said, "Word gets around." To that I replied, "Yes, I guess it does." After that, he asked me, "What type of car are you looking for?" and I said I didn't really know. He told me he had a friend, Butch, who bought old cars and fixed them up, and he had a shop at his home where he did this, and he could take me there if I wanted. Butch also owned the race track out in Langford at the time, "Western Speedway" (now gone). I was fed up with the car I had, the little, white Toyota Corolla, and so I said, "Sure." We started a three-month relationship, and I thought that because he had been married before and had a kid, he couldn't be that bad. However, he hooked me up with someone who sold me a real lemon, an old 1966 white two-door Beaumont with a 327 stick shift, newly painted to hide all the rust, which was unknown to me at the time, but I think Gary knew it was a rust bucket. I thought I had a good deal because I think I only paid one thousand dollars for it, and they told me that it would soon be a collector's item. I saw some of the old cars Butch restored when I went to his house because there were a few of them in his yard when I went there, so I believed this guy knew what he was doing and what he was talking about. I am into old cars, always have been. Well, Gary was living in an apartment in Esquimalt on the corner of Admirals and Esquimalt Road. Gary said he was living in Vancouver but had split up with his wife and was now living over here, taking a Psychology course. I guess I was the subject of his study. He would invite me over to his apartment all the time and make me exotic meals, and we would get high on dope. One night, he gave me a soup to start my meal with, and he wouldn't tell me what kind it was. He kept laughing and saying, "Just taste it, you'll like it." It tasted a bit like pea soup; it was good. After I ate it, Gary told me what it was: turtle soup. He also taught me how to reupholster an old overstuffed chair, and he told me I could have it when we were finished with it, but I never had the opportunity to take it. We used some gold velvet material, which I picked up at a thrift shop, and used the old material from the chair as a pattern. It wasn't as hard as you think. One late night, I was going to his house in my Beaumont, and I rounded this corner, and the roads were all icy when I landed at a bus stop. Luckily, I didn't hit anyone, but if I had done damage to my car that night, I might have found out what a mess it really was and been able to confront the perpetrators with it. At Christmas, Gary bought me a gold necklace with a diamond in it, and I was going to get it engraved, but we never went out long enough. He also bought me a sweater with nice Indian designs on it. Gary introduced me to a friend of his who just happened to be managing the apartment building where he was living. Because I still had to do community hours for that bogus bust the Saanich pigs set up for me, this manager wrote me a letter to give to the pigs explaining I had painted some of the apartments in the building he managed for my community work. Well, all those drugs weren't mine anyway, so I never felt guilty about not doing the community work this guy said I did. This so-called manager of the apartment block was also a teacher at the William Head Prison outside of Victoria in Metchosin, where he said he taught the inmates there the GED. He said he had all the books for it. I told him I didn't have my grade twelve, but I finished grade ten academic. He offered to tutor me for free, so I took him up on this offer. One day, I went over to the apartments for a Tudor session, and my Tudor, Gary's so-called friend, told me that Gary had gone back to his wife in Vancouver. Man, I was ticked then. I never saw either of them again after that. It was about a year later before I got my GED.

I then landed a job as a waitress at the Surf Side through a redhead I met while hanging out there all the time, who got me the job as she started working there too. I wasn't getting many hours at the hospital due to my permanent part-time position in the late afternoons at the Veterans' Hospital, and I thought I might as well work there since I was always there anyway. I wanted to make enough money so I could get the Hell out of Victoria, even if it was only for a holiday. That is when I found out it was owned by one of the Bounty Hunters, a motorcycle gang in Victoria. I only worked there for three nights, and despite making a whole mitt full of tips, it just wasn't worth the aggravation. I'd take an order from the people who didn't have a table, and when I went back to serve them, they were gone. I was stuck with their drinks. And you were allowed to drink the stuff. By the end of the first night working there, I was hammered. Some of the customers would pinch your ass, and I didn't like that either, so I quit. I never realized it then, but the Bounty Hunters were closing in on me, and I was lucky I got out of Victoria when I did.

After Gary took off on me and left me high and dry, I met up with real partyers; Lebor was one of them. This one screwed up broad introduced me to him, Margaret. I knew her from the Red Lion Pub, and she always seemed to be everywhere I hung out, at parties included. She was popular with the guys. Robin's best friend, John, went out with her for a while, and she also went out with my third cousin, Larry, along with numerous other guys from the crowds that frequent the bars and nightclubs I went to. At this time, she was engaged to a guy by the name of Andy, whose brother, Jerry, went out with Patty, my old roommate, and they broke off just before I moved in with Patty. Anyway, Lebor told me that he just broke off an engagement with his childhood sweetheart. He mentioned that if I ever needed work done on my car, he would do it; just come down to Midas's Muffler on Douglas Street, where he was working at the time. I took him up on the offer because my car needed a muffler shortly after I met him. He had a Silver Anniversary Corvette, and while I was waiting for Lebor to fix my car, he allowed me to drive it up and down Douglas Street. He lived in Sooke, and he came to Canada when he was twelve. He was Czechoslovakian. When we first met, he seemed responsible enough, and he was very respectful to me. About a month into the relationship, he took me out to Sooke to meet his parents, and that was when he told me he had over seventy-five points on his license, all for speeding. It was very costly for car insurance, which he owed money for, and he was in debt for the whole amount of the car. However, he was always respectful to me while I was with him in his car. He never drove fast. He would even open the car door for me to get in all the time. And every time we went out, he paid. He wanted to marry me within a month of our courting, and of course, I refused because I didn't know him well enough yet, and what I did know, I was starting to not like. He ended up moving into town and living in an apartment on Pandora Street with a friend. I was over there one night, having a few drinks and tokes, when his roommate came home. I never saw this guy before. Apparently, his wife had given him the boot, and he couldn't accept it. He was in the bathroom for a long time, so Lebor went in to check on him, and I followed. There was blood everywhere, on the walls, on the mirrors, on the floor. This guy had slit his wrists. I couldn't believe it. It really freaked me out. I took him to the Jubilee Hospital, which was only a few minutes away, and they told us that if he had died on the way to the hospital, I would have been held responsible because I drove him there. We should have called an ambulance. I had to replace the new blue carpet, which I had just put in my car, because there was blood all over my car, too. Lebor told me later that his friend was doing acid. I had been going out with Lebor for about three months by this time. I broke it off after this happened, as I realized that Lebor was pretty off the wall himself, snorting cocaine all the time, too.

Shortly after this, I met sweet and innocent Kathy again. She befriended me in the Red Lion Bar one night, sitting right beside me. I couldn't help but notice she was by herself. So we started talking, and in her first sentence, she told me she was only sixteen. She looked a lot older than that, but still not old enough to get away with being in the bar. Boy, our system is in trouble. She was looking for a ride home, and she told me she was going to hitch-hike alone if she had to. It was how she got to the Red Lion. I didn't want her to hitch-hike, so because she lived only a little way down the Island Highway in a trailer park with her parents, ten minutes or so past my house, I offered her a lift. On the way there, she told me she was scared to hitch-hike, really, because she had been raped and the guy who did it was getting out of jail soon. I said, "What the Hell are you doing hitchhiking then?" She didn't answer me. She described in vivid detail what had happened to her and how she was with another girl, and they both got away after being raped, then tied up. When she talked about it, she acted like it was no big deal, though. I suppose I felt sorry for the kid and responsible for her, which was the whole idea. I told her if she needed a ride, I would give her one. After that night, I saw her everywhere Darlene, Diane, and I went, so Darlene started asking her to come out with us to smoke dope. Kathy talked me into taking a self-improvement course with her. She brought out her artwork of the pictures of people that she had drawn when I dropped her off at home one night, and she was a pretty good artist. I was impressed. All the pictures she had drawn were of women with outfits that she had designed herself. Kathy wanted to be a clothing designer. I admired her ambition to make something out of her life at such a young age, so I agreed to take this course with her, picking her up at her place all the time to go to it. The academy was on Cloverdale just before Quadra. She was the last child out of a whole slew of kids, ten or more, one almost twenty years older than she was. Kathy was the only one left living at home. She probably came from a Catholic family. I mentioned this

Self-Improvement course to some of the girls with whom I worked, telling them it was also a course to prepare you for modelling, and that to graduate from it, you needed to get a portfolio made up of your own. One day at work, a building maintenance guy, I can't remember his name, approached me and, in our chat, he said he was going to university. I asked him, "Oh, what are you taking?" and he said, "Photography." I told him I needed to get a portfolio done for this Self-Improvement course I was taking, and he said he would do it for me. It would be good practice, but he only knew how to do black and white photographs. I was never into being a model, but I remembered my aunt Carol's words and how she kept telling me I should be one, so I thought this would be a good opportunity to look into it. But really, I just took the course for Kathy's sake more than anything else. I agreed to have this colleague take the pictures of me for my portfolio, and we made arrangements to meet at Beacon Hill Park. There, he took all kinds of pictures of me in different places all over the park. But I never ended up finishing the program because they had us put on a fashion show, in which you had to participate to get your certificate, and I just couldn't strut my stuff down the aisle in front of a crowd. I knew then that being a model wasn't for me.

I soon found out Kathy would sleep with everyone in sight. She had a hard time finding a decent boyfriend, too. They always seemed to dump her after they got what they wanted, and along with feeling sorry for myself, I felt sorry for her, too. But I thought at least I had John with no last name. He would phone my parents' house and ask me where the girls and I would be going that night. It would almost always be the Surf Side. John would show up and buy me drinks, and he would give me a little bag of real potent pot sometimes. Once out of the blue, he bought me a rust-colored leather vest. It was in the early summer when I got the phone call from him after meeting him for the first time at Karen's, months previous to this. He started taking me water skiing at Shawangan

Lake all the time when I wasn't working at the hospital. I caught onto water skiing right away, always getting out of the water immediately, and soon I was skiing on one ski, crossing over the wake. I went to his house on Whistler Mountain to go snow skiing too. I told my mother about it, and she said, "Well, make sure Kathy or someone goes with you." So John invited Kathy to come too. He had this beautiful A-frame house about a block away from the mountain, and I couldn't help but ask him on the occasion what he did for a living. And his answer was always the same: "I water ski in the summer and snow ski in the winter." At first, when John was in Victoria, he would stay at a friend's called BO, but eventually I would stay with him in his motel room when he came over to visit me, and sometimes he would take me out for breakfast in the mornings. Before this, when John was staying in Vancouver, I thought that because our relationship was so casual on his part, it wasn't going to stop me from going out with other people. Our relationship went on and off for a few months, short of a year, and one time, he just stopped calling me. By this point, I was starting to feel like he was nothing but a "Sugar Daddy." Anyway, it was time to move on and out of the one messed-up town of Victoria and straighten myself out. I guess John, with no last name, disappeared because the plans for our camping trip were all set. Before we left on the trip, Kathy and I went on a blind date with two fishermen. I forget who hooked us up with these people, but they had a lot of money, and they took us out for dinner at the High Steak House. I had only been there one other time, and that was when I first started going out with Robin. They ordered us all this expensive wine to drink when they were already half cut after we met them there. They acted like a couple of pissed up fools throughout dinner, so Kathy and I dumped them after we finished our meal. We planned to meet them at the Surf Side Cabaret, but we didn't go there; we went to some other nightclub instead, and that was the end of those idiots. Kathy said she wanted to get out of this town, too, and live somewhere else, but when push came to shove, she jammed out, and that is because she was just one big setup, which I had no clue about at the time. We planned this trip together, camping in the Interior of British Columbia in July of 1979. We planned it a few months after I took my GED. I still had the books; the guy never asked for them back, so I studied from them, and I finally took the exam and passed in April 1979. It was the start of a new life, I thought. We took Kathy's brand-new Camaro for the trip that she said she bought with the compensation money for the guy raping her. I think, though, she got it for the guy she was going to hook me up with on our camping trip, whose plan was to rape me.

Early summer, on a hot afternoon during the week, just before our camping trip, Kathy and I decided we would go to Beaver Lake, which is one of the two big lakes off the Pat Bay Highway heading towards BC Ferries. We wanted to go somewhere quiet and sunbathe on the beach, at least I did anyway. We were heading down this one-way dirt road leading to the lake, and out of the bush pops this guy in a long trench coat, and he stood right in front of the car. Kathy slammed on the brakes to avoid hitting him. He opened up his coat, and he didn't have anything on underneath, and then he started to masturbate. We both took off our sunglasses, and I immediately locked my car door, as did Kathy. We couldn't believe what we were seeing. At least I couldn't. He wasn't there long when he took off back into the bush somewhere. We drove to the lake to turn around because there was nowhere to turn around on this dirt road. I was freaked out because I thought we were going to have another encounter with this nut case, and this time, who knows what he might do next. I mentioned we should report this to the police, but Kathy said she was afraid to in case this guy would find out who reported him and come after us, so we didn't. This had to be another prank just to make sure I wouldn't change my mind about wanting to get the Hell out of Victoria, and of course, it worked. I had mentioned many times to Kathy and to others that I was getting sick and tired of men, and I wanted to move out of this screwed up city, and when asked where I'd like to live, I said, "Maybe the Okanogan." By this time, I was getting pretty messed up too, and knew I had to do something better with my life. Little did I know I was being stalked and had been since I was about eight years old or maybe even younger.

CHAPTER SIX

My auntie Carol was coming over to my mother's house, still crying on my mother's shoulder, about how her drunken husband Gordie was never home, and she thought he was having an affair. Every chance she got, she continued to tell me I should be a model. By this time, my righteous cousin Raymond Bradford, my aunt Mary's only child, was now a Royal Canadian Mounted Police officer. That was his promotion for having the shit scared out of me, no doubt. I recall going over to my grandparents' for Christmas dinner that year, and he came over dressed in the traditional Royal Canadian Mounted Police uniform. My grandparents made such a fuss over him that it made me sick. My mother's siblings never included my parents nor any of our family in any of the conversations that took place, other than when they got the thrill of asking, "Kimberley, how's your gut? "So, after that Christmas, I refused to go over there anymore. My crazy grandfather was still around, harassing my family, coming over to our house as soon as he saw my Dad coming home from work. I remember when I was twenty, after I left my abusive husband, Steve, I said I was going to get my driver's license, and Gramps said, "Oh, you'll never get it." Well, he was wrong about that, the old fart.

Kathy Stoal and I went on holiday to the Interior of British. Columbia, and the first place we camped was a campsite in Penticton. There was partying going on everywhere, and the people who were camped beside us were really loud. I hadn't talked to Ron since we got pulled over that night by the cops, and out of the blue, there he was with his new East Indian girlfriend. I saw them together in the Red Lion Bar a couple of times. When I saw the two of them at the campsite, I was going to say hi to them, but Ron gave me a really dirty look and kept walking. I guess that was part of the plan to make sure I would leave the campsite. Kathy mentioned that she had a hard time sleeping that night, so we both agreed to find somewhere else to camp. She suggested going to Kelowna because Penticton was known for being a party town, and she knew I was trying to get out of doing that, so we drove until we got to Kelowna. We already set up the tent, and Kathy was sitting at the picnic table rolling a joint when this Ranchero pulled up beside our campsite and dumped two guys out of it and then sped off. It didn't take them long to come over to our table and introduce themselves. We smoked a couple of joints with them. They had some dope, too. They said their names were Mick and John, and they were from Preston, Lancashire, England, and had been hitchhiking all over the United States for the last couple of months. John said he used to be employed with the Merchant Navy back in Britain and worked in the engine room on the ship he was on. He had been to many different places, like Singapore and Australia. Once, he skipped ship to be with a girl in Detroit, and he lived there with her for three months before the relationship ended; he then went back home to England. He worked in a factory making cars in Detroit, and made lots of money doing that. They were both on their way to John's relatives who lived in Alberta because, apparently, they were going to run out of money soon. Kathy and I were intrigued by their accents and what they had to say about their travels. We had never met foreigners before, at least I hadn't. We talked for a while, and then we decided we would go into Kelowna and look for a pub or a nightclub to do some dancing, preferably a pub because it would be cheaper for everyone. We found a pub that had a DJ playing modern music, so we stayed there until closing. I was dancing with Mick when John took over. When we got back to the campsite, it was pouring with rain, and they said that their tent fell out of the back of the Ranchero. Sometimes they have wicked thunder and lightning storms in the summer in the Interior, and we were having one of them then. They wanted to sleep in our tent so they wouldn't get soaking wet, but I didn't like the idea at all. I said, "These storms in the summer up here never last too long." But finally, Kathy and I broke down because the rain wasn't stopping. I told them they could, but they would have to sleep at the bottom of the tent. So, the two of them started off there. However, in the middle of the night, they both worked their way up beside us. John started to rape me. I told him, "I hardly know you." When I said, "I could have some kind of sexually transmitted disease," I thought that would stop him, but he just said, "I don't care," and continued to rape me. By this time, I was so used to this kind of behaviour that I had no idea, or I never thought I was being raped. I kept pushing John off of me and saying "**NO**," but he was too strong, and then he told me, "You like it." I looked over to where Kathy was, and I could see Mick had worked his way over to Kathy, and they were going at it. The next morning, when I woke up, John was sitting by the lake looking at the sunrise, and I went up to him to tell him off for what he had done to me because I was getting sick of being taken advantage of. But he started to ask me if I wanted to go back to England with him for a holiday. He said he had a van which he started to fix up, and we would travel the continent in it. I was dying to get out of the hellhole of a town I was living in, and I thought to myself, I might as well get something good out of the ordeal of being taken advantage of all the time. Just to put the icing on the cake, John also showed me a letter he had from a former employer in Preston, Lancashire, England, explaining he was a hard worker (just like my Dad was). He could go on holiday whenever he wanted, and he would still have a job waiting for him whenever he returned from his travels, and it was signed. He sure impressed me because everyone else that I had a relationship with never did anything much with their lives, and none of them seemed to work on a regular basis, probably because they were too into parting their lives away. I had mentioned I always wanted to travel in Europe when I found out where they were from. I know I had expressed that dream to Kathy, and she always thought it would be something she would like to do too. Of course, they would have to come to the Island first to meet my parents and to see where I lived. Kathy put Victoria in the lights, making it appear she was convincing them both to come because they said their plans were to go to Alberta. I must say I helped butter the Hell hole up, too, because I was so excited about what I thought was an opportunity of a lifetime. We finished our camping trip with them at the same site, then left for Victoria, taking John and Mick with us when we left. As soon as we got back to Victoria, I invited them all into my parents' place so the two of them could meet them and vice versa. My Dad just had another operation, taking some of his intestines out, and was having trouble with the incision, which was held together with these mucky big staples. It kept ripping open. I guess that evil Turd and all his evil doctor buddies wanted my Dad to bleed to death. Anyway, I knew my parents wouldn't allow John to stay at our house. I didn't even ask them because I knew what they were going to say, and I didn't blame them. I said to my parents that they planned to stay in Victoria for a while, and we were going to take them to the Thetis Lake campsite to set up camp. Kathy and I made arrangements to take them around town to see the sights. We took them to some of the bars and introduced them to Darlene and Diane before Nick left for Hawaii. Funny, when I think of it now, they were supposed to be running out of money. All this goes to show you just how gullible young children and young adults are. One night, John and I went to the Juan DE Fuca Arena in Colwood because they were having a big dance there. We stayed to the end, and when we came out, to my white Beaumont, someone had thrown a big boulder through my front window shield. That is when I found out it was nothing but a rust bucket. It was almost hollow throughout the roof. I got it fixed, but that made me make up my mind that I was going to get a plane ticket to England and get the Hell out of here. Good final touch. They must have known I didn't have any money to go travelling, but if I sold the Beaumont,

I would. Deep down, I couldn't stand seeing my Dad sick, and I felt helpless not only in my situation but in his as well. I asked Kathy if she wanted to come with me, but she just got a job at the Toronto Dominion Bank as a teller, so she said she wouldn't be able to get the time off work. Another gift? John eventually started having problems with his leg, which was all infected. He said he had been in a motorcycle accident before he came to North America, and his leg got pretty mangled. He also had internal injuries in this accident. His brother David was hit on his bike in the same accident. He was behind John, who was on his bike, but David only broke his arm. Someone in a car was stopped at a stop sign and just pulled out of nowhere and hit them both. They were apparently, only going around thirty miles per hour down a country road. You could see it was a pretty bad infection because there was this red line going up his entire leg, and there was pus around the big bump of a bone that was now almost sticking out of his leg. I mentioned this to my parents, and they said, "Well, he is not staying here." "We hardly know him." I remember John being pissed off about that. They wanted to do an operation on his leg right away, but when all my so-called friends finally talked him into going to the hospital to get it looked at, John said he would go home and deal with it there. John phoned his parents from a phone booth to tell them he had met a girl and he was bringing her back with him. In the meantime, I tried to get a three month leave of absence from my job but the Dietitian from Memorial, old, crooked eye Miss Stevens, along with Dr Turd who set me up with Robin wouldn't allow me to have one even though I was only two weeks short two years which was needed for a leave of absence if you wanted to travel. I ended up quitting my job because some of my fellow employees had me convinced they would hire me back. I applied for a work visa and passport, and I remember it only taking a few days to come. The passport was stamped with a six-month work visa, too. Which was longer than I asked for. I couldn't get a plane ticket to fly to England with John, so I left three weeks after he did, at the end of September 1979. I had only known him for not quite two months, and my parents were worried about me going over there. My Dad gave me the name and address of his aunt, my great aunt Lilly, who was my Dad's mother's sister. She was living in Birmingham, England, and Dad said I was to look her up if John wasn't at the airport to meet me. Dad also said, "I give you three weeks and you will be back kissing the Canadian soil." I had to give the airline three weeks' notice before I could fly back home once I arrived. Well, when I came back, I did want to kiss the ground, but now, I could gag over that comment.

It wasn't until I was on the plane that I wondered if I was doing the right thing or not. I was pretty scared about travelling so far away from home and landing at one of the largest airports in the world, Heathrow Airport. I noticed right away that everything was so different. There were many signs of foreign languages, and there were so many people all walking and crowded together like sardines in a tin can, it was hard to tell if you were going the right way or not. It took about one hour of walking before I finally got to where my luggage was. After I retrieved my luggage, it was about another hour before I finally spotted John in the crowds on the side of the walkway, which was roped off. I was so glad to see him then. As soon as we spoke, I told him I had to go to the bathroom, so we found a lounge right away. You needed to pay to use it, but John told me to slide underneath the door, so I did. I hadn't exchanged my money yet. When I went to flush the toilet, I couldn't find the handle, and when I looked up, I saw a string dangling above me. I pulled it, and it flushed the toilet. The toilet paper was like wax paper. I thought of my poor mother then. We stopped and saw the sights in London, like Buckingham Palace and Big Ben, and of course, we went to half a dozen pubs that day. I remember being freaked out while standing in front of Big Ben because there were hundreds and hundreds of pigeons flying around, and lots sitting on the cobblestone walkway, and many of them were trying to come and perch on my shoulders. John knew someone living on the outskirts of London, so we stayed the night there, then left to go to John's parents' place, where he was living the next morning. Because of the length of time it took me to get there (eight hours) and the time change (eight hours), it took a few days before I caught up on my sleep. All the houses looked like townhouses, masses of them everywhere in the city and in the small towns we passed through. They called them flats. If you owned a detached house, you were filthy rich; you just didn't see them. It took us about three hours to drive to where John was from in Lostock Hall, Lancaster, Preston England, a town of colleges. I was surprised to see so much barren countryside and rolling green hills off the motorway because I knew there were almost as many people living in London alone as there were in the whole of Canada. In an odd place, you would see a detached house in the middle of a field, but for the most part, I wondered where all the people were. It was weird driving on the other side of the road. John picked me up in his big, maroon American car, which you just didn't see over there, because he said he wanted to make me feel at home.

John's sister, Margaret, was married to Collin, who had been John's best friend for years. Before I came over, and John was visiting Victoria, he told me I looked something like his sister, and after I met her, I realized I did look like her. We were around the same age, too. Margaret and Collin didn't have any children even though they had been married for about five years. They lived in a house considered upper class, semi-detached on a cul-de-sac about ten minutes away from John's Mom and Dad's place. It was bigger and much nicer than his parents. John's parents owned a flat, which was the second-to-last flat in a row of about ten flats. Margaret and Collin actually had a backyard, unlike most, who only had a very small square patch, and they all seemed to be fenced in. Collin worked on planes for a living, and he was into racing motorcycles in his spare time and had loads of trophies for doing so in the attached garage of their home. Collin had so many that he had to put some of them in the living room. John also had a younger brother, David, who was still living at home with his parents. David was attending college to become an engineer. The flat his parents owned was like a miniature three-bedroom townhouse, with all the bedrooms being upstairs, where the only suitable bathroom was. They had central heating. Some folks didn't have central heating because, apparently, it was expensive to have it put in, so they would heat their house with a coal fireplace, which was in their living room. There were doors to all the rooms in the flats, and they'd only heat the room they were in, so if you were to go into another room, you would hurry up and do what you had to do because you'd be freezing your ass off. The heat itself was expensive, too. I also found out some of the flats still had an outhouse attached to their residence, and you would have to go outside and use it because they had nothing else. And you'd pay by the minute when talking on the phone, so you would waste no time chit-chatting on the phone. John's mother used to hang all the clothes she washed all over the house to dry in the winter to save money. She didn't have a dryer; the poor thing—only this old two-barrel washer. On one side, it would wash the clothes, and on the other side, it would wring them out. They had some nice paintings hanging on the walls in their living room. John picked them up for them while in port at various places he went to when he was employed with the Merchant Navy. He worked in the engine room. I slept in Margaret's old bedroom, which was only big enough for a single bed, and that was it. John stayed in a bedroom with his brother. In their room, John's old motorbike, which he had been in an accident with, was strung up all over the bedroom walls in parts, and it was only big enough for two single beds. David was rebuilding John's motorcycle, made up of Norton and Triumph parts, which he was getting chromed. That's what David did in his spare time. They had closets with drawers in them, so there was no need for dressers. Besides, there was no room at all.

   John's Dad, Jack, was brought up Protestant. He worked for Leyland Motors, just outside of Lostock Hall, driving a truck that delivered greeting cards mostly. None of John's family ever had to buy them. Sometimes John's Dad would come home from work with batteries from vehicles. He said he was permitted to take all the stuff he used to go home with. David and John would sell these batteries and keep the money. John's father's Dad was still alive, but his mother wasn't. Jack had a sister he never saw, probably because of religious reasons, but Jack never elaborated when it came to his family. When the war was going on, Jack worked on a farm so he didn't have to go to war. That was the way it was over there; if you worked on a farm, you didn't have to go to war. For most of John's childhood, he lived on this farm. When I was staying with their family, Jack took me to the butcher's, where they got their meat all the time, to show me how they butchered it up. I suppose he wanted to feel educated or important, or who knows, now.

   Francis, John's mother, was brought up a strict Catholic and worked at a slipper factory sewing them. She had a sister whose entire family lived on a farm with their mother. Francis told me that her father had died a long time ago, but she never elaborated on that either. No one has to tell me what most likely happened to him. Francis liked to pretend that her relatives got along with her family, but really, I believe they despised Francis for betraying the Catholic Church when she married Jack. I figured that one out while I was over there. Francis bad-mouthed her sister all the time, saying she was "mooching off of their mother living on the farm with her for all of her married life," as she put it. I guess she was afraid she was going to be left out of the Will, as money-hungry as she was. John and his siblings were forced to attend a Catholic church growing up. I suppose Francis didn't feel she had betrayed the church after all; God forgives, no matter what is one's philosophy. She told me she would tie John up after she got him dressed so she could get the other children ready before she took them to the local Catholic church. She said she wanted to keep him clean. Of course, Jack never went with them. She still attended church faithfully every Sunday while I was over there, righteous as she was. She'd get happy at the Legion with Jack John's Dad every weekend, however. There were many accidents in John's life. Growing up as a child, he used to help his mother deliver milk bottles to various houses. One time, he fell over something in his walkway while carrying a bunch of milk bottles and sliced his hand from the thumb down. He has a fair-sized scar from that. Another time, he was at a farm and someone let a bull out of the barn, and it chased him. John jumped over a barbed wire fence to get away from it and ripped his chest open. He has a big scar about six inches long from that. Now looking back, he was the Devil's child, too, and I believe his mother's sibling may have had something to do with all the so-called accidents he had while John was residing over there. His mother most likely wanted him safe at any cost, and with John being in the Merchant Navy at one time, he was able to figure out just where he wanted to live. So, both evil governments and our families got together and devised a plan to reunite the two of us. After all, they had to keep killing the likes of us off with their sexually transmitted diseases. John was highly qualified in his trades as a diesel mechanic and welder, and good at his work. He started his apprenticeship at the age of fifteen. I also believe now, if you were brought up Catholic and you were a tradesman or the likes, the Canadian Government would recruit you over to our country, thinking we would prosper as a Catholic Nation. The evil British Government just wanted him the Hell out of their country because he was, yes, "the Devil's child." They thought they were both doing each other a favour. Well, look at all the Italians who came over to Canada (the land of free opportunities for all), Gag! when my Dad left the army, and tried to find a job. I say this because I know my mother's younger sister, my aunt Carol, and the Victoria City police officer who lived across the street from my parents' house, Dale, helped bring John over here. That was one of the first things I was told about on my computer when it was hacked in the year 2000.

Anyway, John was collecting unemployment, also known as the dole, while waiting for an operation on his leg. He showed me the farm where he was brought up, and just across the way was a big pond; he said he used to play in it all the time. The schoolhouse where he did all his schooling till he quit and started his trades was only a small, one-room building. It all reminded me of how my mother was brought up, which I always thought was just in the, "olden days." No sooner had I arrived than John's mother was on my case, trying to get me to find a job by looking in their local paper and pointing them all out to me. I asked John if she wanted me to pay for the room and board, and he told me not to worry about it. I could tell John's mother really didn't like me staying with them for free. As a matter of fact, I got the feeling right away she didn't like me much at all, and I picked up on it when I showed her the portfolio from that Self Improvement course I took with Kathy. I brought it along because I thought if worst came to worst, maybe I could get a job modelling. After all, Europe was and still is known to have all the successful models and lots of them. When I showed my portfolio to Francis, she got this disgusted look on her face. I also remember when I was telling her about being married before and divorced, her face looked kind of stern, like she disapproved of that. I got her hint and found a job within three weeks of my arrival. I managed to get a job at a place called Mansfield Shoes. At first, I was stocking the shelves, and then they started to allow me to sell their goods. I worked with a girl who was always dressed in the fifties; you know, the big crinoline skirts and the white Bobbie socks. They called these people Teddy Bears.

Her boyfriend looked like Elvis with the flashy clothes and black, slicked-back hair, etc.. It seemed like they had names for all the people who looked out of the ordinary, like Skin Heads and Punk Rockers, when over here, they didn't so much. By this time, John had the operation on his leg, and they put a plaster (cast) on it, and I couldn't understand why they would do such a thing because it was an open incision, and the wound needed to breathe. Shortly after, they took the plaster off because, like I thought it would, it got infected. Soon, Halloween came around. They called it Guy Fox Day, and of course, England is where Halloween originated. Only a few people put turnips in their window, which would indicate they celebrated it, but most didn't allow kids to their door, and John's parents were no exception. One kid came to John's parents' door saying, "Penny for the Guy?" and John's mother asked the kid in an angry voice, "Does your mother know that you are out mooching?" and then she gave him a ten pence. If they do celebrate it, they give money, not candy. There were only a few fireworks going on here and there; it was nothing like they have here. They had mostly firecrackers. We didn't live with John's parents very long. I never had the opportunity to offer them any rent because after three weeks, there was a blow-up, and John and I both moved out. I hadn't even had a paycheck yet. One day, his Mom and Dad went out somewhere, and when they came back, the door was locked. They are so trusting over there that everyone leaves their door unlocked. I don't think so. But they did apparently, because John and I were upstairs, and I was trying to get ready to go out for the evening, and John kept trying to seduce me. When I went downstairs to get a needle and thread to sew the jacket I had decided I wanted to wear, I noticed that both of John's parents were home and sitting in the living room, as if something was up. I said "hi" to them, then carried on into the kitchen. They said to me that they wanted to talk to me, so I went into the living room to see what they wanted to talk about. John's Dad asked me, "Why was the door locked?" and I said, "John must have locked it,

I guess." Then they said, "We won't have that kind of nonsense going on under our roof." I told them nothing was going on, but they said, "What you do when you're not under this roof is your business, just respect our wishes." I was so upset that I went upstairs crying. John asked me what was wrong, and I told him the conversation I had with his parents, so he went down and gave his parents Hell. We left that night and stayed in his car. Then we stayed with Mick for a short time, who lived with his grandmother in a suite above her flat. After that, we moved into one of John's drinking acquaintances' two-bedroom apartments. It was low-cost housing right in the middle of Preston. It was on the fourteenth floor of this concrete building, and most of the time, I had to walk up the stairs because the elevator never worked. The bloke's name was Ned and he had just split up with his wife. He didn't have a stick of furniture, and he had a big dog that stayed in the living room in his apartment. It was totally disgusting; there was animal feces all over the place, but there just wasn't anywhere else to live. The rumour was that people came from all over to attend the colleges in Preston. Housing was hard to find, apparently. We managed to find a bed for ourselves right after we moved in, and I'll never forget washing the floor over and over again to try and clean it and laying a rug down on this cold, cement floor. I would trip over the corner of the rug sometimes, and a puff of shit would come flying into the air, so I would take the rug up and wash the floor all over again. Ned kept the dog out on the balcony for a short time, but I told him it was cruel to the animal, so he eventually found a good home for his big dog. I wouldn't have it in the apartment, pissing and shitting all over the place. For a long time, all we had was a bed and a rug. It was November when we moved in, and it was so damn cold in there. The heating never worked, but it had piped-in music. Thinking about it now, that was weird, piped-in music. John and I went to bed with layers of clothing on and large plastic pop bottles filled with fairly hot water to keep warm. One time, I got really sick with the flu and a cold, and John's mother sent her favourite son, David, over to see if I was all right. But I knew if she was that concerned, why didn't she come over herself? By this time, John had to have another operation on his leg because his leg had developed gangrene. He was still collecting the dole, and after the second operation on his leg, he started working at Sutcliff's Transport too, training a young mechanic apprentice. I kept working at Mansfield Shoes, so I was able to buy all the kitchenware we needed because there was nothing in this place. Ned literally had nothing but a bed, too. I chipped in on some furniture eventually. Right away, John mentioned he wanted to buy our own place because "This place is such a dump," he would always say. After work, John went out drinking. He said it was the way of life there, having a couple of pints after a hard day's work. I soon questioned myself as to what I had done living so far from home with someone who was never home. Ned was always out with his friends doing the same thing. One time, John was gone the whole weekend. I phoned the airline to make reservations to go back home, but then put the phone down because I thought I had come all this way and it wasn't going to be for nothing. We hadn't really been anywhere yet. I was bound and determined I was going to do some kind of travelling before I left. I had come so far, and it cost me a lot of money. Besides, I was too scared to go home. I remember crying and crying that weekend. John used to tell me to go to the pubs by myself. He said, "All the women do it here and no one thinks anything of it." But there was no way I was going to do that. I mean, he told me once the famous Yorkshire Ripper got his first victim behind a nightclub called, "Clouds" in the alley you could see from the window in the living room of this apartment we were living in. One time, I was looking out the living room window, and all this soapy water and clothes came flying down. I guess they were throwing the water out, they had hand-washed some clothes in, and the clothes accidentally went with it. No sooner did we get everything we needed for the apartment than it wasn't good enough. John bought his own place. I wanted to go to the continent, travelling instead, but he started using his leg as an excuse not to. He bought the flat to get his money's worth out of me, just in case things never worked out for him in Canada.

 John would take me to various bars and nightclubs in Preston, we went to a concert in Preston, too, and one big one near London. You could walk to ten different pubs on one block. No one drove anywhere much; everything you needed was within walking distance. Stocking up on food wasn't heard of because there was no place to store it. People went to the store every day to get what they needed to eat for a day or two. No one would take lunches to work because it was just as cheap to eat at a cafe or pub as it was to make their own lunch. They even had pubs where you could bring your children. Playgrounds were set up for them in a small courtyard with tables so you could keep your eyes on them. Some people would go to the pub for a nip in their lunch hour, and no one thought anything about it. John took me to a wine lodge and he bought me some wine, which I had in a little shot glass, and even though I only had two of them, I was hammered. It was Australian wine, kept in large barrels behind the bar, hanging on the wall, all in a row. A couple of times, I went with Jeff, the son of the owner, who worked with John. Jeff was a good friend of John's, so he took me to various places in his semi-truck or what they called, a Laurie. He took me to Leeds and told me the Yorkshire Ripper got another one of his victims there. John and I went to Blackpool, which was only about half an hour away. They had a procession of lights, "Blackpool Illuminations" all year round, but when we got there one night, it was closing, so I didn't get to see all of them. Another time, we went there because they had a big fairground going on, and it was all year round too. There were lots of little shops on the causeway alongside the ocean, which I was interested in going to, but John was only interested in taking me on a wild ride and to pubs while we were there, so I never got much shopping done. He took me on a ride that required climbing a big bunch of stairs. I hated rides, and I didn't want to go on it, but John dragged me up the stairs and made me go on it. It was like a big wheel which had double seats all around it, and the wheel went forward with great speed, then it went backwards with the same speed, and I thought it would never end. I felt like getting sick afterwards. That was the first and last time I ever went on such a ride. Another time, he talked me into going to what was called the "Trough" for a motorbike ride with his brother-in-law, Collin. They both went full speed for about half an hour, non-stop, around very twisted roads that were narrow enough for only one small vehicle. Sheep were crossing over the road, and I was banging frantically on John's back to stop. When he finally stopped, I couldn't stand up for about fifteen minutes. I sat down on the side of the dirt road, and that is when I noticed my shoes were all worn down from dragging when he went around the corners. On the way home, he did the same thing to me right through the middle of Preston all the way home. They were like two madmen. I never went on a bike with him again. Another time, we were coming back from watching Collin race his bike, and they coaxed me into driving the pig farmer's van back home. I remember going around and around this roundabout, missing the turn off a few times. I drove John's American car once while I was over there, too, and almost got into an accident with it after only going a couple of blocks. I was pretty afraid of driving over there, so I never did again after that. We visited the Lake District once for a weekend, about an hour's drive from Preston. It was a popular place for young people to go to in the summer, and of course, it was nothing but one big piss up.

People were drunk all over the walkways and stumbling around. There were mostly sailboats on the lakes, not many speed boats there, I noticed. Once we went to Liverpool for a weekend, and I saw where the Beatles started in this little tavern. In Liverpool, rows of flats all painted bright red, which resembled their favourite soccer team, lined the streets. Then, a block away, there were rows of flats painted blue. Soccer games would get very violent at times, so we never went to one. I saw the Thames River not too far away from this area, and it was really muddy and choppy, not appealing at all. I managed to visit my great aunt Lilly, too, while I was over there, because I had written her a letter before I left for England and told her I was coming. I wrote her another letter while I was living there to prepare her for the weekend we planned to see her. When we got to Birmingham, she had our rooms all made up for us with heated blankets and supper on the table, but we had already eaten. She immediately took us to her local pub, where she had all her children waiting for us. They were all managers of some big firm and had lots of money from the looks of things. As soon as great aunt Lilly came into the pub, everyone was saying, "Hi" to her. When we found her family and when she sat down, the waitress knew just what she drank and rushed it over to the table. Aunt Lilly threw down a shot of whiskey and then guzzled down a beer, and I was surprised to see such an old lady carry on the way she was. I guess they were all trying to impress us because they wouldn't allow John or me to buy any drinks, and before we left the pub, one of her sons gave me a necklace with a sterling silver locket on it as a gift. When I left, I asked my great aunt Lilly if she had any pictures of my grandfather, my Dad's, Dad, because Dad had asked me to ask her for some. The only one she said she had was a blown-up picture of my grandfather lying in his coffin, and I thought how morbid. I showed my mother this picture when I got back, and Mom thought it was morbid, too. Shocked, she said, "Don't show it to Dad," and I never did. One weekend, we went to Redding, just outside of London. John wanted to go to this heavy metal rock concert, which I didn't enjoy at all. That's the only type of music I was never into. Everyone was drinking and getting high on whatever. People were pissed up all over the place, and they had fires going, and they were falling into these fires. There were so many people that I was afraid I was going to get pushed into one of these fires, so I insisted we leave early. It was totally wild. The first concert I went to was in John's hometown of Preston, and that was as soon as I arrived. Pete Townsend and the Boomtown Rats, and it was in a small school auditorium. They were the only two concerts I went to while I was over there, and neither of them was any good.

My work visa soon expired, and I was pretty lonely all by myself in the apartment, so John took time off work and we took a trip for about a week in his pink pig farmer's van to the very Northern tip of the United Kingdom, as far as you can go, to a place called John O' Groats. When we got there, John said to me, "This is the closest you have been to your home." On our way there, we stopped at various places, and everywhere I went, I collected small, inexpensive souvenirs for my Mom and Dad. I didn't like the countryside in Scotland; it had too many tumbleweeds, and it was really brown and barren. We made a stop in Edinburgh to visit a castle there, (Edinburgh Castle). There was a guard standing at the door wearing the traditional outfit the English guards wear, and there was no way I could make him blink. I tried everything. Then, I forgot where we were, but we were travelling through this little village in Scotland in the middle of nowhere when we saw a whole group of people gathering at this ever-so-small train station, and vehicles parked everywhere along the country road. We wondered what could be going on? We pulled over to ask a bloke (dude) who was walking along the side of this dirt road we'd been travelling on, and he told us the Prince of Wales, Prince Charles, was arriving off the train for a hunting trip. We got out to get a glimpse of what was going on. I was standing behind this rope, only about two feet away from him; however, he never shook my hand, but he did look at me. Of course, John had to take me to see the Lock Nest. I suppose he was hoping we would see the Lock Nest Monster so he could say to all his family and friends I had the shit scared out of me yet again. When we got to the town, we went into a pub beside the lake that this monster was supposed to be in, and we got talking to some patrons of this pub, and they were all on about this Lock Nest Monster. John insisted we stay the night in the alley by the pub. He said there was nowhere else to stay, and as always, he was quite intoxicated, so I agreed. Although I didn't believe all the stories we heard that night, I found it hard to sleep, which was the whole point, I imagine. John and I took another trip in his pig farmer's van for another week. We went down to southern England this time, through Wales. We stopped in Bath and I toured the Roman Baths, which were located in the middle of the town, where there was a big roundabout. I was quite impressed with Bath; it was very well-maintained, unlike some places over there, but it was so small. The roundabout was the town. Of course, John had to take me to see Stonehenge. It was dark when we got there, and a seance was going on with a group of witches. We didn't get out because a police officer came to the door of the van and told us to leave, because sometimes things get out of hand with their gatherings, he said. These witches had a large fire in the middle of the Henge, and I wondered why they were permitted to do so around a historical monument. We stayed the night not too far away from Stone Henge, I believe, in a pub parking lot, and the next morning we went back to Stone Henge so I could get a better look at it. Directly south, we stopped at a farm that made this wine from rotting apples called "Scrumpy". John said, "This will get you hammered just smelling it," and he was right. One small glass and you're out of it for the night. I saved a jug to bring back so my drunken, dope addict friends Darlene, Diane, and Kathy could sample it. John said he didn't think that they would let me bring it on the plane, but they did. He added, "If they do allow you to bring it aboard, it will probably explode on the plane," but it never did. The last trip I took while I was over there was on a train with John's sister, Margaret. We went down south to a place called Bournemouth, right on the coast. While we were on the train, we passed through Nottingham Forest, but the trains over there go so fast; all I could see was a blur of horses running in a small, green, wooded area. We stayed at a bed and breakfast place in Borsmouth, a block or two away from the water's edge. We had booked it beforehand because it gets busy down there in the summer. When we walked along the ocean causeway, you could see the Isle of White, and so we took the little ferry which went over there to check it out. There was nothing but a bunch of pubs. I was surprised to see palm trees growing along the streets down south, because the whole time I was in England, almost a year, I just about froze. I believe along the ocean, the towns consisted of Naval Bases because I saw a lot of Navy ships in the ports we went to pulling up to docks down there. We visited another city called Portsmouth, and later, when I came back home, I found out from my Dad that he was stationed there when he was fighting in the war. I didn't know that before he told me, and it was kind of neat being able to see a place where my Dad had been when he was fighting in the war. My aunt Carol knew he had been there, however. One time when we were getting ready to go out touring, Margaret started to clean herself down in her private area right in front of me, which I thought was brazen. I wondered who the Hell she was trying to impress, my auntie Carol? Then we were out at the pub together, and she talked me into having a Guinness beer. It was a terrible-tasting, dark ale. She told me it was full of vitamins and pregnant women drank it all the time. Despite all this, I feel fortunate to have been able to see what I saw; however, I must say, they sure all took their turn terrorizing me, which I wasn't fully aware of then. Sure, the hell am I now? I guess by this time, I was getting used to it.

 When I stopped working at the Bistro, Mick, the guy who was on the camping trip when I met John, told me I should at least go to the Dole and see if I could get back the money I paid into their unemployment. He said, "Who knows, maybe they will give you another visa to work?" So, I went to the unemployment office in town and told them where I was from. I then asked if I could get my unemployment money back, and they said, "Oh, you can still work." I showed them my passport with the expired work visa, and they told me that because Canada was part of the Commonwealth countries, I didn't need a visa; I could just go and get another job and not worry about it. I assumed maybe the rules here were different than at home, so I quickly found another job at a brand new Wine Lodge and Bistro called "Bodega II", just opening up, not too far away from the apartment where we were still living, which was handy. It was only part-time, a little less than forty hours biweekly, working at the bar, slinging beer and serving shorts, what we call hard drinks. The only thing about working there was that when I worked there at night, John would leave me to walk alone, and I would have to pass the alley where the Yorkshire Ripper got his first victim, going through another alley. I found myself looking around behind my back while running home after work at night. That frightened me a lot. I was a real attraction to the customers who came into the Bistro. They always wanted to shoot the shit with me, and everyone thought I was from the States; they couldn't tell the difference between our accents, just like I couldn't tell the difference between their many different accents they had. You would travel a distance of fifty miles, and they would have a whole different tongue. John would point that out all the time. If someone wanted to tip you, which wasn't often, the customers wouldn't give you money for tips. They would just say, "Have one on me." I never did because I wanted to keep my head together. The shorts were just that, one ounce of booze with one ounce of cordial, which was like very strong pop. I never served many hard drinks. They didn't have anywhere near the ones we have. Where I was working, they served the original tequila sunrises, which would come in a tall glass. Anyone could serve drinks behind the bar; you didn't need a course for that. They called you barmaids. Sometimes I served the food in the Bistro part of this pub. I learned to work the till while working at the Bistro. I believe I made only twenty pounds a week, which was about forty dollars. Peanuts. Most things were more expensive to buy than at home. Only clothes, shoes, and cigarettes were cheaper, much cheaper. Of course, a place to live was really cheap to buy; however, their living quarters were primitive compared to ours, as I have already described. At the time, you could buy a flat for about thirty thousand dollars, compared to our one hundred thousand or more for something somewhat comparable in Canada. The food was quite dear, which was the terminology they used for expensive. Cigarettes were terribly tasting; they tasted like cigars, something like the cigarettes they sell in the States. Nick managed to come up with a bit of dope sometimes, but to my surprise, it was tough to find, so we went without most of the time. It was nice not to have someone shoving drugs in your face all the time. Alcoholism was to the extreme over there, though. Almost the whole year I resided there, I was working and living in that terrible apartment. It wasn't until about a month before it was time for me to go home that John bought himself a flat in Preston, somewhere along the lines of his parents' place. While living there, I bought some jute and made macrame hangers not only for our flat, but I also made a beautiful one for John's greedy mother with a lamp shade which hung over a table. Sitting on the lampshade in places were little stuffed birds. It was the best thing I ever made, and I gave it away. Isn't that always the way? Usually, it is to someone you like, though.

John and I got engaged just before I left. No one had just a diamond ring. The women usually wore sapphires and diamonds or rubies and diamonds for their engagement rings. Mine was sapphire and diamonds. Before the engagement was official, I made it clear to John I would never make England my permanent home. I think I pushed the engagement through because I didn't want to go through any more nightmares like all the ones I had left behind before coming to England, although I never remembered them all. But I just couldn't take the drug scene and the likes anymore. John wasn't able to fly back with me at the same time because he had business to take care of beforehand, and he wasn't able to get it all done before I had to leave. He had an appointment to settle the claim for the motorbike accident he had just before I left, and he wanted the money before he came over. They said he would have the money in a month or two. He ended up leaving his parents to take care of the flat he had just purchased. Little did I know he also left an insurance policy he had purchased when he was in the Merchant Navy in his Catholic mother's name only. I flew home on September 17th, 1980.

CHAPTER SEVEN

John drove me to the airport in his American car. When I got to the luggage check-in at Heathrow Airport, the authorities there told me to open up my luggage so they could check inside. I had one large suitcase full of little souvenirs that I bought from various places in my travels around the United Kingdom. They were all heavily wrapped in thin paper. At the check-in, they unwrapped every single one of them before they sent me on my way. I sat at the very back of the plane, where there were only two seats, and after we had all settled in and were going down the runway, we suddenly started to slow down, and then we came to a stop. Someone said a tire blew on the plane. Because I was sitting at the back, you could really feel the plane sway as it was slowing down. There was a guy sitting beside me from Kuwait who was on his way to Seattle to go to school, and when the plane started to sway going down the runway, he pulled this small suitcase out, which had, what he called, worry beads in it, then gave me one. He held one of them between both his hands and started rubbing it and praying in his foreign language. He told me it was what they were for. When we finally stopped, we had to transfer to the same seats on another plane, and it was quite the procedure. We were way behind schedule by the time we finally took off again. The flight was eight hours, and when I got to Seattle for my connecting flight, I was exhausted. I had been travelling for about thirteen hours. Then, on top of that, I had to wait six hours at the airport in Seattle before flying to Victoria. I fell asleep for a while on the chairs in the airport, and then when I woke up, I looked around. When I arrived at Victoria airport, I caught the airport bus to a bus stop and then another bus to my parents' house. After showing my parents what I brought back for them, I went to sleep. I'd lost much weight because I never liked the food over there, and Mom and Dad kept saying that they thought I was malnourished. I went down from a size twelve to a size seven, and being five foot six, that was skinny.

The next night, I went to the Royal Oak Inn, located just before the lakes off the highway, on my way to the British Columbia Ferries. That was the new hangout for all of my friends. Darlene was still with Ralph, and they were very serious about each other by this time. Kathy was still single. I don't remember if Diane was there that night, but we were sitting at the table when, all of a sudden, I started to get really itchy. I told Kathy what was happening to me, and we both went into the bathroom together. I looked into the mirror, and I had these red blotches like hives all over my face. Then, I went to the toilet, lifted up my shirt, and noticed they were all over my stomach and all over my entire body, too. Kathy took me in her Camaro to the Royal Jubilee Hospital, and they asked me what I had eaten; if it was out of the ordinary? I couldn't think of anything, and I told them that. The doctor who attended to me said it was probably an allergic reaction to something I ate and shot me up with adrenaline. I had to sit in the emergency room for about half an hour until the hives and itchiness subsided. The doctor gave me a prescription for Benadryl and advised me to consult my doctor about it. They allowed me to leave, not even asking if I was driving, and I was wired on adrenaline. It's a good job I wasn't. A few days after that, I went to see Dr. Turd, and he just told me to keep the Benadryl with me in case it should happen again. It never did.

I applied all over the place looking for a job, and finally, shortly after, I got a call back from the hospital. This time, I got hired at the Eric Martin Pavilion in the Food Service Department. Darlene, Diane, and Kathy had been going to the Crown and Eye bar at the Imperial Inn downtown before going to the Royal Oak nightclub, and Ralph was always going along. Darlene was still living with her Chinese husband, but was never home; she was always staying at Ralph's house on Sumas Street, which was just off of Jutland before town. He was renting a house from his Dad. I didn't like going to the Crown and Eye because Robin and all of his friends were hanging out there too, and I didn't want anything to do with any of them. They never went to the Royal Oak Inn, so we'd go out late and go to the Nightclub there. Once in a while, we went to the pub there beforehand. We saved the "Scrumpy" that I brought back from the southern part of England for John after my friends and I had sampled it. Even they thought it was too potent. The night John arrived, on December 5, 1980, a big snowstorm hit, and the roads were icy. Even the buses and cabs weren't running. He knew I was going to be at Darlene's house, so when he got in, he phoned there for me to come and pick him up because he had no other way of getting in. I was too scared to drive, plus I had a shot of that powerful wine. John was mad as Hell at me because I refused to go and pick him up, even though we arranged for Doug, Diane's X-boyfriend, to go and get him from the airport. John got back to Darlene's house safe and sound, and we all got tanked on the Scrumpy and stoned on Darlene's pot. Doug didn't stay. I don't believe Doug and Diane were going out anymore. They were just friends, and he was doing her a favour by picking John up. Besides, I think he learned his lesson when it came to drinking and driving when he killed the family on the Malahat and got seriously injured that night himself.

John refused to stay at my parents' place, so I didn't even ask my parents if he could. He had phoned me before he left England and told me he got his money from the claim he had when he was in that motorbike accident, and he said, "I'll stay in a hotel when I come over." He stayed at the Ingraham Hotel on Douglas Street. We got married at the Justice of the Peace on December 24th, 1980, my brother Brian's birthday. Darlene and Ralph were the Matron of Honour and the Best Man. My father refused to go. He wasn't well, but my mother attended. It was a short ceremony, and I had to break John's arm to wear some dress pants to the wedding. He wanted to go in his jeans. It was the first and last time I ever saw him in dress pants. Darlene and my mother took a few pictures, and we left for Waikiki, Hawaii, on our honeymoon right after we got married. We had booked this hotel in advance, which is one of the high-rises in the central core. We chose it because you could prepare your own meals in a kitchenette, which I thought would help us save money. We discovered that it was more cost-effective to eat out for our meals. The first time at the beach, I stayed out too long and I got a second-degree sunburn. I had fallen asleep, and John never woke me up. He never fell asleep. I couldn't even wear any clothes because it hurt so much. For the first week, I was laid up in the hotel room, so I made John suntan out on the little balcony off of our hotel room. One night after that, we went to a pub where we sat right at the bar. John was on his second beer when he told me to look around, but do it in the mirror, which was behind the bar. I looked, but it didn't dawn on me what he had noticed. I asked, "Where?" He said, "Everywhere," and then said, "Turn around and look in our right-hand corner." When I did, I noticed two guys were mugging each other, and as I looked around the bar, I saw some more doing the same thing. I soon became aware we were in a gay bar when I saw that a couple of them were grouping each other by the front entrance, too. John had to order another beer, though, before we left. Eventually, we found a nightclub that played rock and roll music, and we stayed there for the rest of the night. We were in Waikiki for New Year's Eve in our hotel lounge. Just before midnight, we decided we would try to find somewhere to party. All of a sudden, as we were walking down the street, firecrackers and fireworks started flying out of all the hotel windows. It freaked me out, so we covered our heads and ran back to our hotel room, where we thought we'd stay until it was all over with. We were watching the fireworks from our hotel window for about half an hour, and all the roads soon became covered in a thick carpet of red from the display. After it had quieted down, we carried on our way to find somewhere to celebrate the New Year. We must have checked out all the pubs and nightclubs in town. Everywhere we went, nothing was going on, no dancing, nothing. And there was hardly a soul out anywhere. "Dead as a door nail." I commented, "For a famous vacationing spot, it sure is weird to see nothing going on for New Year's." After searching for a long time, we finally came across a nightclub with people dancing and having a good time, so we stayed there till closing. Our honeymoon in Waikiki lasted for three weeks before we went back to Victoria, where we made that our home.

I still had all my furniture from my first marriage stored at my parents' place. We didn't have to get anything for our apartment, which we found on Pembroke Street. It was a few blocks away from the hospital where I had found employment again. And for a while, I walked to and from work. I sold my white Beaumont to go to England, so John bought a 1979 Dodge Charger Special Edition with some of the $16,000 in insurance money he came over with. Our trip to Hawaii was also paid for out of that money. He wanted to use the rest of the money to put down on a rig and go out on his own, he said, but it was apparent he couldn't do that because he didn't have any connections for that type of work yet. I thought to myself, you're dreaming. Besides, I said, "You could build a house for the cost of a rig." John didn't like the idea of working for someone. My Dad had told him to apply at the mill, and with his qualifications, he would get on right away, but he refused. That's because there was a job lined up already for him before he even came over, but he put on the act that there wasn't to help cover up his tracks and everyone else involved in this.

A few months after we got married, I broke out in sores, and I went to the evil doctor, Dr Turd, and he told me, "You have a mild case of herpes." I asked him if they were contagious, and he said,

"Yes." I asked him, "How?" and he said, "By towels." Then I asked, "Can I have kids?" and he said I could. Well, I knew right away who gave them to me, Robin, because his friend Cameron told me one night that I had herpes, and he laughed after he told me this. I knew you could get herpes, cold sores on the mouth, and at first I thought that was what he was talking about, but then I never had any, so I didn't know what the Hell he meant, and because I was drunk at the time he said this, I never gave it another thought. Eventually, after I broke out in these sores, I knew it had to have come from Robin because I remembered then what Cameron had said to me one night. Of course, I had to tell John about it, and he didn't know what they were either, so I told him precisely what Dr. Turd told me. John didn't seem too concerned about me having them, and so we never really talked about it again after that.

One day, in February 1981, my mother phoned us, telling me that she had read in the paper about a welding job in Langford and that John should apply for it. Unknown to me at the time, it was a setup job my aunt Carol arranged for John. When her husband, Gordie, was stationed in Halifax, New Brunswick, Canada, they met a couple named Bill and Sue, and they kept in touch with each other after they both moved back to Victoria. Sue's husband Bill was working for the Coast Guard when they met my aunt Carol, whose husband Gordie was still in the Navy then, but I do not believe Bill and Sue were married yet. Bill and Sue were around our age. At the time, though, Sue's brother Gary owned the welding shop, "Bemester Welding" in Langford, and that was the job my mother saw in the paper that day. Bill, Sue's husband, was now working there too. So, John, of course, got the job. We became friends with Bill and Sue, who had two boys, Bill and Ben, and Sue was pregnant with another. She had another boy whom they called Tommy. In April, we decided to put the rest of the money, ten thousand dollars from John's motorcycle accident, on a half-acre of property out in East Sooke in a newly developed subdivision. It was about half an hour away from Langford, where John was working, and about one hour away from where I was working. John also bought a truck and camper because he didn't want to drive his Charger back and forth to work, as he felt it would be worth money one day. John said they only made a few of these cars in the year it was manufactured. In November of 1981, I found out I was pregnant. At the time, I found out I was taking a Mixology course at Camosun College. I liked working as a bartender, or what was called a barmaid in England. I guess socializing with the different people you meet all the time attracted me. I thought maybe I could get a job doing that at night to earn some extra money, so we could start building our house. But it never happened. Within a year, we had the property in East Sooke paid off. We only borrowed eighteen thousand dollars. We ended up selling the camper on the truck to pay off the loan on the property. This truck became the workhorse for the house we were planning to build out in East Sooke. I was making more money as a labourer at the hospital than John was at his trade, and that pissed him off big time. But in the first few years John worked for Bemester's, he was getting a lot of overtime work; but then again, so was I. I asked my Dad if he would build us a house, and of course, he said he would. He knew the mill was going to close down soon, so he said we should wait until that happened before starting on our house. John and I went out to our property to where we wanted to build our home, and with a hand saw, we cut the trees down and cleared the brush out. That summer, a girl by the name of Corrine came over while we were working on our property, and John pulled out a joint to smoke with her. Her boyfriend's name was Bill. They just bought the property next to us, and she wanted to introduce herself. Our property was the last parcel in a residential subdivision, and the properties on the other side of our property were considered rural. By this time, there was a road roughed in going up to where John's shop would eventually be, and the area was all cleared there, and it was cleared where the house was going to be built, too. We had machines coming in by this time, doing work. John and I had decided that we wanted our home to be built on top of this huge rock face at the rear of the property, so we could see the Sooke Basin. My brother came and drilled the holes to put the dynamite in because we had to do some blasting. Brian worked like a dog doing that, and it was all for free. Bill and Corrine were going to teach themselves everything they needed to know about building houses and do it themselves. They had the big dream of building energy-efficient houses and making big money. The two of them both made money with another guy in Vancouver, buying and selling a home, each making a huge profit by doing so. I thought we were going to be friends, and we were for a while.

During the year and a half we were living on Pembroke Street, John's parents came over for a visit. They stayed with us in our small one-bedroom apartment. We gave them our bed to sleep in, and we slept on the hide-a-bed couch I had bought, just so there were other sleeping quarters when his whole clan came over from time to time. His mother insisted on going to the Catholic church on Sunday when she visited; that's how dedicated she wanted to look to her faith. I took her once to the one on Quadra Street, and I felt so out of place, like I didn't belong there, so I never went again with her. John's sister, Margaret, and her husband, Collin, came over to visit us, too. When they came over, they said that Collin had a good job opportunity in the Los Angeles area, and they thought about going there for a holiday to check it out before making any decision. They stayed with us in the apartment and slept on the hide-a-bed. I remember being pissed off because I would come home from work tired and hot, and so would John, and they would both be taking turns having a shower, which is what we would want to do. They would eat our food and never once prepare it for us. Before they left after their first holiday to America, Margaret and Collin decided it was "a nice place to visit, but they didn't want to live here." They stayed living in England. Shortly after they left, John's younger brother, David, came over on his own, despite having a girlfriend, and stayed with us. Kathy was over at our house, and she ended up sleeping with David the same night. Love at first sight, or was it another opportunity for a promotion? After that, she tried talking David into moving here, but David said he didn't like it much either. One day, Kathy showed up at our house with a man named Don, whom she had met ,and he was from Montreal. John and I weren't associating with my old gang because we were always working and too tired to go anywhere. We were all talking, and out of the blue, this guy sat on John's lap and put his arms around him, then he gave him a big kiss on the cheek. After they both left, John and I talked about how we thought he was a "fag" English terms for being gay, and wondered what he was doing with a woman if he was. Kathy ended up marrying this Don guy. I didn't see Kathy, Darlene, or Diane for a long while after that. Later, after Kathy's husband, Don, fathered two kids with Kathy, I heard through the grapevine that he left her and went back to Montreal, Quebec.

The mill closed down for a year at the beginning of July.
In 1982, my Dad and his friend Russ, who he worked with at BC Forest Products, started building our house. My mother and father had lent us thirty thousand dollars to start building because the interest rates were out of this world, prime rate plus two percent, which amounted to seventeen and a half percent. That's how my parents made some of their money. They borrowed some from the bank, invested it, so they could earn interest on it, then quickly paid it off when the interest rates went down again. We only paid my parents the monthly interest they would have gotten if their money were in the bank while we were building the house with their money. When we moved into the house, the interest rates had gone down substantially, and so we went to the bank, borrowed money, and then paid my Mom and Dad back with it. We gave my

Dad the sum of a lousy $2,000 for building the whole house, and for ten years after that, he continued to come over in his spare time to do work for us, and he never took another dime.

I worked at the hospital for a month before I had the baby in July. In June, we rented a twenty-foot silver stream trailer to live in on our property while we were building the house. There was one place in town you could rent them from, just off the Island highway. John helped my Dad put the septic field in, which they did right away, so that we could hook the trailer up to it. When my Dad first started building the forms for the foundation, I would stack rocks alongside them to keep them in place. My Dad would come and pull me up off the ground because I was so pregnant. Brian did all the cement work for the house at the cost of the cement, as by this time, he had his own cement finishing company. Because the house was built on a huge rock face, the foundation on the side facing Bill and Corrine was sixteen feet high. My Dad drew up the plans for our house and also built the trusses for the roof. John was working at Bemester, but a recession had set in, and he wasn't working all the time, so he also helped enclose the house. We contracted out the electrical, and a plumber from BC Forest, whom Dad knew, did the plumbing. Russ and John did the drywall. And when my son was sleeping, I helped with the insulation. I didn't want my Dad to do the drywall or insulation because of his illness, so he was busy doing something else. It was a good time to build as the building materials and the labour were cheap. A short time after we started building our house, the couple on the rural property next to us, Bill and Corrine, started to build. They knew the plans for our property, but they dug a hole and put their house in it right beside the location where we said John's shop was going to be built. Bill came over once and looked in amazement at my father's skills after Dad had put up the trusses for the roof, which he made himself. Bill was such a long-haired freak; literally, he never said a word when he came over to look at them. After the framing was finished, the building inspector came out, and I asked, "Well, aren't you going to go in?" He was standing at the bottom of the drive looking up, and he said to me, "I can see from here it has passed."

John was into drinking excessively. About a few weeks before I was due to have the baby, I went and stayed with my folks at their house so I would be closer to the hospital. It was arranged that when the baby was coming, I would phone up Corrine, and she would notify John, and John would come and take me to the Victoria General Hospital, where Dr. Turd had doctor privileges. It closed down shortly after I had my son. Well, it was midnight when my water broke, and I phoned Corrine, and she couldn't wake John. Meanwhile, I locked myself out of my parents' house when I thought John should be arriving soon, which was about an hour after I had called Corrine. I paced the streets for approximately two hours, panicking because the contractions were only a few minutes apart from the word go. He finally showed up just as I was thinking of waking my parents. At the hospital, John fell asleep in the bed beside me, waiting for me to have the baby because he was so drunk. And in the morning, a lady from housekeeping had to wake him a few times to get him out of the bed he was in. She needed to make it for someone. I, however, hadn't been asleep at all. The first thing he said, in his usual sarcastic voice, when this woman got him to get up, was, "Have you had it yet?" As if the baby were some kind of object. I was wondering, and I kept asking where my doctor was. They all knew my water had broken because I told them. I was aware that if you didn't have the baby soon after your water broke, you could have a dry birth, but no one seemed concerned. It was nineteen hours later before I had my son. When the Turd finally did arrive, a few hours before the baby was born, he kept telling me the baby kept going to sleep, and that's why it was taking so long. I had to be induced, and it was unbelievably painful after that, so I think I was having a dry birth, thanks again to the good old Turd. During most of my labour, John was getting pissed at a bar in the Empress Hotel called, the "Beaver." He was there for the birth, though, and while I was taking H2O and no one was in the room, John was demanding, "Give me some of that." Of course, I told him to bugger off in no uncertain terms. My son was born three hours after I was induced at 6:19 PM, and just as he arrived, there was a clap of thunder and a streak of lightning that bolted into this new and modern birthing room I had my baby in. My son was born weighing seven pounds two ounces. It seemed like it took forever to get him to breathe. He was turning blue, and Turd had him upside down, patting him on the back and putting his finger down his throat. I was scared there was something wrong. For the week I was in the hospital, my son was in an incubator because he was jaundiced. They said his liver wasn't fully developed. A couple of times that I went into the nursery to see him, he would be lying in his feces. I got really upset when I saw this, and I remember crying in a rocking chair beside his incubator, thinking no one cared about him. I didn't want to leave his side. I was so worried about him.

The baby had to remain in the hospital when I got released because he was still jaundiced. I stayed with my parents and went to visit him every day until he was well enough to leave, a few days later. I had to take him to the hospital every week to check on his condition, and it was easier staying with my parents until I was given the all clear with my son's condition. My aunt Saint Mary gave him a silver piggy bank when he was born, but I guess she will be needing that now. The honest cop from across the street from my parents' place, Dale, gave him a pair of Indian moccasins, and I wonder now what gesture he was trying to make. Was he trying to remind me of what Robin told me after we broke up? "I liked being with Indians." The bunch of mental abusers. I used to wet my finger and put it up to my son's mouth to see if he was still breathing because I was so afraid of crib death. One night, we

were all sleeping, and John's pillow fell to the floor from the
pull-out bed we were sleeping in and landed on the propane heater,
which was missing a grate. It caught on fire, and I was going
under. If it weren't for John waking up, we probably wouldn't be
here right now. The whole trailer was filled with smoke, and I
quickly grabbed the baby and ran out the door with him when I
realized what was going on. John threw the smouldering pillow out
the door. I was so worried about our son. I woke him up to make
sure he was all right every so often that night. After this happened,
he started to cry every evening at six, and he'd continue to cry until
well after midnight. I was thinking it was because I was
breastfeeding him, and it was something I ate, and he had colic.
That is what the book Corrine had given me about being a new
mother said. There was nowhere to walk with him, but I would
pace back and forth in the trailer or just hold him to try to comfort
him. Then I swore it was the lime green and bright yellow curtains
that affected him, and the cramped quarters, trying to make a joke
of it. Around ten, after four hours of non-stop crying, I would start
to lose my patience, and so I would put him into the Charger and
drive around the subdivision. As soon as the car started moving, he
would stop crying just like they said in the book, so I would drive
around long enough to get myself together again, or until I thought
he was sound asleep. But he would wake up as soon as we stopped.
There were no street lights as this area was just being developed,
and it was out in the middle of "No man's land," which is where
my Dad said we lived. I didn't know where the Hell I was going,
and there was only one other house in the whole subdivision at the
time. When we moved into the house, my son continued to cry in
his regular routine. John's Dad came over alone to visit us soon
after we were settled in, and that was when my son stopped crying
at night. John's Dad told me to "Leave a light on; maybe he is
afraid of the dark." After we got a dimmer switch for his bedroom,
his suggestion worked. The baby stopped crying. It never even
dawned on me before this that maybe he was afraid of the dark; he

was only a few months old. But it did cross my mind that maybe it was because of the fire in the trailer.

Well, Dad and Russ worked like crazy building the house, and within four months from the start of the framing, we moved in. Although it wasn't nearly finished, my father made sure it was comfortable for me and his new grandson, whom he was extremely proud of. I don't think he could stand the thought of us living in that trailer, especially after what had happened in there. Everything was done legally right to the bitter end. We were told you didn't need an occupancy permit to move in. Dad thought maybe we might need one, so before we moved in, John went to the Capital Regional District in Sooke and asked about it. John said that they told him we didn't need one. There were no rails around the sun deck, and there wasn't an insert for the fireplace. Come to think of it now, what is the purpose of having building inspections when they don't enforce the building codes? That kind of thing still goes on here today. Anyway, we thought it may have something to do with living in what was mostly a rural area at this time. The basement was nothing but a big hole, too, but it was no big deal because upstairs was suitable for living in, and you couldn't get to the basement from the main living area yet. John was still working at Bemester's, and because the place was going downhill, John made the handrails and the insert for the fireplace at the welding shop when there was no work coming in the door. By this time, Gary, the boss, had to find a job to keep the place afloat. He had become a cocaine freak, according to the rumour, which didn't help his situation much. Dad continued to come to our house to work on it. He trimmed all the windows and doors and installed cupboards and closet doors himself, as none of that had been done when we moved in. And I painted it all. The house just had one undercoat on it. The living room and halls had two coats, though. I managed to do most of the painting in the bedrooms as well. Mom and Dad got new cupboards, and they gave us their old ones, which

Dad had made, so I painted them all up too. I wouldn't allow my Dad to do any painting because of his illness. I was busy with the baby, but I'd do all this while he was sleeping. I had the six months maternity leave allotted, and no sooner did I go back to work at my permanent position in one of the kitchens at Eric Martin, the Fairfield Hospital, which used to be the Victoria General, was closing down, and the employees from there were bumping people out of their positions. When I got bumped, I was told I could do the same or take a layoff for a year, then come back on-call. Because I wanted to be with my son, I took a leave for a year. Sue was looking after my boy when I first went back to work. She would always rub it into me when he progressed to a certain stage, like she saw him when he first sat up. I didn't like that one bit either. When it was time for me to go back to work, I was pregnant with my daughter and due any time. I phoned my employer to see if I could get maternity leave for that. They told me that if I got a note from my doctor, they would allow it, so I went to doctor Turd and he gave me a note requesting it. I had two years off with pay, thanks to the evil doctor Turd. I guess he was trying to make himself look good to me.

The relationship with our new neighbours, Bill and Corrine, like I said, started on a good foot. Corrine wanted me to join the Ratepayers Society with her, but I was too busy with my new baby and painting the house, so I said I didn't have the time. Corrine told me they ran out of money, and I suppose she was looking to cut corners wherever she could. She found herself working at a job in town just to make ends meet, and eventually, Bill was doing work out in the community. It was September 1993 when I found out I was pregnant again. I had just gotten the news when I was out doing some gardening beside my son's bedroom window. Corrine approached me and asked, "How about a fence between you and us?" John had just done some work for a guy named Randy, and he was building a mechanic's pit for John. I guess she thought that we were starting to build the shop, which we weren't. Anyway, I said "Sure," thinking we would go in on it together. She said, "No, I was thinking of you putting it up and paying for it." Then she added, "I don't think I will be able to stand listening to John's AM music from his truck all the time." Well, I was completely flabbergasted because by this time, I had her looking after my son, and this was right out of the blue. John had helped them put the shingles on their roof, and he'd have lunch with them sometimes, too. John would say, "They eat like a couple of shrubs." I think they were vegetarians. I also invited Corrine and Bill to come and use our shower because they were still building their house and living in this dump of a trailer, which was rat-infested. They were going to Bill's sister's house in town to clean up because they never had any cleaning facilities. As far as I know, they didn't even have an outhouse. They took me up on my offer, and every time they came over, they wouldn't even have the decency to clean the tub afterwards; they left it filthy. When she said that, I said, "Well, you will be waiting a long time for a fence." "We have a basement to fill and a shop to build first; a fence is the last thing on the list." She said, "Well, we'll see about that." From that time on, when John talked about them, he referred to them as the "Shrubs." These people helped make my life a living Hell.

CHAPTER EIGHT

I had just joined the Mother's Group out in East Sooke and was starting to attend their meetings. When I first started attending the Group, I was surprised to see such high attendance for a small community. Jan, who loved drinking, lived in a cottage on about a half an acre just up the hill from my house. She was the one who told me about the group when I was out for a walk one day with my son. She said she could hear my boy crying in the trailer when she went past my place and felt sorry for me. I thought that was a weird comment, seeing the type of house we were building. I never felt sorry for myself. She was from a big Catholic family back in Ontario, and she liked her booze. She told me she had moved from a beautiful brick house to this "dump," which was her word. She had a small boy, around four years old, Luke, and it seemed like she didn't have much patience with him. Her husband was in jail back East for selling drugs and was getting out soon. She told everyone that. They were going to make a fresh start here. Jan worked on and off for the government, and just before we moved out of East Sooke, she got a job as the manager of the Sally Anne in Sooke. Gary, her husband, well, let's say he liked to smoke lots of pot, but he was a plumber by trade, and before we moved out of East Sooke, he got on at the Dockyards. She and her husband became our friends. Down the road from us lived a couple by the name of Dorothy and Larry who had two small children, a boy about four, Morgan, and a girl around two, Tessa. Dorothy was a school teacher, but couldn't get a job working as one, so she found employment with the government, and Larry, well, who knows what he did. It was always something different. I knew somehow they were trouble when I first met them. I later found out that, along with smoking pot, they were cocaine addicts. They had a cottage too, they were extending on the corner of a road called

Seaguirt. Sometime after I moved out of East Sooke and after I left John, I heard that Larry was teaching some boys to make pipe bombs, and one of them, not theirs, got seriously injured. The accident happened in their garage. Shortly after that happened, Dorothy left Larry. Another couple, Uta and Don, had a young boy, Adam, the same age as my son. They pretended they were righteous, going to church on Sundays, but they would have big summer bashes at their house every year with all kinds of goings on at them. That, too, I found out about after I left John. Uta delivered the mail for Canada Post, and Don also landed a government job through Dorothy. They also split up after I left John. At the end of Seaguirt lived Barb and Randy, who also had a small boy the same age as my boy, Paul, and she was actually the first one I became friendly with. Barb worked for Spraut Shaw teaching typing, but later got hired on at Edward Milne High School in Sooke. Randy was a bricklayer working for a company. They were adding on to a cottage as well. Randy drowned shortly before we moved out of East Sooke. He drowned in the ocean in Oak Bay. Barb eventually remarried sometime after I left John. Then there were Marion and John, who had two small girls, around two and five. John was working for the Volunteer Fire Department in East Sooke for most of the time. Marion was a stay-at-home Mom, but later she ended up getting a job as an interpreter in sign language for the Sooke School District. That was after she left her husband, John, and after I left mine. Marion's husband worked in the computer department at a store somewhere in town at the time. They were also extending a cottage at the other end of East Sooke Road. The only house in the subdivision belonged to a nurse and her husband, Irene and Paul, and they had a small boy around three or four years old. I believe Paul was a plumber and worked for the Dockyards too, but I'm not sure about that. There were three or four more couples in the group at this time, but they didn't really affect my life, so I won't mention them. One time, while we were building our house, a couple from Edmonton was out camping on the rural property beside Bill and Corrine. They came over, introduced themselves, and told us that they were teachers who had bought the property for their retirement, planning to spend time at it every chance they got. From that time on, every time they came out, they would come over to visit.

I felt on top of the world, I was going to have the family I always wanted and a brand new waterview home, which I never dreamed of ever having. The only problem was that John was still drinking, and because he was working so hard all the time, I thought his irresponsibility was starting to show, so I started to make sure he didn't look after the children. He still had the green truck he bought when we were living in the Pembroke Street apartment, and over the years, it proved handy hauling things for the house regularly. One day, John came home with a little blue Chevy for me to run around in, and I liked it. I thought it was the ideal car, but that was short-lived because John ended up buying a beige lemon that I drove for a very short time. I didn't like the Charger; it was too fast, with a four-hundred-horsepower engine, and I thought it was nothing but a gas-guzzling machine. John was trying to preserve it anyway. Once, I was going down Sooke Road. My son was in the back seat of the Charger, eating an ice cream cone with it all over his face and clothes, when I got pulled over by the Royal Canadian Mounted Police for travelling too fast, but when the cop saw my boy and noticed I was pregnant, he let me go. However, I decided then John deserved to keep the Charger if he wanted. Now I think he deserves a swift kick back to England so they can lock him up and throw the key away.

Barb, Randy's wife, and I would get together so the kids could play. She smoked cigarettes while she was pregnant and was trying to get me to smoke them near the end of my pregnancy with my daughter. Smoking nauseated me when I was pregnant with both children, so I never indulged in it. Coffee did the same thing. As

soon as I smelled it, I wanted to go and throw up. Barb was also
pregnant with her second child. Her kid, Paul, was a brat, always
going after my son for toys and biting him. She would then hold
Paul on her lap and tell him he couldn't play with other children if
he was going to do that. He would squirm, hit Barb, and bite her to
get away. My boy soon realized what this kid was like, so he
would quickly give Paul the toy and run away from him. It was a
Sunday morning, and I started to get contractions, and then my
water broke shortly after. John phoned Barb and told her it was
time for me to go to the hospital to have the baby, and could she
take the boy for us? We had arranged this beforehand, so she said,
"Sure." We drove over there and dropped my boy off. That was the
only time I saw her without makeup, which she said took an hour
to do. She looked ten years older than she was. I think that is one
of the reasons why I seldom wear the stuff. By this time, they had
just built a new hospital off the Island Highway, about a half an
hour drive from East Sooke, the new Victoria General. Turd had
privileges there now. I had been doing Jane Fonda's workout for
pregnant women with Jan, who was also pregnant with her second
child. She invited me over to do the exercises on the tape she had,
which I think helped a lot. The contractions were less painful than
with my son. After six hours of labour, I had my daughter. She
came flying out, screaming her lungs out, and had all this dark hair
sticking up, which was bleached at the ends from being in the
womb too long. She reminded me of a punk rocker, and I couldn't
help but laugh when I saw her. Not only was I elated that I had a
girl because this was going to be my last child. She also looked just
like my grandmother, my mother's, mother. I was surprised to see
the dark hair because both John and I were fair-haired. I thought I
was going to have her on my birthday, June 6th, because I started
to get contractions then, but they soon went away. I arranged to
have my tubes tied right after I had my daughter, and it was so
painful that they were giving me morphine for the pain afterwards.
I was begging for them to give me more shortly after they gave me

a shot of it, but they were only allowed to give me so much. It was all timed, too, apparently. I couldn't believe the pain I was in. Turd could have ordered more because that amount of morphine ordered did nothing for the pain, and he probably knew it wouldn't. The pain was almost as bad as when that bastard burnt the shit out of me. John was there putting on the act that he was so concerned for me. With everything the Turd had already done to me, though, he might not have given me anything for the pain if John wasn't there. Of all things, John said to me, "Maybe you shouldn't have had it done." I suppose it was the Catholic coming out of him then. But he picked a Hell of a time to suggest that, didn't he? He didn't want to have an operation because I asked him if he would. But things were working fine for him; that's what his response to that was. He raped me from time to time, but Hell, I was ignorant of that by then. Ironically enough, my old Junior High School buddy Teresa was in the next bed beside me, having her daughter. My sister-in-law, who is a nurse, asked me, "Didn't your doctor tell you it would be worse than labour if you had it done right after the birth?" The bloody Turd just didn't give up making my life painful and miserable. He never told me anything, as usual. Shortly after having my daughter, I found another doctor, Dr. Leon, closer to where we were living at the St. Anthony's clinic in Langford. He was Chinese, and I really liked him. He seemed efficient. I only saw him a few times, and then he suddenly disappeared, leaving another doctor, Shifty, to replace him. The Chinese doctor, Dr. Leon, was only supposed to be on a holiday, but he never came back after I started questioning him about my health. I understand why he left now, but I didn't then. He didn't want anything to do with being a GP in an evil health care system. My doctor, Shifty, turned out to be just as bad as Turd. Anyway, Barb came to the hospital with a plush, pink teddy bear for my daughter, and she told me that she was hoping to have a girl, too, but she had a boy, Mark, a month or two after me. Jan had another boy, Mathew, and my daughter and he was only a couple of weeks apart. It was weird because they both had the exact same birthmark in the same place on their backs. The two of them became good buddies for a while. Uta, whom I never saw much other than at the Mother's Group, was also pregnant at the same time, and she had a girl, too. Laura. Once again, I was surrounded by greedy, evil Catholics. Three weeks after my daughter was born, my grandmother died of cancer. I wanted to bring my daughter to the hospital so grandma could see her before she died, but my aunt Carol must have thought it might trigger something, so she told my mother she didn't think it was a very good idea, so I never did. I regret that now. My grandmother would not allow her crazy old man to be in the hospital room with her, and she seemed so angry when she mentioned this, my Mom said. She wasn't only angry towards him, but she also expressed the same feelings towards John when I was talking to her privately. She asked me, "Do you still make homemade fries for John all the time?" and I said, "Yes." Then she said in a very bitter tone and stern face, "I would make him make his own." I wonder now if she knew what was going on? After grandma died, gramps would always be sitting on a lawn chair in his front yard as if he was looking for sympathy. I remember feeling sorry for him then. My evil gramps died three weeks after grandma died of cancer, too, and other complications. Right after he died, all my mother's siblings took off with what they thought was their share of the Will, deliberately ripping my parents off. Never to be heard from again. Maxi apparently owed the Will money because my mother told me many times how my grandmother would come over, angry that Maxi had not paid them the money they loaned him when he first got married. Also, my parents were always openly promised that Dad would get paid from their Will for the house he built them, but that never happened either. Mom and Dad saw a lawyer about it, who said they would have a good case, but Dad said it wouldn't be worth the trouble; his health was more important, so they never bothered about it. When I look back now on everything that went on in my life, I find it all so hard to believe. I blame myself most of the time for everything you can think of. I should have caught onto all this long before now, I tell myself on a regular basis, but then look how many other people all over the world who are suffering with this curable yet devastating disease called Crohn's and are ignorant about it all too. As disgusting as my story is, remember I am not my STORY. And some may not understand what I did to survive, but that is why I am speaking out, because this kind of unbelievable emotional and physical pain, deceit, and trauma orchestrated by the evil Catholic government and their "International Underground Network" has got to stop.

My daughter hardly ever slept. One time, as an infant, she was awake for thirteen hours. When she started to cut teeth, that's when the trouble really began. Her first two teeth came in at the same time, and they were joined together. I always knew when she was going to get another tooth because she would cry a lot. My boy was very jealous of her. So when I was breastfeeding my daughter, I would read him a book so he wouldn't feel left out. My son, on the other hand, was plagued with ear infections from the time he was four months old right up until he was about eight years old. The poor little guy would get a high fever, crying in pain, and I would have to rush him half an hour away to the hospital or clinic in Langford at all hours of the day and night to get treated. Eventually, when he was four, doctor Shifty got a specialist to put tubes in his ears to prolong the agony some more. The tubes would soon work their way out, and he would be ill with ear infections again. I'd put earplugs in his ears when he had a bath or if I took him swimming so his ears wouldn't get wet inside. The boy worshiped his Dad, and his first word was "light" because he would look out the window, searching for his dad. On the rare occasion when his Dad was home, he would see the lights on his truck outside. He would stand on the couch and turn the light on and off repeatedly. It was sad because John never made time for either one of them. He only made time for them when he wanted to traumatize them.

There were many unexplained accidents in the children's lives. One time, when my boy was about one and a half, he was playing in the small swimming pool on the sun deck, and the bar to the gate was locked because I always made sure of that. In a split second, someone had opened the gate, let him out, put him on top of this beige car by John's mechanic pit, and he fell off the car onto some rebar and slit his forehead open right between the eyes. I heard him crying, so I looked out just as he was scrambling up the side of the house with blood gushing out of his forehead. I took him to the pool to try to clean it up, but it was pulsating into the pool. So, I put pressure on it to try to stop the bleeding and took him to the clinic right away. He had to get stitches for that. I found out through the Mom's group that there was a retired doctor in Beacher Bay about ten minutes away who would take emergencies, so I phoned Jan to take my daughter for me because she was the closest and on our way, so I could take my son there. I realize now that there was no way a child of that age could open that gate and climb onto a car by himself. John must have put him there. Another time, when my son was about two and a half, he found the right key out of many, at least twenty, which were on John's key chain, and started the beige car we had, then took it out of gear, and it rolled back down our steep drive, which we had now on the other side of the house. The car went over a cliff and landed on a rock halfway down a twenty-foot drop. I was standing on the sun deck with my daughter in my arms when it happened. I'll never forget his little face as he cried Mom… mmy. I quickly gave the baby to John, who was standing there laughing, and by the time the car landed on the rock, I was there in bare feet to rescue him. Just as that happened, ironically enough, a friend of Randy's, Barb's husband, came down East Sooke Road with his backhoe, and John flagged him down to pull the car back to the drive. John would still leave his keys on the table after that, and I would constantly put them out of reach of the children. I now realize that the boy had to be taught to do that.

My daughter was two and my son was four when we got some bad news about Randy, Barb's husband. He had drowned in a so-called boating accident out in Oak Bay in Victoria. Apparently, they all had been drinking, and Randy, who couldn't swim, didn't have a life jacket on, and he was leaning against the guard rail of the boat he was on when it broke. He fell into the frigid, rough water and couldn't be rescued. Now I wonder if it was an accident? He was protestant. There was a funeral for him in the community hall beside the fire hall on Copper Mine Road in the subdivision which had just been built, and I went to it to give Barb my deepest sympathy. She didn't even acknowledge or look at me when I told her how sorry I was about what happened to Randy, and if she ever needed anything, just let me know. I really liked Randy and Barb, for that matter. Randy was a good, hard-working man who, to my knowledge, didn't drink that much. Their house was completed, but the yard hadn't been worked on. The community got together and fixed the yard up for her, and everyone came over for a while, giving her casseroles, me included. Our friendship was never the same after that.

It was around this time that John got into an accident with his green truck, which he had bought while we were living in the apartment on Pembroke Street. He was pissed one night, and coming home, he put it into a tree and totaled it. He was lucky he wasn't killed, as it was quite the mess. Gary, John's employer, was starting to sell things from his welding shop, getting ready to close the doors soon. John bought a truck and a welding machine from him because he planned to start his own portable welding business when Gary closed his doors. John had already acquired a few customers who only allowed him to work on their machinery, but things were slow everywhere. I was worried about how we were going to make ends meet. I became his bookkeeper. I went to this accountant, Eva Banks, who lived in the subdivision, and she showed me how to do his books. We both went to her to get our taxes done every year after that. I had gone back to work and was working a lot, but the babysitter, Nicky, who was a friend of Jan's and had gone to school to be a child care worker, was making more money than I was. I remember one time I couldn't make it home in the big old Oldsmobile, fully loaded, another one of John's toys, which I was now driving. Because of the snow, I had to stay at my mother's house. As usual, John never showed up till about eleven that night, and Nicky made a bundle of money. I ended up getting a weekend and stats position in the housekeeping department of the hospital just so I could stay employed. It worked out because of tax reasons, too. I was making more money to take home than I would in a full-time position. So I did that for a few years.

When John's employer, Gary, finally closed his shop in the summer of 1985, he gave John a fence that was going to come down and be destroyed. I had a vegetable garden growing beside Bill and Corrine's property, and Bill came out when John was putting it up and told him it was on his property. That was the first thing that happened with Bill and Corrine after Corrine had come over that day with her threat of a fence. A little while after John started his business, he decided he would advertise his company by racing Demos at Western Speedway in Langford. We still had the Charger, but it was uninsured, and when he got this race car, Bill and Corrine started to complain about too many unlicensed vehicles on our property. The by-law officer at this time just told John to put the race car on the licensed utility trailer, that he used to transport it to the track, and then the property would be legal. One day, Norm, John's main employer, was doing some excavating out in East Sooke, and he had to get rid of a whole lot of dirt, so John told him he could dump it on our property. Norm used to come into Gary's shop all the time and only allowed John to work on his machines, and he was continually buttering me up over the phone. All day long, dump trucks were coming to the house, unloading this dirt. I think this really pissed off Bill and Corrine because now our property was higher than theirs. John also had some huge boulders dropped off to make a retaining wall where the shop was going, and the shrub came out one day complaining this huge boulder was on his property; he even went as far as to get his land surveyed to get us to move this boulder. John brought Norm's machine home and moved it one day to keep him quiet, but that didn't please him. One day, I was planting some daisies along our property line, and Bill came out of his house yelling like a madman for me to get off of his property. His face was beet red, and he was mad as Hell. John had the shop built by my Dad's friend Russ. John, Marion's husband, was the chief of the fire department in East Sooke when Bill started a fire in his incinerator and tried to smoke Russ off the roof. I called fire chief John about it because it was in the middle of summer and everything was dry, so he had Bill put it out. John, the fire chief, invited us to come over to his house and have a sauna whenever we wanted, and we took him up on his offer once, only to find him and his wife, Marion bearing their ass. I refused to be acquainted with them again. After this, we were always getting calls from the by-law officer about something Bill and Corrine had complained about, like John's stash of metal or noise from the demo car that John would do work on at the house occasionally, but because it was only them complaining, nothing was done about it. The by-law officer would just say," Put your metal behind your shop and out of sight and try to keep the noise down". One day, a guy by the name of Nick, who volunteered for the fire department, too, came over to my house, and he was concerned about a table saw running for hours with no boards being cut. He thought someone was hurt, but it was Wild Bill. He would do this when he knew I'd be lying down with the kids for a nap. I think the guy needed some professional help, but good luck finding it. Corrine was forced to go to work after a couple of years because they got as far as boarding the house up and covering it with tar paper, and then they ran out of money. That is the way it stayed for years. But Bill stayed at home all the time, and no one would come over, and he never went out. For years, there were no windows in their house, and Bill made it his hobby to terrorize me. When they finally got some windows, he started to take pictures of our every move from one of them facing in our direction. When another couple moved into the house behind ours, Armin and Petra, they joined in on the harassment by getting another by-law officer involved, whose name was Tim. And he was a bloody asshole.

One day, John was coming home in his shiny red welding rig, and he went off East Sooke Road, coming home late, pissed, and rammed into a tree once again. The guy who lived in the house behind us before Armin and Petra moved in was a hunter, and he gave him some fur to put in the grill of the truck before John took it to the Insurance Corporation of British Columbia. John said he hit a deer, and so the insurance paid for it to get fixed. One night, he came home pissed and decided the supper which I had saved for him wasn't enough, and so he fried up some bacon. Well, he fell asleep and I woke up to the house full of smoke and the bacon as black as Toby's ass. I gave him a shove as he was sound asleep on the couch, and told him off. I said, "You could have burnt us all down." The whole time we were married, he never came home before eleven o'clock at night. He was either working, getting pissed, or God only knows what else he was doing. The Mom's Group would have dances on special occasions at the community hall in East Sooke, and John would always show up late or not at all, and I would have to go there with Jan and Gary. A couple of times, I went to the local pub, the Seventeen Mile House on Sooke Road, with Jan and Gary, Dot and Larry, but they were all such piss tanks I never really wanted to go out with them. John would be invited, and as always, he would show up late or not at all. Dot and her husband, by this time, I found out, were bad news because we went to what was supposed to be a hot tub and sauna party at their house one night, and they were all in the kitchen snorting cocaine, John included. I was so mad at him, and I thought he knew better, seeing that his boss lost everything partly because of this apparent cocaine habit. John promised he wouldn't do it again, but sometimes I would see him come home from that direction, and he wouldn't really have an excuse for being there. John would buy me sleazy clothes to wear in the garden. I say that because he never took me out anywhere. For my birthday, he once bought me some cow dung for my rose bushes, and another time, he bought me a weed eater, which he never used. John was very verbally abusive toward me. He was constantly telling me that I needed to lose weight, and I was only a size nine/ten. He would tell me I should dye my hair purple and style it like a punk rocker. He also told me I was like part of the furniture that he could sit on whenever he liked, and numerous other bizarre phrases. I was a bitch when I wanted to discuss his drinking problem, and he had the nerve to tell me I was spoiled and nothing would ever make me happy. And I was happy just to have food on my table and a roof over my head. He never came out and told me he loved me, either, and it was not like I didn't look for reassurance.

The children were only about two and four when I first started thinking about leaving John. It was right after the so-called accident he had with the truck. Mom and I were talking on the phone when I mentioned it to her, and she said, "Well, whatever you do, don't get involved with another man." I told my mother I had my fill of them. But the evil government had something else in mind because shortly after this, I got a phone call from Dave, Ron's friend, who, along with Ron, used to escort me to all of the parties. Ron was involved with the Saanich cops' setup, their bogus drug bust, but I didn't know this at that time. Dave started coming around with a bag of pot and some booze, and John met him a few times. I just thought he was touching base with me, but now I wonder what he was really up to. He never made any moves on me because I guess he could see he would just be wasting his time. Shortly after this, Margaret came around to my house in her yellow Camaro. She had broken off the engagement with Andy, and I heard from someone that she had been with a friend of my old Junior High School buddy, Theresa, and got into a fight with him. She hit him over the head with something and killed him, but I didn't know this when she came over. I wonder now if she is looking for someone to blame it on?

It was around this time that I started to have very vivid nightmares of myself dying in different ways. I was swimming, and I swam out too far, and I started to go under many times. I woke up gasping for air because I couldn't breathe; I was drowning in my dream. Then I had a dream that my mother and I went to Hawaii on vacation, and we were on the eleventh floor in our room when there was an earthquake. The high-rise we were in was coming down, moving back and forth. I was pressed up against the sliding glass window as it was toppling. I hit the ground, and I woke up, and I couldn't breathe. I felt all this pressure on me as I kept gasping for air. Another dream I had, I was in quicksand, and in the dream, there was someone around trying to get me out. They were holding a stick out, telling me not to squirm. I was going under in that dream, too, and I again woke up gulping for air. I didn't know this at the time, but now I think all of these dreams were my subconscious telling me about how much danger my family and I were in.

Well, I made up my mind that I was going to prepare to leave John. It was obvious his drinking was getting right out of hand, and he was never going to change. That is when Diane from work and Darlene came back into the picture again. I hadn't seen her or

Darlene for a long time, since long before my son was born. The two of them showed up out of nowhere with a shit load of clothes for my daughter. They never showed up when my son was born with anything, so I thought this was weird. Diane, by this time, had finished her Food Service Supervisor course and was working over in Memorial Pavilion. I was applying for all kinds of jobs, and I got one in housekeeping with more hours, but not full-time. I didn't have enough seniority for that. It was working in the Memorial Pavilion basement. She had just finished the course, and she told me I should take it, and if I did, I could use her books. I was fed up with working like a dog and decided that it would be a good idea, so she gave me all the information, and I soon started taking it. I asked her for the books one day, and she apologized, saying she gave them to this other girl who was already in the position of supervisor but didn't have the qualifications for it. In the meantime, I applied for a weekend porter job at Eric Martin because I had decided to take this course, and I didn't want that many hours. I'd be too busy doing the program. You couldn't take it here in BC at the time, so I was doing it through correspondence from the Southern Alberta Institute of Technology. Most of the supervisors were from out of province. I took the first year of the program, which was, according to Diane, the hardest part of it. There were Dietitians in the cafeteria who would leave their books behind just for me, and in my lunch hour, I would go in there and get information out of their books. I didn't do the last year because they told me I wouldn't get a job because I had been there too long and I knew too many people. Diane had to quit because of that, and she lost all her seniority, she said. But now I wonder about that, given that they hired her back again. I guess so she could continue being their detective. I didn't want to take that chance, and I didn't know what to do with the kids when I had to go to SAIT (Southern Alberta Institute of Technology) to take the in-service in the second year. By this time, my Dad was so ill, and John couldn't be trusted with the children. I thought that at least with having the first year, it qualified me to be a short-order cook by trade, get that hay, and it put me up a notch in the hospital. However, they were reluctant to give me a chance at any position. I had taken the exam for it in front of the friendly cop, Dale Milan, and got As on all of my assignments, but when I took the test, I barely passed. I wonder why? Did Dale the cop demon change my answers? Anyway, I got a little card for that in 1986.

I was taking the kids into Langford for Sue to look after, and it was becoming a real hassle all the time, so we decided we would fix the basement into a suite. In the meantime, I was looking for a weekend babysitter. John was busy filling the hole in the basement with rocks by hand with a wheelbarrow. It took a year in his spare time to do it, and right after it was done, we got my brother to come over to do the cement work. It was around this time that Armin and Petra moved in behind us. They had two girls, Tessa, a year older than my son, and Lydia, who was a year younger than my daughter. Armin worked for the CRD (Capital Regional District) Parks, and I would see him come home in his truck with building materials, which he was using for a garage he was building. I could tell it came from his work. Another time, he came home in his lunch hour with some gravel. I assume for his road. His wife, Petra, never worked and had joined the Mom's Group. Her kids would come down to my house to play with my kids all the time. I took them outside on the sundeck to finger paint once. Tessa had problems in school right away, and I could tell she was emotionally distraught about something. She never wanted to put her fingers in the paint, and if she did, she would run into the bathroom and wash her hands right away. She wouldn't even do any painting. I told Petra about this, and she said that when she was a baby, she would take her diaper off and smear her feces all over the wall, and she had a discipline problem with her. Sometimes they would go off the sundeck and play in the Charger, which was stored on the property, and I didn't like the idea, but

John convinced me they could get hurt more at a playground. I told this to Armin one day when he came over to complain about them playing in the Charger. He said he was worried about them getting their fingers caught in the door. John continued to work on his demo car in his shop. Armin came down to complain about the noise early one evening after I talked to him about it, saying, "We never had any noise complaints from the people who used to live in your house." I noticed him going over to Bill and Corrine's place all the time. After that, we started to get phone calls from the new by-law officer, Tim, and when our nanny moved in, he would come around unannounced all the time, looking in the basement windows.

It seemed John was always working on the weekends, mostly because the machinery would need work done, and he would do it on the weekends when it wasn't operating. Anyway, my first, at-home, weekend babysitter was a girl by the name of Olivia. She lived near the dead end of East Sooke Rd, and her stepfather and mother were both teachers. Denise, her stepfather, taught a STEP parenting (Systematic Training for Effective Parenting) class to the Mom's Group hosted at my house when my kids were about four and six, and he recommended her to me. He was a principal at a school for children with behavioural problems off the Pat Bay Highway. Petra didn't come to the STEP parenting program, which she needed to because she had big problems. Jan never attended either, and I believe she could have benefited from the course, too. If her kids got hurt, she would be in a panic, yelling at them. It was the best thing I ever did for my kids. Olivia was thirteen when she first started babysitting for me, and she was really good to the kids. She would bring over her clarinet and play it for them, but by the time she was sixteen, she would punish them; she would put them in the corner for a long time. My son would tell me little things like not eating their food. I told her that they get just as much nutrition from their dessert and not to make a big deal out of it. She never used the proper consequences for their actions at all. Denise phoned me up one day and asked me if I would clean their house for them during the week, as he knew I had worked in housekeeping at the hospital, and I said, "Sure." They gave me cash and told me it was a gift. My daughter would come with me, and I would do it in the mornings while my son was at kindergarten. It was only on a bi-weekly basis, and even though Olivia's parents were untidy, I enjoyed going there because they had these big windows all around their house, which looked out onto the water. I would have to clean them every time I went there. It gave me peace of mind somehow. One day, I saw some downers on the bedroom end table, and Dana, Olivia's mother, said she was taking them because her mother died, but I know they liked their booze, and I started to wonder if she was hooked on them. Soon, I was working for their friend, another teacher up in the subdivision, cleaning her house, but she would pay me by check, and I worked like a dog there, too. She didn't have any kids at home, so it wasn't really dirty, but she sure kept me busy. She had antique dining room furniture that she would get me to polish every week, along with numerous other chores. When they remodeled their basement, I had to go down there too and clean it, and they didn't give me extra money or time to do it.

-No sooner did we have the house and shop finished than John decided he wanted the laundry room enclosed. It was too loud for him, so my Dad came over and did that. He also put a huge wall up to make a closet in the kitchen for us and a small linen closet in the bathroom. There were no stairs leading to the basement, and John wanted some, so of course, my Dad volunteered to do that for us. John was always finding work for my Dad. After all that, we slowly began to get the basement ready to make into a suite because I was getting fed up with Olivia, and I couldn't seem to find anyone else reliable. Gary, Jan's husband, came over and did all the plumbing because he was out of work at the time and needed a job. The basement was already wired. We got a local to come and do the drywall and spray it with an undercoat, and I started to paint the place, but by this time, I had tendons from all the painting I had done. My \Dad, as always, had been busy at his house making cupboards for the suite, and he had installed them, and I had just given them three coats of paint. Before that, I had finished painting all the rails around the deck with three coats of paint, and it was a big deck. We ended up hiring a sixteen-year-old boy to paint the walls in the suite. John showed up with a whole slew of rugs, which were in a hotel, and the hotel was being remodelled, so he got them for free. We were working on the suite in the basement, and at the same time, there were a couple of cops building a house on the other side of us. One was a Saanich cop who was doing the electrical, and the organizer was an Esquimalt cop who was building the house for his perverted Christian minister father, and they were using our hydro, which ended up being for free, so they could go and snoop around. I wonder if this was under the table.

They came out with a noise by law in Sooke, I believe, just for a cover-up for John. We got a call from the Capital Regional District by-law enforcement to come down to their office. John and I both went, and the guy we talked to, I can't remember his name now, showed us a picture of a piece of industrial equipment they said John was working on at our property. This guy had a stack of pictures, but he wouldn't show us anymore. We told him John had a mobile welding unit and that it doesn't make any sense to bring equipment all the way out to East Sooke to work on, it just isn't feasible. He works on-site. He went on and on about all the noise that apparently was going on at our place, and I myself told him John was never home, maybe once a month he may work on his demo car just before a race, and that was it. We had kids at home. I wanted a copy of the by-law book, but he told me they didn't have any. I asked, "Well, where can I get one?" He said, I would have to go to the downtown Victoria office. So that's what I did right away, and the old By-law officer who was working there now gave me one. Well, John got pissed off about that, and one day, when his parents, his brother, and his wife, Andrea, were over from England, he devised a plan. He brought home one of Norm's excavator buckets and put it in his shop, and then we all went to the May Day Parade with his family. While at the parade, John took a picture of the clock on the corner of Douglas and Hillside downtown. That same weekend, his brother David took the Charger out for a spin down East Sooke Road as John had insured it just for his screwed-up family and laid a bit of rubber in front of the house. His family was over for three weeks, and they were always coming over and being ignorant. So, my mother, who had never been anywhere, and I planned a four-day trip to Disneyland while they were over. Mom even paid for it. I thought they would be forced to do something for the kids, plus I needed a break, and they sure never gave me one. The only help they ever gave me was his mother used a dishcloth to wipe the kid's face with, and that kind of help you don't need. They would all go for long walks while I would make their meals, and they wouldn't even do their own laundry because they claimed they didn't know how to work the washing machine, even after I showed them how. Margaret, however, knew how to work one because she had one just like the one I had. John's mother would instruct me to go and get John's food for him when he came home from work late, and it was all ready for him in the fridge; all he had to do was put it in the microwave. Well, they were all pissed off about me leaving, except for John's Dad. He understood the stress I was under because we told them all about everything that had been going on, and John's Dad was the only one who told me to have a good time. David, mamma's boy, said, "How could you do this to us?" "We came all this way and you're taking off?" He had me in tears because John was supposed to tell them beforehand, but didn't. Well, coming back, I had bought so many souvenirs for everyone, I forgot about the white leather coat I was wearing and had picked up when Mom and I went on a day trip to Mexico, and they ended up searching our bags. They only give you a few minutes to fill out the forms, and I was racking my brain as to all that I bought everyone. I phoned John to tell him this and that we would be late coming home, and the evil demon thought it was hilarious. Shortly after John's family left, the by-law officer, Tim, came to the door, serving us with legal papers to go to court over noise and working on industrial equipment in a residential area. They were taking me to court, too, but later decided it didn't involve me. I guess they didn't want me to have something against this one screwed up system. That was just what John was hoping would happen. By this time, we had the suite rented to a young vegetarian mother, May, and her three-year-old daughter, in exchange for her babysitting my kids. We called her our nanny. Apparently, the father of her child molested the baby, and she was going through court procedures for that. She would give us some money towards the hydro because it was so expensive in the winter. May was the one who told me to take my son off of meat products, and the ear infections will probably go away. I took my son off meat for a couple of months, and he never got another ear infection after that. Anyway, the prick, By-Law officer, mentioned to me once that we had an illegal basement suite too, and that he was going to get us for that as well, but I soon straightened him out. It went to court, and even though May, the nanny, testified about her not being able to hear any noise and her living right beside the shop, John still got fined for the squealing of tires. I suppose May was trying to make it look like she liked men. John didn't get fined for working on the industrial equipment, but he did get fined for bringing it to a residential property. The total fine was five hundred dollars, and John said it was worth every penny of it. This was to make it look like he was home with the family, which he never was. **Never.** By the way, there was someone working on that bucket that weekend.

It was Jamie, John's old boss's younger brother. That was the type of man he was: DECEITFUL and EVIL.

CHAPTER NINE

Jan and I had come up with the idea to form a group we called Contact for Kids. It was a group for preschoolers so they could come with their Mom or Dad and get together with each other to socialize. My son was getting on the bus and travelling a half an hour to Sasseno's Elementary School in Sooke for kindergarten class in the mornings, so we had the program then. We asked for donations of toys, and we set up art activities in the community hall for them. It was only ten dollars a month to rent the hall for this. There was a little park with a playground, so when it was nice out or they got restless, they could go outside and get some fresh air and exercise. I was elected president of the group, and by this time, there were quite a few preschoolers around. However, I was disappointed with the attendance. The only ones who seemed to come all the time were Jan and her youngest boy, Matthew, and Uta, who had a little girl, Laura, the same age as my daughter, and the cop's wife, Donna, who was the secretary of the group and her only kid, who was a couple of years younger than the rest. The group went on for a couple of years, and then we later changed it to the Youth Club, because there seemed to be more of a demand for something for the older kids. We were still living in the house my Dad built when they put on a Soap Box Derby, and of course, John, being so greedy for money, didn't have the time to make a soap box for his son so my brother had one for his boy Jeff, who was a couple of years older than my boy he said he could use.

They closed off East Sooke Road by the Copper mine, where you turned off to go into the subdivision, and used the big hill in front of our house for the race. My son was so excited about it, and he just about won, but someone had made one for Paul, Barb's boy, and he beat him by a hair.

John's parents' continued to come over, and Francis would sit on her big ass and visit every year because John had sold the flat in England and had given the money he made from it to his parents for all the so-called troubles they had with it. John said to them, "Use it to come and visit us." I believe the kids were around seven and five when they came over again. They wanted to see another part of Canada, particularly the Rockies, so his mother got in contact with her cousin, who was a bachelor living in Edmonton, and told him they were coming out for a visit. They had been communicating with each other over the years, and I wonder now if this cousin knew the couple from Edmonton, Alberta, who said they bought the property next to Bill and Corrine. Well, it was arranged so we would catch the train to Edmonton and meet his parents there. My son got sick with an ear infection again just before we left for the train trip. I was ever so worried about him. I had even taken a Sign Language course because I thought he could go deaf. Anyway, this cousin had a small house on what used to be a farm, so he had quite a bit of land. He paid for absolutely everything. He paid for the hotel for all of us. He met us for breakfast every morning and paid for it. While we were in Edmonton, we went to the Edmonton Mall, but her cousin never came that day. I remember we went to the big, wave pool, and my daughter was on John's back, and she got sucked under, and I had to pull her to the surface. John let my boy go down the big slide by himself, and I waited at the bottom, panicking about it. We stayed in Edmonton, Alberta, for about a week so his evil mother could meet all of her family. We all drove back to Victoria in this Winnebago, John's mother's rich relative rented. This cousin drove us back home because he wanted to see where John lived, and it was going to be a nice holiday for him, too, he said. We stayed in hotels on the way back, and this guy paid for the whole shot, meals and all. While we were driving through the Rockies, I decided I wanted to lie down in the bed at the very back, where I had told the children to stay. John's Dad was sitting in the front, and John and his mother were in seats in the back. My son was asleep when I fell asleep for a while, and when I woke up, I woke up just in time to see my daughter with her hand on the door handle, opening the door to the Winnebago. I immediately jumped up, then bent over John's mother and pulled the door closed. I was so upset, I said, "Why weren't you watching her?" "She was supposed to be lying down in the back bed with me." Now I think Francis wanted her to fall out because that bitch of a mother-in-law didn't even stop my daughter from opening the door, and we were driving down the bloody highway through the Rookies. A real evil demon.

By this time, I was getting tired of being harassed all the time by our neighbours, and John and I had gone to a lawyer in Langford about it because I started to document everything that was going on with them. We took it to him, and he said to us that there wasn't a harassment law, and there was nothing we could do about it but move—the liar. We should have gone to someone else, but we didn't; not that it would have made a difference.

Meanwhile, the crazy Bill was doing work from his place, making barstools for some establishment in town, Corrine told me, and making all kinds of noise and harassing me to boot. One day, John and I were arguing about the neighbours because they had once again complained about something, and it was the first time John ever raised a fist at me and tried to hit me. He let on that he was furious about the neighbours and their harassment, and he said, **"For a couple of thousand dollars, that will be the end of them and anyone else that tries to fuck my business." "It may be ten years from now, and no one will be able to tell."** This scared the hell right out of me. I was also fed up with the drunken state he would come home in all the time, and we were arguing about that, too. He looked pretty serious when he made those statements, and his face was beet-red with his veins popping out of his head. He enjoyed being a troublemaker as far as I was concerned. One time, John was coming home from work, and apparently, he tried to run

Armin, the neighbour who lived behind us, off of Gillespie Road as he was riding his motorcycle home. He told me about it, and when I confronted John, he said, "I just gave him a little shove." Charges were laid, and John went to court, but because the Sooke cops conveniently lost the paperwork and the cop never showed up, it got thrown out of court. I think it was all a big scam, myself, to make it look like John never got along with the neighbours. After he said, "and anyone else who tries to fuck my business, etc." I started to stash away my money. I wanted to make sure I had enough money for a separation and to have a roof over our heads. Little did I know that the system had paid for the separation back then. That was after my lawyer I had for the separation took my entire life savings of five thousand dollars, and left me without a penny.

Very rarely did I allow John to look after the kids. John had bought my son a small motorbike to kill himself on when he was about six. One day, he was looking after the kids, and he made a ramp for the boy to go over with his motorbike, and he allowed my daughter to go on the back with him. They weren't even wearing any motorcycle helmets. He took a picture of them because he thought it was great fun. Around the same time, a guy John knew from Gary's shop, Pat, came over to pay a visit. He was on his motorbike and had just driven in from town, over half an hour away, so his bike muffler was really hot. My son was intrigued with motorbikes, and as we were talking, the boy was beside me, and before I knew it, he was screaming. He had put his hand on the muffler of the bike and burned it really badly. Now I wonder who sent him over? I phoned Irene up, who was a nurse, to ask her if I should take my son to the hospital. She told me they wouldn't do anything for him, so I comforted him for about six hours while he was screaming in pain. I ran his hand under cold water for a while, and then I gave him some Tylenol, but I know now I should have taken him to the hospital. Good nurse, Hay? Another time, John was supposed to be looking after my son, but as always, he was working in his shop. He had told the boy to get some wood from underneath the sun desk and bring it for the stove he had in his garage. He was doing what he was told when, out of nowhere, two big dogs came and attacked him. I heard the sounds of the dogs growling, and I came out, and one of them had a hold of my son's ski outfit and was trying to bite him. I started screaming for John, and when he saw the dogs, he got a crowbar and started towards the animals. He scared them off, and I took my son into the house to see if he was hurt. Luckily, he was wearing a lot of clothes along with a ski suit. John got in his truck with the crowbar to try to track the dogs down, he said. When he came back, he mentioned he killed one of the dogs, but the other one got away, and he met up with the RCMP cop, Mike, Donna's husband, who was living in the subdivision, and he was going to find the owner. The cop came over a little while later and said he found the owner, and if it happens again, they would put the other dog down. As far as I'm concerned, the dog should have been put down right away. What was John and this cop up to? Hats off to them. Shortly after this, the couple from Edmonton who owned the property next to Bill and Corrine came out to camp on their property. They were over at my house, and John was at work. I thought the kids were in the house, but somehow they had gone into this dangerous playground that the big man John made in the back yard we had. All of a sudden, I heard this screaming, and just as I was going to run out the back door, my daughter came in crying, saying they had stepped on a bee's nest and she got stung. The boy was still standing in the same spot, yelling his head off and stamping his feet on the ground, so I ran up to him in bare feet and took him into the house. They had stepped on a mud wasp nest, and I wonder now how it got there. The couple from Alberta phoned 911 when I told them what had happened while I tried to find something to treat them with because they had been stung many times all over the place. My son was worse because he didn't move from the spot they were in. I was really worried about this because the boy had been stung by a bee before on his hand, and it got pretty swollen. I knew you could die if you were allergic to them. The only thing I had to treat them with was deodorant and antihistamines, which were recommended by the person on the phone. To this day, I'm puzzled how they got out of that gate. I always kept it closed. I believe now John was trying to arrange his own kid's death, which ended up being true. He knew my son may be allergic to bees, and apparently, I was told over my computer that John had put the mud wasp nest there.

Before Shifty, when I had the Chinese doctor, Dr. Leon, around 1985, I went to have my annual check-up, like I did every year. The Chinese doctor told me my pap was in the third stage, and the next stage was cancer. I remember asking him if I could have an AIDS test, and he asked me, "Why do you want one?" I said, "Because you never know who your partner has been with last." After that, I never saw him again, and Doctor Shifty took his place. When I saw doctor Shifty to see about my pap test because I made him give me another right after the Chinese doctor left, he said, "Your pap turned out normal." I told him about what the Chinese doctor had told me about my pap test, and that is when he said, "There is nothing to worry about." I noticed Shifty wrote his notes in pencil, but I never thought anything about it then. Like everyone else, I trusted our health care system. Shifty got a lot of business with the kids and me. Every year, when I went for my annual check-up, I would mention to John that he should go in for one, as he hadn't seen a doctor yet. I told Shifty my history, too, and who my previous doctors were, and he pretended he was looking after my kids and me, but he ended up being as evil as Dr. Turd. Once, my daughter had to get treated for Impetigo because John let the little dog we had, "Chase," out, and he had gone into the ditch in front of our house and contracted it and gave it to my daughter. I suppose they were trying to make me look dirty. People were living and extending these cottages, and they weren't upgrading their septic fields. The septic field contents would all come down the hill and settle in front of our house. Everyone complained about it for years, and the Capital Regional District even tried blaming it on us once, but finally, they started making people upgrade their septic fields. Anyway, I had female complaints, but good old Shifty would just brush them off, saying it was a yeast infection, and told me what to get from the drug store, and I did. But really, it was from years of infection unknown to me at the time. I was in agony with herpes often, and he told me to have hot baths and put hydrogen peroxide on the sores. Once, I went in because of a mole on my rear, and Shifty said it was nothing to worry about after he had taken it off in the clinic. After we had gone to the lawyer in Langford about the harassment the neighbour was putting us through, I decided I would tell my doctor about it. I needed someone to talk to because I just couldn't understand why this was all happening. Doctor Shifty asked me if I wanted to talk to a psychiatrist about it, and I said, "Sure, if you think it will help me." That was the first time I had ever seen a psychiatrist. He sent me to see someone at the Health Center on Goldstream Road, the same clinic my doctor was in, and I went to three sessions with him, but John wouldn't go with me. This shrink gave me the creeps. He had this big, black, bushy mustache, which he kept twirling around in his fingers while I was talking to him. I told him everything that had been going on, and when I told him about the neighbours taking pictures of our every move, he asked me. "Well, what do they want?" "Do they want your body or do they want your husband's body?" I said, "I don't know, that's why I'm here." And then I asked him, "Do you think I'm crazy?" he said, "No," and I asked him. "Do I have to come back again?" I asked, and he said, "No, you don't have to come back again." I guess doctor Shifty wanted to make it look like he was helping me, but he didn't give two shits about me or my two, innocent, little children. While I was doing my supervisor's course, I noticed I was starting to have problems with my eyesight too, so I went to Sooke to an eye doctor there who was supposed to be reputable. I told him the problems I had when I was little, skipping lines, but he never commented about it. He said my eyesight was weak in the left eye, and if I covered the other eye and practiced reading with the poor eye, I might get my eyesight back. He fitted me with some glasses, but I ended up taking them back because I didn't think they made a difference at the time.

One day, Petra came over, and I had mentioned to her I needed to buy a new bathing suit because we got on the subject of it. She offered one of hers to me, and I told her it wasn't important. I was going out to buy one, but she insisted and went to her house and brought one down. Well, I tried it on and a little while later, I gave it back to her. Shortly after that day, Armin came over asking if I would look after their kids because he had to take Petra to the hospital. I asked him, "What's wrong?" He just said they didn't know, but they needed to go to the emergency room. I said, "Of course I will." A few hours later, I got a phone call, and it was Petra. She phoned to tell me she had herpes, and it sounded like she was crying. I said, "Well, there must be some sort of mistake." You and Armin have been together forever. I asked her who her doctor was, and she told me. Well, that was the same doctor who did my abortion—the fitting name of Dr. Rippington. Anyway, I told her not to worry about the kids. I would look after them for as long as they needed, and we hung up. I didn't know what to think about the whole thing at the time. I found it all so weird and kind of frightening at the same time. However, I did wash her bathing suit after trying it on. When John came home, I told him about it and he laughed. He thought it was funny. After John was home one day, we were both outside, and Petra had been out for her daily walk. John, the evil demon, yells out to her, laughing, "Ha Ha, you've got herpes." I told John to shut up; it wasn't a very nice thing to say. But he said it even louder and was laughing his fool head off even more. What a scam that was. I guess it was meant to freak me out about trying on her bathing suit, but it didn't work, and I suppose that doctor she had was trying to save his crooked ass somehow.

I was so distraught over what all the neighbours had done, I ended up going over to the minister's house to tell him about some of the neighbours' harassment and to give him one of the Christmas baskets I had made. The Mom's group had just put on a Christmas fair at the community hall, and I had all these leftover Christmas baskets that never sold. I felt sorry for him because I was told by someone that his wife was dying of cancer at home, and he was travelling an hour all the way from East Sooke to the Jubilee Hospital twice a week for kidney dialysis. I went over, and his wife never came out of the bedroom, and I thought to myself, she must be pretty sick. He took me into his garage, and there was a huge white cupboard filled with food, he said, that was there to give to the poor. If that was so, what the hell was it doing in his house way out in East Sooke? I don't think so. He took the basket, and we sat on the couch in his living room and started talking. I told him about what was going on with the two other neighbours we had, and I thought, being a minister, he would understand what I was going through, but to my surprise, he was sicker than the rest of them. He had moved closer to me on the couch, and I was uncomfortable with that, and then he started to rub his hand up my leg while his wife lay dying in their bed. I got up after that and said, "I have to go." The next thing I know, he grabbed me and started to French kiss me, and I pulled away from him and ran into the house, where John and Nick, from the fire department, were sitting at the kitchen table. I told them about it, and John started to laugh. Nick said, "That's pretty sick." No one told me I should report it, even when I told Jan about it. All she said was, "Oh, he is just a sick old man." And I left it at that.

John had a friend, Angus, who was a diesel mechanic and had his own business, and they were always spending time together. One day, I got fed up and took John's yellow work truck, which he had as a spare, and filled it up with all of his belongings. Nick's girlfriend, who came over to see me from time to time, helped me, then followed me in her car, and I took the truck with all of John's stuff from the house and dropped it off there at Angus's house. I should have changed the locks on the door, and I thought about it, but then I was afraid of what John might do. Before I could do anything else that night, John came home with his yellow truck and brought all his stuff back. I thought the children and I were trapped. He told me all our problems were because of the neighbours, and we should find somewhere else to live with more property, so this kind of thing wouldn't happen again. There was no way I wanted to move from the house my Dad had built and go through building another house, and my Dad couldn't do it again. He was getting sicker and sicker as time went by. I agreed to look around for a place already built, which we didn't do, as I knew there was nowhere as nice as what we had to live in. I didn't want to go into debt either. Then again, I didn't want to stay in East Sooke. I had gotten the drift one day when I took my daughter over to see if she could play with Matthew; they had been up to no good. I wandered in their backyard looking for them, and everywhere I looked, there were these huge pot plants. I'd never seen so many before. I had been wondering where they were getting all their money to fix up their place because Gary still wasn't working. I knew then what they had been doing, and I didn't want any part of it. I asked her in surprise, "What the Hell are you doing with all those pot plants?" Jan, whom I never saw smoke a joint, I guess because she was being careful around me, said, "Oh, we're just keeping them for someone." Yea right. The next thing I know, they went in on one hundred acres with her friend, Nicky, and her husband, Ivan. How did they get a mortgage with only a Sally Anne income?

Meanwhile, the couple from Alberta had bought a cabin by a lake in Edmonton, Alberta, to live in, and they decided they wanted to sell the property they had next to the shrubs in East Sooke and put the money towards their new cabin. John convinced me to buy the property as an investment, he said, because "It is such a good deal." They sold it to us for eighteen thousand dollars, and we put it in John's name because he said that way I wouldn't be involved if the neighbours were to complain about what he was doing on this property. It was designated a rural property, similar to Bill and Corrine's, and since there wasn't any water going to it, it was still a steal of a deal. We had paid off our house by this time, so this was the only debt we had, which is why I agreed to it. Within a year, we had that paid off too, and he was going over there clearing and cutting all the big trees down, which pissed the whole community off, especially Bill and Corrine, who then moved their camera over to a window on the other side of their house. Steve, who was from Wales and lived up in the subdivision, had become friends with John and had just gone into the backhoe business as a hobby, he said. Steve came over to practice on the property at first, and later, when he needed welding work on his machine, John did it for him.

One day, John came home and said to me he had found some property, ten acres, and had put a thousand dollars down on it. Weird as it was at the time, Mom told me Dad bought property once behind her back, too. John told me we would sell the house and then put a trailer on the property next to the shrubs to live in while he built a new house. He said, we will use the money from the house my Dad built to pay off the property. Then he would get the land cleared and a road built, which he said would take a while, get another mortgage, and then, after the house was built, we would use the money we made from selling the trailer to pay for the new house. I didn't have much of a choice at that point because a deal had already been made. It wasn't easy selling the house my Dad built. The real estate agent, one of Jan's friends, eventually sold it for us after she told us to buy some white living room furniture and paint the living room stark white so it would make the place look brighter. I still had the same stuff I bought when I was seventeen with my first husband, Steve, and the couch had big tomato tins for legs. Ironically enough, in the meantime, John bumped into the guy I used to go out with, Lebor. John had met him when he first came over. We got invited to his wedding as he was marrying Dawn Lee, the girl I met some time ago, who went out with my first crazy husband, and who went out with Robin's friend Wayne when I started going out with Robin. They were splitting up, and they had a trailer together in Sooke, which he wanted to sell, and it was going cheaply. John said Lebor was really into cocaine and selling it all over the place, and it was probably why they were splitting up. We ended up buying the trailer for cash and had it placed on the property next to the shrubs. The trailer we put in my name, as the property we had it on, was in John's name. We had the water board come out and run city water to the property, and had it installed to the trailer, and had a septic field installed with my Dad's help. It was barely livable when we had to move into the trailer. We sold the house just before Christmas, and it was in February 1989, the rainy season, when we moved into the trailer. When we were still in the house, but the trailer was on the property, a big wind storm hit, and our property was now bare. The property on the other side of us belonged to BC Tel at the time, (now Telus), which had all their spindly, alder trees really swaying in the breeze. One day, John noticed a big branch that was right over the bedroom where he and I were going to sleep, and John said, "If it comes down, we will be killed." So, he decided to cut the branch down without informing the owner. Well, the next thing you know, I got a phone call from BC Tel's manager saying they got a call telling them John was trespassing on their property, cutting down their trees. I explained the situation to them, and the guy over the phone seemed to understand. He told me to put it in writing and not to worry about it, which I did. I told John about it first because I wondered if I should write a letter, and John said, "Do what you want." I thought that was the end of it, but no, the next thing you know, while we were living in the trailer, they got all these BC Tel employees to come and cut all the trees down, and then they slapped John with a lawsuit because the property was in his name only. Of course, like everything, his actions were my fault. Now, I realize this was all because of the release of false information about me. Shortly after I left John BC, Tel changed its name to Telus; I guess they were afraid of a lawsuit. I bet they are shaking in their boots now.

No sooner did we get moved into the trailer, than the phone rang in the middle of the night. I answered it, and it was John's mother from England wanting to talk to John. His Dad had died while he was in Liverpool dropping a load off. He was backing up in his semi-truck and had a heart attack, apparently. When John got off the phone, he put his head down on the kitchen table as if he were crying, but he wasn't, and then he told me, "My Dad died." I could see he was pretending to cry. We arranged for him to fly back there right away so he could be with his family, and now I find out his evil bitch of a mother had him murdered. I suppose because they all knew I was close to dying, it was time to kick Jack off, too, and they would all be one big happy Catholic family. Shortly after Jack died, John's mother informed us that her flat had been broken into and all of his identification had gone missing. About ten years later, after finding out there had been a twenty-year investigation into this case, I figured that explained the break in. I thought John would be back after a week because he left me and the kids in a real dilemma, floating in the mud with no laundry facilities. Everything went wrong that could go wrong. I was running back and forth to my parents with our laundry. Then the plumbing went, it was all plugged up, and Gary had to come over with a snake and wallow under the trailer in the mud to unplug it. Next, the hot water tank went, and Gary got a new one and installed it for me.

By this time, I was fed up with the mess John left me in, and he had been gone almost three weeks, and I hadn't heard from him at all, so I phoned England to tell him everything that had happened, and I wanted him home now. His whole evil family was pissed off with me for phoning him to come home while they were all grieving. This is what John told me when I phoned. Grieving my ass; they were all IN THE PUBS every chance they got. Celebrating their apparent success, knowing full well what I was probably going through. Well, my Dad hurried and put on a sun deck and a laundry room for me. He still had a little green truck he bought so he could help us out. He always knew John didn't give a damn about me or the kids. Shortly after John returned home from his apparent holiday in England, the bank he had ploughed in between BC Tel and our property failed. There was a big lake that had accumulated in this gully at the very back of BC Tel's land, and all this water came rushing over to our property. Matthew was over, and he and my daughter were playing with trucks in the bank when it gave way. The water was soon rising and was almost to the top of the deck my father had built onto the trailer. I was panicking, and I didn't know what else to do but to phone Jan and see if Gary was home. I couldn't get a hold of John; he always made sure of that, so I thought maybe Gary would know what to do. Jan and Gary came over with shovels, and for the rest of the day, we dug trenches in the rain to divert the water away from the trailer. Gary had to go on BC Tel's property to dig trenches from the lake so that most of the water would stay on BC Tel's property.

John had started excavating the ten-acre property out in Metchosin. He was working for his business, apparently, and after that, he would work on that property. One summer night, as he was coming home late from work, he was stopped by the Sooke RCMP on Gillespie Road for drinking and driving and possession of marijuana. John told me they didn't give him a breathalyzer; they just did a road test. But I wonder about that entire situation now.

The Sooke cops eventually dropped the charges for possession of marijuana and took him to court for drinking and driving, which he got off for when it went to court because of his stupid leg, which he used as a defence. The night he got busted, they released him the same night, still pissed to the gills, and let him drive home. When he woke me up to tell me about it, I could tell he was smashed out of his mind, and he reeked of booze. This confirmed I was going to leave this son of a bitch, it was just a matter of time now.

CHAPTER TEN

As usual, my Dad did a good job on the skirting of the single-wide
trailer, the sun deck, and the laundry room. I painted all of it. My
Dad had made us a big picnic table, and we had my daughter's
birthday party on the sun deck with a tarp over the picnic table
because it started to pour buckets. John was too busy ploughing a
road with five switch blacks in it, ten acres up the mountain on the
Metchosin property. He wanted the house to have a view of the
Straits and of Metchosin Valley. John did work in exchange for the
use of Norm's excavator, and in the following two years, he never
made much on paper, and I was so worried about what he was
doing. I thought it was defrauding the government, but little did I
know, the government was defrauding itself. Big time. He even
bought an old 1959 Caterpillar so he could later grade the drive
with it. The day I saw the marijuana plants at Jan's house was the
day I stopped going over to her house. I used to go there in the
morning and have coffee with her after taking my son to the bus
stop for school, and she would always offer me some booze for my
coffee. It was Irish cream liquor, usually, and sometimes I did have
some. Jan and Gary always had a twenty-sixer of different kinds of
booze and would have drinks at all hours of the day or night. One
night, we went over to her house, and John and Gary talked Jan
into smoking some pot. Gary always had his own supply of pot,
and sometimes John would buy some from his so-called personal
stash. That was the only time I ever saw her smoke up. Jan never
came over to my house, except just before a function at the
community hall. When she started working at Sally Anne's, she got
me to shop there. I told her the Salvation Army was for the poor,
but she said, "You'd be helping the poor if you shopped there."
She had two rooms downstairs in her house, piled with stuff she
got from Sally Anne, and her house was always a disaster area,

piled high with clothes, dirty dishes, and toys scattered all over the place. Those kids had every toy going. One day, I went to Sally Ann's, and she was in the back rummaging through all the stuff looking for deals. She said she could do that. No wonder there was never anything good on the shelves. I used to look for Blue Mountain Pottery because my mother collected it, and you couldn't find it in the stores anymore, and I told Jan that, and I told her I thought it might be a collector's item one day. After that, you never saw the stuff on the shelves anymore in any of the Sally Ann Stores in town. At the Halloween dances in the community hall every year, she came up with some really good costumes to wear, which she got for deals at Sally Anne's, and she gave me a costume of a saloon girl to wear one year. She should have been that. I helped serve the drinks at the dances in the community hall when I knew John wasn't going to come. I continued to go to the Mom's Group whenever I fit in, and I soon noticed there was a younger crowd going, so I started to spend more time with the "Youth Club." Besides, my son was getting older and wanted to socialize more and needed an outlet. The last thing I did for the "Mom's Group" was help out with a Fashion show for the community, and of course, I wasn't picked to be a model; that was just for all the raving beauties. I helped make some silk flowered wall hangings out of wicker plates to sell at the show. They also got me to help get these fashionable ladies ready to strut their stuff down the aisle, but they were all so busy helping themselves that I never really did much. I paid for my mother to attend because it was on Mother's Day, and I sat with her. She seemed to have a good time, and she bought one of the wall hangings that I had made. The "Youth Club" put on an Air Band Concert one evening, and it turned out to be a great success. The parents were involved by making instruments for the kids to pretend they were playing, but John never made time to get involved. We also didn't have any instruments that my son could use, so he didn't participate. He wasn't too bothered about it anyway. "I just want to watch," he said. One of the parents brought over an expensive stereo and set it up in the hall, and the kids chose their favourite band to mimic, one group, imitating the Beatles. They even had fake microphones to use and Stage props and strobe lights. I helped put on the makeup for the kids before they went on stage, and they were all so excited about the concert. It was good fun for everyone.

That is when I met this girl by the name of Vivian, who also helped with the makeup. She was an on-call school teacher at Edward Milne High School in Sooke, and she and her drunken husband, Gary, were Scottish. Her husband was a so-called architect and ended up drawing up the demented house plans for out in Metchosin, which John eventually had people build. As a matter of fact, everyone involved in building that house for John was nothing but piss tanks. Vivian was always complaining about how the cops would find her Gary passed out on the side of Gillespie Road on his way home from the Seventeen Mile pub. She had a boy the same age as mine, with whom my son never got along, a girl about four years older, and a girl younger than my children. I told her I had the same problem with John, and as soon as the house in Metchosin was finished, I was going to leave him. I said to her I wanted to make sure there was an occupancy permit issued first before I left him, so it could be sold, and in the meantime, I was saving all of my money for the day I was going to leave him. She said she was going to do the same thing, but she ended up pregnant again, and so she was going to "hack" it out, she said, and that was the last time I saw her.

My son was having problems in school, and in grade one, he had this teacher, who had more problems than he did. I was going to the school to help out once a week, and one time I arrived to see the teacher slamming her fist down on a child's desk, yelling, "How many times do I have to tell you…" This teacher decided my son needed to see the school psychologist. He did a battery of tests, and then the psychologist told me I should take him to see a neurologist. So I took him to a neurologist. All he did was tap on his knees, look into his eyes with an instrument, and get him to put out his arms, then touch his nose. He asked me a few questions about his father, and that was all the evaluation consisted of. When he made up his report, it said my son had "Attention Deficit Disorder" and his father should spend more time with him, which, of course, never happened. He wasn't telling me something I didn't already know anyway. They finally put him in the learning assistance class at school, which seemed to help him, but every year, I had to fight to get him some help.

When we were settled in the trailer, I was working as the late weekend porter in the dish room at Eric Martin, and I decided to put my name down on the call too. They would call me at the last minute, first thing in the morning, and I would have to fly in to work. When I got there, the supervisors would be doing the work, and I would take over, and later the nurses would complain to the supervisors that the job wasn't done properly, and they would try to blame it on me. One time, while I was in the weekend porter position, a cook who was new to the hospital told me I had nice legs. It made me feel uncomfortable working with him. He soon left to go to Vancouver to take the Food Service Supervisor's course over there because it was now offered at the British Columbia Institute of Technology. I guess it was his promotion for sexually harassing me in the workplace.

My Dad was finished helping us out, so he decided he was going to make wooden lawn ornaments. I told him I could probably get rid of them at work, so I ended up getting a bunch of orders for them. He got busy and had like a little factory going on, making donkeys and carts and road runners whose feet would go around and around in the wind. I took them to work and sold them for basically what it cost my Dad to make them, and all the greedy

Catholics of Eric Martin Institution got a good deal on them. Twenty-five dollars for the donkey and cart, and fifteen dollars for the road runner. He also made my mother a beautiful wishing well and a bunch of other lawn ornaments to keep himself busy. He could never be idle, even as sick as he was all the time.

One time, I was forced to leave the kids with John on the weekend when I went to work, and he was burning some stumps and brush, and I was informed that the ass told my daughter to get a pop bottle out of the hot embers, and she burnt her hand really badly. He took her to the hospital, and they gave her some liquid codeine. When I got home, her hand was all bandaged up, and she was dopey. I guess that made John look good; he did something for the little girl, got her treated, but I was pissed off with him because at the time, I put it down to him not watching her. My Dad had put some tiles in the doorway of the trailer instead of the dirty rug that was there. One day, my daughter came in from the snow, slipped on the floor, and hit her head on the coffee table, and I had to take her to the clinic to get stitches.

A job came up in the main kitchen of Eric Martin. "Meals on Wheels" for the elderly, and I got it. It was ideal Monday to Friday, from eight to noon. My daughter started kindergarten, attending in the mornings. I would be home by the time she got home, and John had the big job of making sure the kids got on the bus in the mornings. I did all the yard work on the property while we were living in the trailer. I built stone walls around a flower garden in the middle of a roundabout, and it turned out pretty nice. I remember when we first put the trailer on the property, people from the community would drive by, give us the finger, and yell at us as we worked on it. They were pissed off that John had cut every single tree down on that property, and it had some pretty big old trees. When we borrowed the money from the bank to start building the house, we bought a Subaru four-wheel-drive with some of it because it was what I needed to get up the drive. I drove the

Oldsmobile for a while, but the heat never turned off. In the summer, driving home, which took almost an hour, I was just sweltering. Then the engine started to sputter, and when I stopped at a stoplight, you wouldn't be able to see me for all the fumes, and I was so embarrassed. I kept nagging John to do something about it; after all, he is a mechanic. I was afraid one day I'd be driving home with the kids at night and we would be left stranded in the middle of "No Man's Land." I drove the car like that for some time, then one day, as I started to go to work, it crapped out right in front of our house, Dad had built us on East Sooke Road. After the car went, and I had the Subaru for three weeks, I came home from shopping, put the emergency brake on, and parked it in neutral. Well, the emergency brake gave way, and it rolled down the little hill it was parked on, and it smashed into a tree. I went to the Subaru dealership to try to get them to pay for the repair because I suspected the emergency brake was faulty; it was really stiff and rigid to engage. However, they wouldn't do anything for me, so much for having a brand-new car. Nine hundred dollars later.

I wanted nothing to do with building the house out in Metchosin, and it became obvious to me that John wanted all the credit for doing it. To this day, he'll say he built the house, and I want to ask him where he got his carpenter training from, in England, where they have nothing but brick flats. He never did a damn thing on it, except eventually he made the rails around the decks. It was the weirdest design I have ever seen. The kids' bedrooms were downstairs, and there was a bathroom between them and a spare bedroom with a wood stove in it. You could never use the room for anything because it would get too hot in there. It was always messy, and of all things, he had a rug put in this room. There was a utility room downstairs, and when you came in the door, you would find a cloakroom and stairs that led up to the second level. On the second level, there was the living room, a huge dining room, and a kitchen. Then you would go up another set of stairs to the master bedroom, and off of it, there was a recreation room which overlooked the living room, and the living room had a vaulted ceiling. In the same room as the master bedroom, there was a toilet, sink, and a hot tub. Twenty-eight hundred square feet, and there were forty-eight windows in the house, as if I hadn't gone through enough work in my time, and of course, I was left to do all the yard work too, which really consisted of planting rock plants everywhere because it was what we were on, a big rock. You couldn't have a vegetable garden because the weather up there wasn't suited for it. Beside our property was the Vancouver Island Motocross Society, and you could hear motorcycles roaring through their property all the time. We sold the trailer for $80,000, but we had run out of money, even after selling the property with the trailer on it. We had to go into debt for $70,000 to finish it. I knew from the start it would end up being that way because John always did have big dreams. He had to have the best of everything, and he also had to be the center of attention. Because there was no city water, he had to drill for it, which cost a pretty penny. He wasted so much money on blasting for the road; he even had a future swimming pool blasted in the rock next to the house, and it was nothing but a health hazard and a danger to the kids. He didn't even have anyone install cupboards or closet doors, so my Dad, who was having trouble breathing by this time, had to come and install some so we would have somewhere to put our clothes and bedding, etc. Dad also put the closet doors on, too. When we first moved into the house, there were no rails on the huge deck, which surrounded three sides of the place, and there were balconies off the master bedroom and the recreation room, too, which didn't have any rails, but the building inspector allowed us to move in regardless. If John wasn't sick enough by this time, he had really lost his mind to the booze, and I noticed there was a huge increase in the personal column of his books for his business. He was using a thousand dollars a month on what I don't know, but now I believe it was for cocaine. One time, we went over to an East Indian friend of John's, Kete, for dinner. I asked Kete if he was in my home room in Junior High school, but he said he wasn't. I wonder about that, though. I knew this guy was bad news and never allowed him in my house, but I agreed to go because I knew John liked curry, and I had a liking for it by this time myself. His wife, Pam, was very nice. That year, they invited us to their New Year's party and Kete's brother, I found out, lived across the street from him. I noticed John was missing from the party, so I asked Pam where he could be, and she told me they had all gone across the street. When I got over there, I saw Kete's brother snorting cocaine, and I presumed it was what they were all up to, but I never stayed long enough to find out. As soon as I saw the blow, I left. John told me he never did any that night, but I could tell he was lying. John was continually intoxicated, and I think building this house just gave him another excuse to drink even more and socialize with all the druggies whom he hired to build the house. I was always having to deal with Norm, the contractor, who would seduce me over the phone. One time, he invited John and me to go to a dinner and dance at the Ranger's Station, and Bill and Sue were invited to go too. John said he would meet me there. I was to go with Bill and Sue. They served the weirdest food that night, like cougars and bears. I had a little of the cougar, and it tasted something like pork. That night, Norm kept coming over to the table in a drunken state and insisting I dance with him. Eventually, I got sick of his continual presence at our table and told Bill and Sue I was leaving. I got out of the building and into the parking lot, and who did I see, the Dot and her husband Larry and some other people, all up to no good, I would imagine. I asked them if they had seen John, and they hadn't, so I got in my car to leave. Just as I got to my car, the drunken Norm came running over, grabbing and groping me, telling me not to leave. I got in my car, and he tried to open the door, but I managed to lock it. I just sped off home and left him in the dust. I would tell John about the way Norm acted towards me all the time, and over the phone, and he said it was in his nature. I also told John what he tried to do that night at the Ranger's Station when he never showed up, and he said Norm was just pissed and didn't know what he was doing.

Well, Bill and Sue had been our friends throughout the years, and they would come out to East Sooke and spend the weekend with me, hoping to see John in the process. Bill was always looking for extra work, and occasionally John would get him to work on the Metchosin property. Tommy, their youngest boy, was only a year older than my son, and Ben, the second oldest, was three years older than my son. Then there was little Bill, who was about five years older than my son. When they were young, they all got along pretty well together, and my daughter learned to keep right up with all the boys when they came over on the odd weekend. They would bring their booze, a bag of pot, and some food, and it was company for me. As usual, John would show up late and pissed up, and one time he fell asleep right away at the table, and we put an unlit cigarette in his mouth, stacked empty beer cans on his head, and took a picture of him like that. I wanted to show him how ridiculous he looked. I was always so embarrassed at his drunken state; he would come home in, and I thought if I showed him what he looked like, he would tame down, but he never did. He just got worse. Before we rented the basement suite to May, the vegetarian, we let Bill, Sue, and the kids live in it for free for about two months because they sold the little house they lived in to Gary, Sue's older brother, John's old boss, who fixed it up and eventually sold it to his younger brother Jamie and his wife. Bill and Sue purchased a house that had a basement suite for Sue's parents. They couldn't move in there right away, so they moved downstairs with us. I thought Sue and I were good friends, but when I was dying, unknown to me at the time, I found out who my real friends were, and that was me. Only me. The greedy bitch sided with John at the divorce hearing, writing an affidavit saying that if John got custody of the kids, she would look after them for him.

We moved into the house in late 1991, and during this time, John started to have some accidents at work and when he was at home working. One day, he was at Agnes's house working on his truck by himself, and the truck came down from the hoist onto his finger and took the end of it right off. He took himself to the hospital with the end of the finger, and they operated on him and were able to attach the end of it back on. He had a steel post in it for a while to hold the finger in place. Another time, he was working at home, moving some big rocks from the entrance way, and I had the front door locked, which for years, was a habit I got into. John took a different finger almost off when a huge boulder rolled over it. He was banging at the door to be let in, and he was so mad at me because I had the door locked and he couldn't get in right away; he had to wait for me to open the door. He had that finger sewn back on at the St. Anthony's Clinic in Langford. John was always lighting big bomb fires on the property when we first moved in, and once he went down after supper to keep an eye on the fire, and he said he would be back in about an hour. More than two hours passed by, and he didn't come up, and as always, he was drinking while he was working on the property, so I went down there to check up on him. He was about twenty feet away from the fire in his welding truck full of propane, with it running, and he was fast asleep. I had a Hell of a time waking him up. I kept yelling at him, "You are going to blow yourself up in the truck!" Finally, he woke up and drove somehow up to the house. Needless to say, I was worried about the fire he made and couldn't sleep that night, so I ended up going down there for a while to keep an eye on it myself. Another incident was when we still didn't have the rails on the deck, and he came home pissed to the gills, and I woke up just in time to see him heading out of the sliding glass door we had in our bedroom three stories up. I pulled him in, and he looked like he needed to go to the bathroom, so I pointed him in the right direction, and the next thing you know, he was going on the bloody floor in the corner of the room. One day, my Mom and Dad were over, and my son was with his Dad. The next thing you know, the boy came up in John's yellow truck, which he had as a spare, driving it. It looked like there was no one operating the truck because he was so small you couldn't even see him, and he couldn't see over the hood as he drove recklessly up the mountain. He was only ten. My Mom and Dad couldn't believe what they were seeing, and neither could I. John never came up to the house to visit my Mom and Dad when they came over, which wasn't very often unless Dad came to do some work. John would also let my son operate the excavator alone when he had it on the property to do more work. There was no stopping this maniac, and it was hard now that my son was getting older, only eleven, to keep him away from John. I was constantly worried about the children on this property. My son would get on his motorcycle and ride up and down the driveway, and I couldn't see him to supervise him. They would throw stones in the stagnant pool water all the time, and I was afraid that they were going to fall in and get some sort of disease or fall and hit their head on a rock. John made me a nervous wreck. Just after we got the occupancy permit, a girl by the name of Anne, who did salad prep in the main kitchen at work, was befriending me. I was coaching my son's fastball team for the second year, and she would come out with her husband, Russ, and watch his games all the time. I found out that Russ had just taken the Realtor's exam, so I asked her husband to come out to our house to give an estimate as to how much the house would be worth. I told her things weren't going too well for me in my marriage, and I was thinking of leaving my husband, but not to say anything to John about it because he didn't know that. I told John it would be nice to see how much it was worth and that they were coming out. I remember another co-worker of mine, Debbie, asking me if I had a shower before I came to work, which I thought was a rather personal question to ask me. Of course, I said yes. One day, John was working for Norm, and Norm had told him I could come over to his house and pick his blueberries, which he had in his yard, so I took him up on the offer on my way home from work one day. Norm's business was operated from his home in Langford, and that's when I met this guy who just got hired to pour septic tank forms. John invited this guy and his wife over to our house one night, and he told us that he used to work for the Jubilee Hospital in the disease control department. His wife never came through. He was a real piss tank and pot smoker too, and I can't remember his name because I only met him maybe two or three times.

By the beginning of the summer of 1992, I was continually tired. I would come home from doing "Meals on Wheels," and I would fall asleep a couple of times. I was supposed to pick the kids up from the bus stop, but I would sleep through it, and I would wake up with them knocking at the front door to come in. The mole on my rear grew, and it started to bleed, so I went to doctor Shifty and he took it off in the St. Anthony's Clinic below his office. I wanted him to have the mole tested because I heard from somewhere that moles could be cancerous. Later, I asked him if it was cancerous, and he told me that it wasn't. I also told him about how tired I was all the time, and Shifty said it was probably due to stress, and I knew that experiencing stress was true. Little did I know, I really did have cancer, and Shifty, my doctor, didn't want to treat me for it. In July of that year, John planned a trip back to England to see his screwed-up family, and I just didn't want to go. I was so exhausted, and I thought it would be a good break for me to stay behind. Besides, his mother was paying for it, and I didn't want to take her money because she was always complaining about how little she had. I'll never forget when I dropped them off at the ferry. The kids were only ten and eight at the time and were following him like two, lost, little sheep. I had just reminded John to keep a close eye on them, but John walked around half the time like he was in a trance, or if he wasn't in a trance, he walked around in life like he was too good to be associated with the majority of the population, which included his own kids and wife. While they were gone, all I did was sleep, it seemed, and I was starting to feel worse, not better. Apparently, while they were in England, the Leyland Parade was going on. That only happened every twenty years, and John took them to that. John also took them to the fairgrounds and let them go on wicked rides, apparently, and my son told me his Dad was with a girl by the name of Kathy and was with her at pubs most of the time they were there. While they were in England, I phoned them and talked to John's mother, and she told me her concerns about John and his drinking, and I said I was concerned about it too. I knew when I dropped them off at the ferry, I shouldn't have allowed the kids to go there alone with him, but I also knew I was not well, and I was finding it hard to get through the day.

Come September, I was starting to cry all the time, especially when I looked at my daughter, and I knew something was definitely wrong with me, so I made an appointment to see Dr. Shifty. I told him I couldn't stop crying all the time, and I wondered if he could give me something. He said to me, "I was wondering when you were going to ask me that." He prescribed 75 milligrams of Deserial to take every day, but I didn't feel physically fine either. I guess Shifty was hoping I would take some antidepressants, so it would look like he was treating me, in case I committed suicide from all the physical pain I was in because he refused to treat me. I eventually made Shifty do complete physicals on me and the children, run blood tests, urine tests, and the whole nine yards, I said to him. Something was telling me there was something wrong with the children, too, but he checked us all out and said we were all fine. One day, I stopped at Norm's shop in Langford and was talking to the new guy who used to work at the hospital in "disease control dept.". I told him what I was going through and that I wasn't getting any answers from my doctor, and he said he had some medical books that I could borrow. He dropped them off at the house one night. I looked through all of them, trying to find symptoms that resembled what I was going through, and I got some information about "attention deficit disorder" too. No one could convince me that I wasn't physically sick. As it turns out, I was dying of bladder Carcinoma In situ and having a severe episode of Pelvic Inflammatory Disease. Still, it was never confirmed for me until seven years later. I went to see Doctor Shifty again. I told him I was getting unexplained aches and pains, and I thought I found a small lump in my breast. He checked me out and decided maybe I should have the lump removed, the mental abuser. In October of 1992, I had an operation to remove this lump on my breast, and I made John come with me, and he took me there, but he couldn't stay because working was more important to him. The last thing I remember before going under was telling this Chinese doctor how I broke out in an allergic reaction once, and they said it was due to something I ate. They had asked me if I was allergic to anything. After it was over and I was in the recovery room, waking up was when the Chinese doctor came up to me and said, "You wanted to die, didn't you?" and he walked away. I couldn't believe what I was hearing; it really upset me. The lump wasn't cancerous, but it still didn't convince me there was nothing physically wrong with me. It got to the point where I couldn't sleep, and I would wake up pacing the floors, having panic attacks, and I called the ambulance to my home three times; I remember because I thought I was having a heart attack.

As soon as I got to the hospital, the panic attacks would go away. One time, I drove to the hospital because I hadn't had a bowel movement in over a week, and all they did for me at the hospital was take an X-ray and show me how full I was. Then, they sent me home with an enema, but I was too ill to use it. Just before I called the ambulance to my home for the last time, I was bedridden and couldn't get out of bed. My stomach felt like it was on fire, and I was getting sharp stabbing pains everywhere in my guts. There was a phone on the bedside table, and I phoned up Doctor Shifty and told him that my stomach was on fire, and about what was happening to me, and he said there was nothing wrong with me, and what did I want him to do about it. I couldn't stand the pain I was in, so I phoned the ambulance to my home, and when I got to the hospital, the pain went away again, and I was once more told to go home. It was the middle of the night, and I phoned John to come and pick me up, who, by this time, was really pissed off with me. While I was waiting for him, I was crying my eyes out, and a nurse took pity on me and told me to go to Eric Martin, "They will help you there," she said. John picked me up at the hospital after much coaxing and took me home, complaining all the way there that he had work the next day and I had woken him up for nothing. He went to work in the morning, and I was so ill and my eyes were beet-red and stinging because I had not slept for a long time. One night, I woke up to this excruciating pain in the lower part of my leg, something like a charley horse, but much, so much worse. I sat up abruptly in bed from a dead sleep and looked towards my closet. As I held onto my leg, I saw what appeared to be a ghost. I thought I was dreaming, but I wasn't. A few seconds after I saw the ghost, it vanished into the closet, which had no doors. A few seconds after that, the excruciating pain in my leg went away, and I was left completely traumatized, still suffering from the sharp stabbing pains and burning in my stomach. I forgot about it almost immediately. I guess because it was so traumatic, and I was so physically ill. It was November 16th, 1992, and I decided to phone my brother up, who I hadn't really seen since he did the cement work at our house in East Sooke around 1986, and had given John a box full of old Playboy books, telling him they might be worth money one day. I asked him if he would take me to the Eric Martin

Pavilion. I just couldn't stand any more pain. I was pacing the floors at the hospital, and I couldn't see very well. Everything was blurry, and my eyes were burning, my stomach was on fire, and I had stabbing pains everywhere, too. The lady at the desk of the waiting room who took my information felt bad for me, and I remember her saying, "Oh, you poor thing." My brother waited there with me until I got admitted, which is more than John ever did for me. That is when the nightmare really began for me, and it still hasn't ended.

CHAPTER ELEVEN

At the emergency room, I was put in a private room with a bed until a doctor came in and saw me. I told him over and over again I couldn't see very well, and I saw this sore on my husband just before I came in. By this time, I was really freaked out. I was disoriented and in excruciating pain, and the doctor in the emergency room that day told me to write down what I saw. And I did, but they most likely changed it or threw it away. After all, this one fucked up system wanted me dead, which was the whole point of hooking me up with one hell of a loony. They wanted to keep me from knowing what I had been carrying around for twelve years. I was in the hospital for about a month, and they were sending me to lectures and exercise classes, and I was so ill I couldn't comprehend what was going on. I was finally bedridden again, and the nurses would all come in and harass me when I told them about my physical complaints. They brought another doctor in to assess me, and I didn't even say anything to him. He sat on a chair in my room with all these so-called attentive nurses around me, then left, saying something about me hallucinating. I couldn't understand why he said such a thing. Well, I guess the cancer went into recession because I started to feel somewhat normal. However, I still had the odd sharp pain in my stomach. When I was disoriented, I remember seeing a poster they put up just for me about sexual abuse. I broke down crying when I saw it because I started to remember the sexual abuse, so a nurse took me into my bedroom. She asked me what I remember, and I said I remember falling off the bed and my abuser saying, "I will kill you if you tell." That was the first recollection of the incident that I had ever remembered having. However, one time, just after my daughter was born, I do recall thinking I had been sexually abused, but it was just a thought that quickly went away. I told John about it, and he just said, "Really."

When I started to feel better, I asked my attending psychiatrist, Doctor Bore, when the pain would go away, and he said, "When you confront your problems." I got on the phone right away and called my abuser and confronted him. I asked, "How old was your daughter when you had those pains in your stomach and had to go to the hospital?" He said she was around eight. I said that's how old I was when you molested me. He then said, "I don't know what you are talking about," so I left it at that. I thought all the pain that I was having was psychological, and it had gone now, and it wasn't going to come back, just like what happened to my abuser that day. Suddenly, I remembered seeing the ghost, and I told the nurse at the time about it. "I think I saw a ghost when I woke up in the middle of the night one night," I said. She told me, "Sometimes people hallucinate when they are really sick," and I left it at that, and I never told anyone else about it again because it completely left my mind for a while after. Even now, only my family and my former physician know. I hadn't related it to the Holy Ghost yet because this nurse convinced me it was a hallucination. I know different now. The shrink Bore gave me some medication, Luvox, which I thought made my stomach burn even more, and then he decided to put me back on 75 milligrams of Deserial after I told them what I thought it was doing to me. I also told them I thought I might have Crohn's Disease and I wanted all the tests for that. They gave me a series of tests and tried to assure me that I didn't have Crohn's Disease, and there was nothing wrong with me; it was all just in my head. The social worker had called a meeting with my husband, John, because I believed he was part of the reason why I was in the type of hospital I was in, so I told him, in front of the social worker, Jack, that I wanted him to get help for his alcohol problem. John said to me, "You have the problem, that is why you are in here and I am out there." There was no talking to

John, and the social worker was trying to be the liaison between us, but John wouldn't listen to anything I said to him, so I told him, "Well, I am going to leave you then." We had discussed my leaving before, when I wanted him to get help for his alcohol problem. I told him that if I made the move and I left, I would never come running back to him. We had been married eleven years. I went to a lawyer who took every penny I had in the bank, five thousand dollars, for the separation and custody of my two children. I had a psychiatric evaluation done in order to get custody of my kids, which my lawyer told me cost three thousand dollars, and I only went to the psychologist three times. She was the same psychologist my son saw. Before I was discharged, a nurse by the name of Wendy, who walked with a limp, came up and asked me if I was having any suicidal thoughts. I said "No," but I just got this vision of a woman who walked into the ocean at sunset, never to come back again. A little while later, my mother told me she heard on the news that they found this thirty-eight-year-old woman, who was the same age I was at the time, had left Eric Martin and drowned in the ocean at Willows Beach. As soon as my mother told me this, I remembered my vision and told her about it, but I never mentioned it to anyone again for quite a few years after. Maybe God was warning me about that place. I was discharged on December 18th, and I asked the shrink Bore for a letter of my diagnosis, so he wrote down that I had a "Major Depressive Episode" with an "Obsessive Compulsive" personality and marital discord.

Many things happened before I left the hospital. John called his mother up in England and told her what was going on, and she flew out to help. Right. All she did was verbally abuse me every chance she got, telling me, "Lots of people have nervous breakdowns and they don't go running off on their families." When I had passes from the hospital to go home, I was left to do all the work, make dinner, do the dishes, etc.. She did bugger all for me, and I was so ill my ears were ringing from her abuse. It was around Christmas, and the kids wanted to go shopping at the mall, and I had promised I would take them. John wasn't home from work yet when we were getting ready to leave. One of my son's friends, Gary, was coming with us, and just as we got into the car to leave, the evil demon got home, and he was pissed up as usual. He said to me, "Where the Hell do you think you are going?" I said, "I'm taking the kids to Mayfair Mall to do some Christmas shopping." He staggered and said, "Oh no, you're not." "You just got out of the loony bin." I tried to shut the door to the car, but he pulled it open, then tried to drag me out of the car by the legs. The kids were yelling, "Please don't fight." "Please don't fight." Somehow, I managed to push him off of me and shut the driver's door to the car, but he managed to get into the back door and into the back seat with the kids. I started on my way to the mall, and he was in the back verbally abusing me the whole time and wrestling with the kids. I thought I would drive straight to the RCMP station in Colwood, but then I was afraid that John would attack me while I was driving the car, so I continued in the direction of the mall. As we were going down Sooke Road, I noticed a roadblock had been set up, so I quickly pulled over. I was in shock when I told the police officer who came to my door that I wanted John out of my car because he was drunk and making a scene. They told him to get out of the car and for me to wait. The next thing you know, an officer got on the phone in one of the cruisers and phoned up the Institution for the Less Fortunate and spoke with my attending psychiatrist. I heard John tell the cops I just got out of the Nut House. Well, a short time later, the police officer came to my car door and told me I could leave. I couldn't wait to get away from John. I saw John get into the police car, and when I got back to the house, I learned they had just taken him home. No one asked me if I was hurt or if he did anything to the kids, and I was in so much shock I could hardly speak, plus I was dying. My daughter was then worried about how she was going to get to her soccer games, so I assured her I would take her. At eight, she knew she couldn't rely on anyone but me. I got a weekend pass for when she was supposed to play soccer, and I was coming up the driveway, and the evil demon John jumped out of nowhere with a running chainsaw in his hand; he scared the Hell right out of me as he stood in front of the car so I couldn't go anywhere. I immediately locked the car doors and rolled up the window. He walked up to the front door of the car, and then he said to me, "There is something wrong with the car. Open the hood up." As I drove up the steep drive, steam started coming out of the hood, so I thought something might be wrong. I cracked the hood open so he could take a look. He then took the spark plugs out of the car, and it stopped running. After he did that, he came up to the door with the chainsaw still running, saying, "Now you'll talk." The doors were still locked, and the window was still up. I had no idea what to do, so I just stayed in the car until he left. He went down the hill towards his shop. I got out of the car, ran into the house, and phoned the police. Two male officers came to the house, and I told them what John had done. They asked me, "Well, what do you want us to do about it?" I told them I had to take my daughter to a soccer game, and we were going to be late now. I also wanted the spark plugs put back into the car. I told them I wanted a police report made out on John, and they assured me they would have it on record. But they didn't. Another time, the loony came to the hospital and took my car, and I had to report it missing. He told the officer he needed it for his mother because she couldn't get into the truck, the bitch. So I phoned Jan and Gary to come to pick me up from the hospital so I could go and see my children. I thought maybe they would make sure John gave me my car back, but they never stayed. Neither John nor his mother ever had the decency to bring the children to the hospital so I could see them, nor did they come to see me. I guess they thought I was a goner. I recall Gary asking me, "Do they have good drugs in there?" I looked at him and said, "Not really.

" Well, I got my car back by going through the police. They did something for me for a change, probably because the car was in my name too. It was the 15th of December, and there was no Christmas tree up. The kids kept asking me when they were going to have one, so the next time I was out on a pass, I asked John to get one. He came into the house with this huge, ugly Christmas tree. It must have been at least twenty feet tall, and threw it on the floor in the living room and walked out the door. Like he had just done us a big favour. I didn't know how I was supposed to put it up, and I told John that, but he told me, "You figure it out." The kids were crying because we couldn't get it to stand up. I got a bucket of rocks and put the tree in it and tied it up to the lever on one of the windows, but it still kept falling over. I had to leave without the kids decorating it, and they were so disappointed. Whenever I could, I would pick them up from the Metchosin School on Happy Valley Road, where they were both attending. One time, my daughter decided she was going to slide down the handrail of the steep staircase outside. As soon as I saw what she was going to do, I told her not to do that; it was dangerous. It was about twenty feet or more down from the top. She did it anyway, and when she got to the bottom of the staircase, I gave her one slap on the bottom because I was in fear for her life. According to the STEP parenting program, which I had taken, one slap was okay. And to me, in a case like that, it became a natural instinct for a parent to react that way. Another time, just before I admitted myself to the Institution of the Unfortunate, Eric Martin, the kids were fighting, and my son hit his ear on the bookcase handle, and it instantly went black and blue. I suppose the children could tell I was ill, and they were always acting out. I pulled my son by the hair and took him downstairs for a time-out, and that is the only time I ever laid a hand on that kid. Anyway, just after that, the evil demon shrink, Bore, discharged me from the hospital on 75 milligrams of Deserial instead of a clinical dose of 200 milligrams. John was being verbally abusive to the kids and me. I bought a relaxing tape of a running waterfall, which one of the nurses at the hospital suggested I get to listen to. My son wanted to hear it, so I let him, and John snatched it out of his hand, then asked, "Is this the crap the shrinks give to you at the Nut House?" I was fed up with all he had done to me and his mother had done to me, and of both of their verbal abuse, so I phoned the RCMP to come and have him at least removed from the house. The kids were both sick with a cold, and I guess they couldn't understand what was wrong with me, so they were acting up. When the police arrived, I was trying to treat my daughter's cold, give her some Dimetapp, and talk to them simultaneously. Of course, John's mother wasn't going to lift a hand to help out, so I looked in the bottle of Dimetapp and noticed there was only about a teaspoon of it left, so I gave it to my daughter to take. The next thing you know, they were suggesting they should phone up the medical team, the Mod Squad from the Eric Martin Institution, and see what they thought of the whole matter. I thought it was a good idea, thinking they were helping me. I told a nurse in the hospital, "I was afraid of John," and she could see the terror in my eyes, so she told me that I could go to the "Transition House" with my kids. I never even heard of this place before, but if I had, I would have left him a long time ago. Anyway, the female officer who was there phoned the squad up, and they came out and took me off to the recreation room upstairs to badger me. I remember shaking their hands after they walked up the first stairwell. I was so glad to see them, and I thought they would stick up for me, but they didn't. They were asking me what happened at the school the other day, and I had no idea what they were talking about. It didn't occur to me that someone had reported the one slap on the rear I gave my daughter for sliding down the dangerous outside banister at the school. I suppose it was what they were referring to. I had to leave my own house, leaving the kids behind. This female police officer told me to go to my mother's for the rest of the weekend. I had to leave my kids with an abusive man and his mother, who was just as bad. On the way to my mother's, I saw the female officer standing outside her police car on the side of Happy Valley Road, so I pulled over to talk to her. I asked her, "Why did you make me leave my children with an abusive man?" She told me it was only for the weekend, and I said, "They have been with him too long as it is," and I left crying. My parents couldn't believe they had made me leave my children.

One day, I went to the house to get the kids so I could take them to the Transition House, and only my daughter was there with her grandmother. My son was with his Dad at work. I told my daughter to pack her suitcase; we were leaving. I had prepared both of the kids beforehand, telling them it wasn't safe anymore for us to stay here because their Dad couldn't stop drinking alcohol. I told them that for him to stop drinking, we would have to leave and live somewhere else, but they would still be able to see him if they wanted to. I also explained to them how I was feeling. I told them that "I feel like I have a big headache all over my body." I explained to them, "None of this is your fault, and don't ever think that it is." After my daughter and I packed some clothes in a suitcase, I gave John's mother some pamphlets on alcoholism I had collected and told her her son had a big problem, and it was why we were leaving. As we were going down the stairs to leave, John's evil demon mother stood at the top of the stairs and called me a "tramp" right in front of my daughter. I looked at my daughter, and since she had her back turned, I spat in her direction and left. I didn't even think before I did it, but I am sure glad now that I did because she deserves to be spit on.. She got the idea of being a tramp from the RCMP officers that night, when they came and told me to go to my mother's house for the weekend. I took my daughter to my Mom and Dad's, and although I had custody of both children, John would not give my boy to me, and there was nothing I could do about it because I didn't have the custody papers yet. I tried to track my boy down once after school. I found out where his friend Gary lived and went to his house to see if my boy was there. My daughter was with me. Gary's mother, whom I had never spoken to before, must have called John on the phone when she said she was going to ask Gary if she had seen my son. Later, she came out and said Gary didn't know where he was. Then just as we were going to leave, John drove up their drive. I was trying to talk to John about giving my son to me when my daughter got into his truck and was sitting in the driver's seat. When John noticed this, he grabbed her by the hand and bent her fingers back, trying to get her out of the truck. I told my lawyer about all the trouble I was having trying to get my son, and she devised a plan because she said the papers were held up in the courts. She told me to befriend John and get him to allow me to take the boy to my Mom and Dad's house for supper. She didn't tell me to take the kids to the Transition House despite her knowing what kind of man he was, but I did. I had phoned up the Transition House and told them what was going on with me, and I won't be coming until I have my son. That night, when I told them I was coming, as I started driving to the Transition House, my son asked me, "Where are we going?" and I reminded him of the conversation we had at home about his Dad drinking. I told him we were going to be with friends. When we got there, it took a while for my son to settle down, but he eventually did. At first, he kept running out of the front door in tears, saying, "I don't want to stay here." I heard John tell the kids many times that we would be living on welfare if they went to live with me, and I don't know if they were old enough to understand that concept, but I think the boy got the drift: it wouldn't be a very nice experience. The RCMP phoned the Transition House and said John had told them that he had custody of the kids. I had the papers by this time, after waiting for over three weeks, and I had to show them the papers so they would believe me. I was coming home from Dr. Shifty's office one day, and I noticed John's yellow truck following me as I left the parking lot. When I got back to the Transition House, I decided I should tell my counsellor I saw John, and I thought he was trying to follow me, but I managed to ditch him. Once, my son had a stomachache, and John said in front of the boy, I wasn't feeding the kids, and he wrote a five-hundred-dollar check out in anger, which said on the bottom of it, "Food for Kids." I showed the check to my counsellor at the Transition House. That was what the judge initially awarded me for child maintenance. Another time, he phoned the cops, claiming I had stolen some money from him when I came to the house, which I didn't. I brought a girl from the Transition House with me up to the house as a witness that day. I remember seeing some change in the window seal by the front door as we were leaving. I guess that was his excuse for changing the locks on the doors to the house. Just after I thought everything had settled down, the phone rang, and it was John. This old lady of a councillor, Norma, gave the phone to my son so he could talk to his dad. However, he started to tell John where we were, so Norma took the phone away from him. John had told me the RCMP let him know where we were. In my confusion, I let this lady, Norma, talk me into giving my son to his Dad. I could see the police were defending John. Norma told me that's where the boy wanted to be, and my son had made it unsafe for everyone living here. They couldn't take a chance on John knowing where we were. I know now that it was all a bunch of bull. I remember a group of so-called professionals coming to the Transition House, so maybe it was the squad from the Institution for the Less Fortunate (Eric Martin), and they had something to do with it. No doubt after everything else, the evil demons ended up doing to me. The Transition House told me I had to leave, so my daughter and I were thrown out into the cold. I thought once I found my own place, I would get my son back again. They could have transferred us to "Hill House," another Transition House, which I didn't know about at the time, but they didn't. I guess they pick and choose who they want to save. Before I left, they gave me an application form to fill out for a program called the "Second Stage Program for Battered

Women," which was just as bad. And to make themselves appear as though they were helping me, they also provided me with numerous other low-cost housing applications and informed me that women who come to the Transition House receive priority for low-cost housing, being moved to the top of the list. However, this didn't benefit me at the time. I thought to myself, after everything I had gone through to try and get my boy here, they should have known that I wanted my children safe away from that nut case. I had made the biggest mistake of my life. If it wasn't for my parents, I don't know what I would have done with no money being thrown out in the cold in the middle of January.

We lived at my parents' place for a couple of months while I was dying. I continued to take my daughter to school every morning, a half hour away. One morning, she forgot her pencil crayons at home, so I turned around in a driveway off of Burnside Road, and just as I pulled onto the road, out of nowhere, a milk truck pulled out, and I backed into it. There wasn't any damage to the milk truck, but I had about $900 worth of damage done again to my Subaru, and I paid for it rather than go through my insurance and get penalized. I wonder now if it was intentional. I still never stopped trying to get my son back. Dad even tried to talk some sense into John about how I got custody of the boy and showed him the custody papers. Still, John told him, "I don't give a damn about those papers." He also told my dad I was crazy, and this was right in the Metchosin Cafe, all concerned for the boy, but all he was concerned about was the money he was having to dish out. He also knew it would drive me over the edge, him having the kids.

He told me my parents' house was unstable in front of my son. Before I admitted myself to the Institution for the Less Fortunate, I had arranged for my boy to get into a special education class, which was recommended by his teacher at that time. There were psychological forms to fill out again, and John refused to fill them out, saying there was nothing wrong with his kid and was offended that they all thought there was. He said, "I'm sick of all of this psychological bullshit and ripped the paper up." You couldn't tell him my son just learns differently from the other kids. There was no talking to him. Really, though, I knew he was the biggest problem the boy had. He was always beyond reasoning, alcoholics all are. He was not in touch with reality whatsoever. He should be in the, as he called it, the "Loony Bin." Not me. Meanwhile, my son was getting headaches and stomach aches, having to lie down in the school office all the time. At the time, I thought it was psychological, but now I know it was more than that: Crohn's disease. He was supposed to go to the doctor's about it and missed his appointment, not that the doctor would do anything for him. I already had the children all checked out by him. I found this out after the fact. One time, I asked my Dad to come with me to the school to see if he could get his grandson to come with him. They were always really close. Papa was the only real father he ever knew, and I thought he would listen to his papa, but by this time, John had poisoned the boy with so much evil about my family, and the kid was afraid of what his Dad might do if he went with his papa. My Dad came to the school, and his grandson got in the car with him, but Dad ended up driving him up to the house in Metchosin because he told his papa it was where he wanted to go. John phoned the RCMP in Colwood about my Dad, and they phoned my parents' house, accusing my Dad of kidnapping the boy, and John wanted to lay charges against my Dad because of it. At this point, I still had custody of my son.

Come the end of February, I got a phone call from the councillor at the "Second Stage Program for Battered Women" telling me they had a two-bedroom townhouse for me and my daughter to move into, and I could start the program at the beginning of March if I wanted. I felt really lucky since I didn't have to pay for this townhouse, and the program was free too. The program was run out of the old orphanage, which my grandfather used to tell me I'd go to if I was bad, and the son of a bitch was right. Only I wasn't the bad one. It was now called the Cridge Center for the Family, and there was a small row of townhouses, right across from the center, where battered women got to live while they were taking this program. A deception pretending to help women and children, but in reality, they are worse than the orphanage was. My place was furnished, and I wondered why all the others weren't. And now I guess this unit was for women who they were going to harass, which they had no intentions of helping, and knew they wouldn't be staying long because they were, as I was later told, one of their "Victims of the System." I transferred my daughter to an elementary school nearby, Oakland's. The judge had made an order which stated John could see the kids every other weekend, provided he refrained from the use of alcohol. I talked to the children's counsellor, who was a male, about getting my son back because I still had the custody papers, and he said No, I couldn't. It was too late to get him back now, and he had a look of anger on his face. I wondered about what he said because I thought these people were supposed to help you. Well, I had to allow John to see the girl, and one time he refused to bring her back to me. He asked her where we were living, and then he asked me, but I refused to tell him. I could hear my daughter making a fuss in the background when I was talking to him on the phone in the Hillside parking lot because they hadn't arrived yet, so finally we arranged for them to meet me there at the Hillside Mall, a few blocks away from the Cridge Center, and he would give the girl to me then. He followed us home that night, and I couldn't ditch him. When we arrived at the townhouse, my daughter and I ran out of the car and around the buildings until we saw the evil demon leave. He didn't find out which townhouse we were living in, but he knew where we were. One time, John took the children to Western Speedway and left them there alone. Then, when I went to bed at night, I would hear the police outside in the parking lot talking on their loudspeaker, saying, "The lights just went out," whenever I shut off my lights to go to bed. I didn't know what to think about that. I felt like the police were watching my every move, and I started to get freaked out about it. I phoned up Robin, the second intimate relationship I had, and got him to meet me at the soccer field one weekend when my daughter had a game. I had seen Robin there with his kids, and he reminded me of what my psychiatrist Bore had told me about confronting my problems, and the pain would go away. I guess the recession was over because my guts started hurting again, stabbing pains and burning. I confronted him with the sexually transmitted diseases he had given me, and he said he never had them. I said, "Well, you were only the second one I had ever been with, so I know you gave them to me." Well, his dirty mouth fell wide open. I left the demon standing there after I said that and went and watched the rest of the soccer game.

I was trying to figure out why the cops were coming here at night, patrolling the place, plus I was getting confused due to my illness. I thought I had done something wrong. I was trying to do the program, and I got the feeling someone was coming into my townhouse all the time, too. One of the exercises we had to do was to think up as many names as we could for our abuser. Someone had put all kinds of nasty names down in my book. I guess they thought I was full of anger or something, but I found this hard to do. Memories started to come back to me, and I started writing them down. When I would go back to what I wrote, it looked like someone had been at it, but I wasn't sure. I recall telling the male counsellor about where I used to work when I first started working for the hospital because he asked, and he asked me, "Was Miss Stevens there?" and I asked him right away, "How did you know that?" and he walked out the door without answering. I felt I was losing it. I was asked if I wanted someone to come and help me out with housework, and I said, "Please, it would be nice. Well, this lady came from Nitaka Home Care, and she made a salad out of eggs that were black, rotten, and soggy, and I had to throw it all out. She did the laundry and put my underwear in my daughter's drawer, so I told her about it and said I didn't need any more help. After that, I was in so much pain, fear, and confusion that I just wanted to go to sleep, and when I woke up, the pain, fear, and confusion would all be gone, so I took the rest of the sleeping pills the evil demon Bore had prescribed for me. Because Bore let me out on only 75 milligrams of antidepressant instead of a clinical dose, I was quickly going downhill. He also told me to quit smoking. I guess to make himself look good, the mental abuser. I took about fifteen sleeping pills, and as soon as I took them, I knew I shouldn't have done it, so I called up the male counsellor because he had given me his pager number in case I needed him at any time, he said, but no one came. I even phoned up the emergency squad, but they never came either. The next morning, my daughter managed to get me up, and I took her to school in my car, but no way I should have been driving. I was right out of it, and even now, I barely remember that. When I got back from school, the so-called Family Violence Counsellor, Jane, who was supposed to be available for me at any time, too, was at the townhouse, and I told her what I did, and she took me to the hospital. I remember being in bed in the emergency room and my Dad coming in to see me. I told him, "I just wanted to die." I didn't tell him how much pain I was in, though, because just as I said that, I heard a doctor ask me, "Who gave you the sleeping pills?" and I told him, and then he made a disgusted-like sigh, and I heard him walk away like he was mad. It is hard for me to describe how I felt after that. I remember very little, but I do remember a nurse talking to me about all the abusive relationships I had in my life, and when I came to Mike, I couldn't remember his last name, and after that, I went blind, and I recall telling her I couldn't see. I still can't remember his name, probably because I was doing so much cocaine back then and never thought to ask him. I must have gone unconscious after that because the next thing I remember is being helped down the hall by this same nurse, unable to walk. A little while later, the same nurse harassed me by condescendingly asking if I had remembered Mike's name yet. Then they were rolling me in and out of the operating room at the Institution for the Less Fortunate, giving me electric shock treatments, which I remember saying I didn't want. Apparently, my evil demon of an ex-husband didn't want me to have them either. But that again was just to make him look good. I was there for three months, and I had eight electric shock treatments. I imagine the evil demon Bore got a thrill seeing me dying without any painkillers as he gave me ECT (Electric Convulsive Therapy). I recall some of my fellow employees coming to the floor I was on to visit me, like Debbie and Lorraine, who I worked with when I was doing Meals on Wheels, and they telling me how skinny I looked. Overnight, I had lost eleven pounds, and I was already thin. Anne, the fat salad girl, would come too and bring me special things from the kitchen. I was told that if you knew someone in the Institution for the Less Fortunate, you were not supposed to acknowledge them at all, never mind visit them. Sometime during the ECT treatments, Dr. Shifty decided he would send me to a urologist. He did a cauterization on me, and when I asked him what it was, he said "Carcinoma In situ," and I knew that was cancer, I guess, from working in the hospital, but like everything else traumatic, I just threw it into the back of my mind again. Besides, I was getting ECT, which screws up your memory for a while. They treated me for the cancer, but not the cause of it. I only realized that eight years later, the son of a bitches. After the ECT was all over, the male counsellor came to the Institution for the Less Fortunate to see if I could continue with the program. A male nurse named Norm was present at this interview. He started talking about sexually transmitted diseases. I started to cry. At this time, the male counsellor allowed me to continue. After that, I found out my loony-tune husband took the matter of custody of my son back to court and won while I lay dying in the hospital. He also tried to get custody of my daughter, but my parents stepped in, and the judge granted temporary custody to them. The bitch of a lawyer I had then, whose name I got from the Transition House, a legal aid lawyer, and I was now paying for her, phoned up my parents late Friday afternoon and told them they should get a lawyer for Monday morning because it was going to court then. That was impossible, so they went there alone, and John never even showed up. That's how interested he was. Besides that, knowing his arrogance, he most likely thought it was a slam dunk. I had the custody papers awarding temporary custody of my daughter to my parents at the Cridge Center townhouse. Someone came into my apartment and stole them and other documents, like the documentation I had of the neighbour's harassment out in East Sooke and the note from the evil demon Turd who gave me illegal permission to have maternity leave with my daughter. Everything was spewing all over the apartment when my health nurse, Collette, came over. She saw the mess and thought I had done it, which I didn't. I told her what was missing, but she wouldn't listen to me. I had transferred doctors to Dr Turd because it hadn't dawned on me he was behind all of this. Who would figure all this out? I was just beginning to remember things. I thought it would be closer, and I knew I was being harassed and found it hard to drive.

One day, my daughter and I were coming back from the Crystal Gardens swimming pool, and I was driving on Quadra Street just before Cook, when a lady in a truck tried to run us down. She cut right in front of us and gave me the finger, and I wasn't even doing anything. I don't know why, but right away I thought Bore had something to do with it. Collette, my health nurse, took me to the doctor's office and then to the Jubilee Hospital because the Turd wanted me admitted. The evil demon Turd and a shrink by the name of Jensen, equally as evil, had me committed, and they threw me in a locked room. First, a rude nurse came in and ordered me to take all my clothes off and put the hospital PJs on. When she spoke to me, she was very abrupt, and it was all so frightening and degrading. Then they put me in a dirty room on the third floor of the Institution for the Less Fortunate. In the hospital, this Jensen came up to me and said he thought I should be taking Haldol because it was for drug addicts. I told him I'm not a drug addict. When I went to have a bath, I had to scrub the tub out over and over before using it, so we could all maintain some sort of dignity. It was so filthy. I then demanded to be put in a clean and private room, as I had paid extra for it, and they accommodated my request. Because my memory was coming back to me, I told Collette, while I was in the hospital, what the evil demon Turd had done to me: "He gave me lazier treatment, and it hurt like hell." She told me lazier treatment doesn't hurt. I said, "Well, I couldn't believe the amount of pain I was in." She asked me if I wanted to confront him with what he did to me, and I said I did. When he came to my room, all I could say to him was one question, "Why did you say that I think I got them all. He said, "I don't remember saying that." It was so long ago, but he must have remembered because why did he say it was so long ago? I suppose they all wanted me to think that I had done something wrong when I hadn't. It didn't work. My admission only lasted the weekend because my shrink doctor, Bore, released me on the following Monday, presumably in case this should come up in a court case. I suppose the theft was all a plan to get me out of the program at the Cridge Center, as I was starting to remember too much, and they wanted it to appear I was crazy to cover all their evil tracks. The lying, evil demon shrink put me on what he said was another antidepressant. It was really an anti-psychotic drug called Loxipine, which allows people to walk all over you, along with the 200 milligrams of Zoloft he then prescribed for me. After that, the male counsellor told me I wasn't able to participate in the program because I had missed too much, and it was one of the mandates to live at the Cridge Center. Again, my daughter and I were thrown out onto the streets. As usual, my parents came to my rescue, and that is when I found out what all they had been through while I was being bounced in and out of the Institution for the Less Fortunate and so-called safe houses.

The day after I was hospitalized for the overdose, John and my son went to my parents' house and started banging on the doors. The boy was at one door and John at another. My parents phoned the Saanich cops on John for that, but as usual, nothing happened. John would continually phone my parents' house, wanting to talk to my daughter, and would always make her upset with his slanderous remarks about my parents and me. He told my daughter her grandmother was nothing but a witch. Of course, the same old line we were all crazy, among numerous other slanderous lines and phrases. One time, he wouldn't bring the girl back to my parents, and she phoned three times, crying her eyes out for Papa to come and pick her up. My Dad called the police about that, too. Again, nothing happened to him. John showed up unannounced once at Oakland's school. Dad would drive his granddaughter every morning and pick her up. John said to my Dad, "I'm going to kick the shit out of you," and he said it right in front of my daughter. Another time, John told my Dad, "I am going to drive you to your grave and spit on it." My parents allowed John to take my daughter camping for the Easter long weekend, and when she came home, Mom said, "You could tell she was ashamed of herself because she was so dirty." My daughter told the male counsellor that there were beer cans stacked high all over the place at the campsite, and she and her brother would go off into the woods on her brother's motorcycle late at night while all the adults were drinking. The evil demon was supposed to refrain from alcohol when around the children, but he didn't care what the courts said, and he didn't care about his own children either. He was going to do what he wanted. Even after all this, once the male counselor asked my daughter, "Would you like to live with your Dad?" And she told him, "No."

he asked her, "Why not?" And she said "Because every time I go there to visit he gets me to do house work and my bed is full of bugs." In June, when I was hospitalized again, John phoned the hospital, harassing me, telling me I was crazy. On my daughter's birthday, he came over to my parents' place, harassing them, and the cops were called. She was only nine, and he came by with a stereo, trying to buy her and threatening to take her. All for the love of money and nothing else. By this time, he was bringing my brother into the picture, slandering his name all over town, and that angered my Dad to no end. John's lawyer and my lawyer had cut off all John's visiting rights to my daughter because John was acting so damn crazy. I thought with all this I'd get my son, but no, that never happened either. John would also make promises to my daughter, such as that if she were to live with him, he would buy her a horse, but the girl wouldn't buy into it. One day, my parents and my daughter came to visit me in the hospital, and John showed up and made a big scene in the lobby, and the police were called. A police officer came up to the ward and asked my daughter if she wanted to go with her Dad, and she said, "No, not now or ever." After my parents left the hospital that day, John tried to run them off the road, and my daughter was hiding in the back seat of the car. My son was in the truck with John. My Mom said she was terrified, and when she looked at John as he tried to run them off the road, she noticed the evil demon's face was beet red, and his head and mouth were moving up and down vigorously. My Dad managed to maneuver around John, and he immediately went to the Saanich cop shop. At the cop shop, this so-called officer told my parents. "Oh, go home and have a cup of coffee," and wouldn't even take down a report. When I got out of the hospital, I found out what this manic had done to my Mom and Dad. I took Dad to the Victoria City Police Station, where the honest Dale, the righteous cop who brought this lunatic over here in the first place, unknown to us, was working. I just couldn't believe nothing was being done about this loony. I wrote out the police report because my Dad, just thinking about it, was visibly shaken. Later, John got charged, so I heard, but Mom and Dad were never called to testify, and so I don't believe anything ever happened to him because of it. Meanwhile, my mother got a little black book and documented every single thing John did to them.

In June 1993, I received a phone call from the British Columbia Housing Association, informing me that I had qualified for a unit in the new Tillicum Terrace apartments on Tillicum Road. It was about five minutes away from my parents' place. We moved in on June 15th with nothing but the clothes on our backs. I thought I was lucky to get a brand-new, low-cost housing unit, but it was only a two-bedroom, and I still wanted my son. It soon became apparent that I wouldn't get my son, and my luck in securing a suite in a BC Housing Complex seemed like another scam to harass people who didn't meet their standards, or rather, Canada's standards. "The land of the free, opportunity for all." For years afterwards, you would hear the spokesman for this organization blabbing over the radio about how they help women and children, when the whole time I lived at Tillicum Terrace, it was another nightmare in itself.

CHAPTER TWELVE

I had a different lawyer, and he was referred to me while I was in the Institution for the Less Fortunate. He came to the hospital to talk to me, and I told him I had gotten a place to live, but I had nothing to put in it. John had everything. He asked me what I wanted, and I told him I had bought the bedroom furniture with my own money, and the computer, which was only a little over a year old at the time, and I wanted that. Mom and Dad gave us an oak desk, which was in the recreation room and was also used as an office. I asked for that too. Of course, I wanted my daughter's bed. As far as I was concerned, I should have gotten all the household furniture and items because I had all of that when I first married John. When it went to court, the judge ordered John to provide us with beds and all of our personal belongings, and that was it. I sent a moving company, "Two Little Men with Big Hearts," out to the house, and when it came back, it was filled with junk. John had done his house cleaning, and I had to tell the movers to take most of it away. There were no beds for either of us. When I left the "Second Stage Program For Battered Women," Jane, the Family Violence Counsellor, provided me with a letter to take to "Women in Need" explaining that my daughter and I didn't have any furniture, linen, or household items, and we would be needing all of this. WIN (Women in Need) came to the apartment with a truck and dropped off an old dresser and a bed for me, but I couldn't sleep in the bed because it smelled so bad. I took it to my parents' place, and my Mom phoned them to come and get it. They didn't want to, but my mother said, "Well, you gave it to her." They eventually came and picked up the smelly thing. They certainly help women in need, but they also harass them. Mom and Dad had bought a bed for my daughter, and they also gave us a love seat, which turned into a hide-a-bed that my daughter and I both slept in at first. It took a while, but eventually, after I got more hours at work, I bought what was supposed to be new furniture; however, I ended up getting ripped off for some of it, too. I had to get my daughter a new mattress to sleep on because, Anne, the fat salad girl, and her fat husband ruined it for her, and that never lasted the length of time it should have. I had to buy yet another mattress for her. And I don't know about my mattress because I had only been sleeping in my bed for a few years, after over ten years of sleeping on the couch. The coffee table I got from Dodd's furniture ended up being a dud. The leg was always wobbly, and eventually it broke off, so I had to throw it away because it couldn't be fixed. I should have taken it back right away, but I didn't, probably because I was so doped up.

A court advocate was appointed by the courts to conduct interviews with the kids. It was ordered while I was still living at the Transition House, and it took years before they finally got around to it. At the time, my daughter was worried about me pulling my son's hair and what this guy was going to say about it, and a counsellor at the Transition House told her she could tell the advocate Mom was sick, then, when that happened. I was surprised they would take a ten-year-old and an eight-year-old's decision as to who they would like to live with, especially in a situation like ours, where there was abuse going on in front of the children, but they did. Not only did they do interviews on all of John's references, but they also didn't do any on mine. They were the RCMP who told me to leave my children behind that night, Sue the greedy bitch who took John's side thinking she would look after the kids if John got custody but that never happened because John is too greedy for money, Doctor Shifty who was going to let me die, Gary's mother who I spoke to once and the Vice principal at Metchosin school who John never had anything to do with. I suppose they were all Catholic. The decision for the children to remain where they were was made in February 1993. John failed to attend the scheduled meetings in January 1994 with the new advocate, Sharon, and she subsequently wrote a report on this fact. John used the excuse that he was away in England with my boy and never got notification of it until a month later, when he got back from England and picked up his mail. This was against the court order to leave the country, but the evil demon was picking up his soon-to-be bride, Kathy, with whom he had committed adultery. It was right at Christmas time. I remember Mom and Dad giving us a few decorations and their fake tree because they went out and bought a smaller one. My daughter and I made some decorations for it because I couldn't afford to buy any. We made stars out of the sticks from the ice cream given out at the hospital, which I collected, and bells out of the coffee creamers. We wrapped them in tin foil and made a garland out of construction paper. Mom and Dad gave us some lights for the tree, too. I had to buy some of my household goods from thrift stores. Well, after we were settled in the apartment, a different court advocate was eventually assigned. He had the same outcome as the first, and I wonder now what they consider mental abuse, or do they even know the meaning of it? I guess they think they do, but only from a book, maybe. He went to my daughter's school, Tillicum Elementary, where my girl had a really good teacher. I had informed the school about John's visiting rights being cut off by our lawyers until the case went back to court again. My daughter's teacher knew that she was having a rough time in her life, and her teacher was really good with her. The following year, this teacher taught a grade four/five split class, and she ensured my daughter was in her class again to maintain communication. I had been going to the school to help out with various functions, so they were beginning to know me there as well. I know the school gave this guy a good review, but it didn't seem to matter to him one bit. I still never got my son.

A woman named Sandra moved into the apartment beside me. We were on the bottom floor of the Tillicum complex, so it was like a townhouse, really. Sandra befriended me. She was a single mother of a boy named Michael, and he was just starting school. Sandra worked at the pantry in Colwood as a waitress, and she was supposed to be Catholic. Her mother was in a home over in Vancouver. Her house was a pigsty. She rarely ate at home, and when she did, she left the food in the pots for weeks. Fuzzy things would grow inside of them, and dishes were stacked everywhere. I have never seen such a dirty, messy place in my life. Clothes and junk were scattered all over. She kept everything that came in the mail. Her son, Michael, had a problem peeing the bed, and she would take the sheets off the bed and throw them in a corner, and there they would stay for weeks. She would keep the window open all day so the mattress would dry. Now I know where clymidea comes from. She wanted me to clean her house and give me money for it, but I never took any money. I said I would help her out once in a while as a friend, and when she insisted on taking my money, I gave it to my daughter. By this time, my daughter was working for an Avon lady and liked the fact that she could make her own money and would help me clean Sandra's place from time to time. Sometimes Sandra would take us out for a meal as a thank-you for helping her. When my daughter eventually got her babysitting course, she would look after Michael under my supervision, and Sandra would pay her for that. I soon had to end the friendship because I just couldn't stomach cleaning her place anymore, and she wasn't making any effort to help herself. Her house was a real health hazard. I would have phoned the authorities about her, but she told me once someone did that, so I didn't bother. She met a really nice guy named Wayne, who worked at a gas station. I didn't know what the Hell he saw in her, but they ended up getting married and moving out of Tillicum Terrace. Later, I found out her mother got transferred to the Memorial Pavilion here in Victoria, so maybe that was her payment for her dirty ass showing up beside me and for trying to get me to take money when I was collecting disability.

Shortly after we moved into Tillicum Terrace, John broke the restraining order issued against each other. Get that hay me who all along had been fighting for her life has a restraining order out against her. Anyway, John harassed me at McDonald's in Colwood on my son's birthday. He told me that if you go after me for maintenance, I will go after your Mom and Dad. I could see the children were being emotionally abused over everything that was going on, and I even went to the Social Services with documentation of all the incidents to try to get my son apprehended. Still, I was unsuccessful with that, too. They said they did an investigation, but when they got to the house, the boy had just gotten out of the shower and appeared to be well looked after, they said. Didn't anyone ever tell them that first impressions can be deceiving? Those people with all their useless book knowledge, in the meantime, the evil demon continued to abuse the children. He wouldn't show up when it was arranged for the kids to be together. Once, he told my daughter we would never see her brother again, and she was really upset about that. John would phone us up and leave rude messages for my daughter on the answering machine when he was all pissed up. When he did see her, he would call her his favourite name, "Beaker." One time, John phoned us seven times in a five-minute period, harassing us.

Then I became friends with a woman in the apartment block named Tammy, who had a girl a couple of years older than my girl, Robin. Doctor Bore asked me when I wanted to go back to work, and because I was settled in the townhouse, I told him as soon as possible. I was only receiving disability from my part-time Meals on Wheels job, and I was finding it hard to make ends meet. While I was off, Meals on Wheels was taken over by Silver Threads, an old folks organization, and was no longer on contract with the hospital, so I had bumping rights. I didn't have to exercise those rights, and I was glad, as it always caused a lot of friction in the workplace. I applied for a job in one of the Memorial Pavilion kitchens, Homer Three, which offered about fifty-six hours bi-weekly. I got it. While I was working there, Anne, the fat salad lady, found out through the Dietitian at Eric Martin where I was working, and came to the kitchen when she was over from Vancouver every chance she got. Her fat husband said he found it hard to sell houses over here, and his Dad was living in Surrey, Vancouver, so he thought he would do better living over there. Fat Anne got a job at the hospital over there, so I guess that was her promotion for befriending and stocking me for two years. She was always looking for a place to stay when she came over. Anne told me her mother was on the Island and was sick, so she didn't have anywhere else to go. I offered to let her stay with me when she came over. She took me up on my offer many times, and she would always want me to phone up the personal ads in the Monday magazine looking for a mate, but I told her I wasn't interested in anyone. A couple of times, we placed an ad just for fun. Later, she started a business selling her homemade dog treats and would enter all the craft fairs here in Victoria, often coming over to stay with me. I thought she was my friend, but I later discovered she was on a mission, just like everyone else I met.

Tammy looked after my daughter when I first went back to work, and I thought she was my friend too, but I found out differently. She had a daughter named Robin, whom I tried to get my girl to play with, as she hadn't made any friends at this point. However, she and Robin never saw eye to eye. One time, my son was visiting, and we all went out together. When we came back, I parked my car in my underground parking spot. We all got out of the car, and my boy noticed there was a wallet on the ground in the underground parking lot. He ran for it and looked in it, and there were forty dollars in there. Of course, my girl wanted to see, and they were fighting over the wallet. Tammy and her daughter just went into their apartment as soon as the argument began. I guess they didn't want Tammy to be a witness to how I wanted to find the owner. I told my son, "You can't keep the money, we have to find the owner," and there was a male student's picture identification in the wallet, and my daughter said the boy didn't live here, but she knew where this boy went to visit. The kids and I took the argument to my place, where I told them to go knock on the door and see if they could find this person. They did, but no one was home. My son was making such a fuss about keeping the money; he kept saying, "Finders, keepers; losers weepers." I tried phoning the managers, Tina and Tom, about it, but no one was home there either. Well, eventually, I told my boy he could keep the money as a gift from me, and I would replace it the next day when I went to the bank. I then got him to put the wallet into the manager's box by the front entrance. The next morning, around 9:00 AM, as I was getting out of the shower, the phone rang. It was Tina, one of the managers of the complex, asking me to come up to the office. When I arrived, a cop was with her, and they were accusing me of theft under one thousand dollars. I told them my son, who was visiting me, took the money, and I was just going to go to the bank to replace it. We also looked for the owner first and tried to contact the managers, but no one was home anywhere. Then I said, I told my son it was a gift from me because he insisted on keeping the money. The cop asked, "Don't you have any control over your children?" The two of them had me in tears about it, and I said to them, "You should be after the real criminal, my ex-husband." Well, now I see it was a well-thought-out plan, which, as far as I'm concerned, didn't work. Seeing my phone has been tapped for almost forty years, probably longer, it's proof that it didn't work.

All I wanted to do was work, support my daughter, and get my son back. There were a lot of cutbacks going on at work, and they decided to get rid of my job I had on Homer Three, so again I was granted bumping rights. Instead of bumping, I took a temporary position in the cafeteria of the Memorial Pavilion because the lady was on holiday for a month, and there was word that she was retiring. I thought if I did her job when it came up on the board, I would have a better chance of getting it. I really liked it. I was preparing all the desserts and salads for the displays and dishing out the food at meal time. It was Christmas, and all the bigwigs were having meetings, and I would have to cater for them, making sandwiches, arranging goodies on trays, and making coffee. There would be around thirty or more people at these meetings, and this was almost every day; what the meetings were about is beyond me. I'd also have to do my own job. None of the bigwigs ever knew what the Hell was going on in the food department. While I was in this job, I saw the crooked eye, Stevens, who was now long-time retired, and she came waltzing into the cafeteria with the Dietitian who took her place. I wondered what the heck she was doing back, but I had just been zapped, so it didn't occur to me that maybe she was worried about being busted for the sexual con she and Turd hooked me up with. Not only that, who would have figured it out anyway? It's all so bizarre. After the job was over, they decided to eliminate my position in the cafeteria. A job in the Eric Martin Pavilion came up on the board, working in the kitchen on the third floor full-time. Since I had worked in this kitchen before, I applied for it and got it. No sooner was I in the job than the girl who had it before me decided she wanted her job back. She had applied for the dish room porter job at Eric Martin and didn't like it, but that was an about-face because she told me she liked it. It was Monday to Friday, with weekends off. Well, the dish room porter job came up on the board, and since I had done that job before, I applied for it and got it. What was supposed to be a permanent job turned out to be temporary when I applied for it. I suppose they were getting ready to faze me out or something worse.

On Mother's Day 1994, my son came to visit me, but I had to meet them at the bike shop on Cloverdale. My son wanted a bike that cost a couple of thousand dollars, and his Dad told him to come to me. I told him there was no way I could afford a bike like that, and he was really upset about it. Later on, he said he needed to get some cream for his feet, which cost four hundred dollars, but his Dad bought a stereo for his Dodge Charger instead. He wondered why his Dad always got whatever he wanted. I looked at his feet, which were all red and raw, so I rubbed some cream on them, and my daughter helped. He eventually fell asleep on my lap, and when he woke up, he told me he had a dream that the mountain had collapsed. Well, he told me the evil demon Saffery said to him, it was some kind of fungus he had on his feet. It never occurred to me at the time that John had fungus on his hands long before I met him. He couldn't get rid of it, and it would occasionally act up. I kept telling him to go to the doctor about it. This was the same thing. He directed him to a dermatologist who prescribed some cream for him. It was just before I got sick. Other than the accidents he had, it was the one and only time he ever went to the doctor's while he was here. I was told John had an untreated sexually transmitted disease that he had to give to me, which eventually he got treated for, and I almost died of cancer from it. The kids, well, the doctors didn't give two shits about them. They would just have to suffer from Crohn's disease because of it. On my daughter's tenth birthday, John sent her a thousand-dollar check in the mail inside a birthday card. I invested it for her, along with a bit more, and it was supposed to go towards her education, but it was so little that I decided to put it towards a small wedding for her. He was still trying to buy her then. I threw her a party in the community room of Tillicum Terrace that year and got a clown to come because I felt so guilty about all she had been through. She used to tell everyone she wanted to be a clown when she grew up. She had quite a sense of humour, most likely to hide her real feelings of confusion and fear. It was Father's Day, and my daughter and I had been to a garage sale. We saw John's truck, and I think my daughter thought maybe he had a birthday present for her, so I asked her if she wanted to go and see him. I also wanted to get the donkey and cart my Dad had made for me. We went to the house, and on our way up there, we stopped because we noticed John was at his work area, where he had a twenty-foot trailer he had converted into a shop. He was okay at first, but then he started talking about maintenance, so I changed the subject. I told him I wanted to go up to the house to get the donkey and cart my Dad had made for me. I also wanted to see my son, but he said, "he isn't home." He told me, "You can't go up there," and as I tried to drive off, my car door window was open, and the evil demon began to turn the wheel in the direction of the cliff. I struggled to close the window, but I managed to do so, and then I continued up to the house. When I got there, I noticed his wife, Kathy, lying in the nude, and my son was right there working on his motorcycle. My daughter saw her too. No wonder he didn't want me to go up to the house. When I noticed this, I flipped and ran into the house to confront her with what she was doing in front of my son, but she ran into the bedroom upstairs. I ran up after her and started banging on the door, trying to get her to come out, but then John came up to the house and went up the stairs. When I saw the evil demon, I panicked and ran down the stairs and out the door to my car. I then drove to the RCMP station to make out a report on what I saw. My daughter was even questioned by the RCMP officer, and she told him what Kathy looked like and the fact that she didn't have any clothes on. But of course, nothing ever became of that either.

My daughter was beginning to make a lot of friends at her new school. She got involved in all the sports activities in and outside of school. I enrolled her in baseball at Hampton Park, about a 15-minute walk away from our apartment. They didn't have a girls' fast-ball team, I guess, because they knew I was coming, so she played hard-ball on a mostly boys' team. There were different rules for hardball, and I wasn't aware of all of them. They were always looking for someone to keep score. That is when I met up with my old fastball buddy, Gail, who, along with the Federal Government and other government agencies, set my life up to be a living Hell. Not only, they want me dead. Gail introduced me to the drug scene and to my first husband, Steve. She and her husband were on the executive board for the park, and I ended up going to a meeting to learn how to keep score for my daughter's team, and Gail was the one who taught everyone there. My daughter had an umpire who was being unfair to her, and I piped up with my disapproval. When I turned around in the stands, I noticed Gail was sitting behind me with her husband, giving me a dirty look. I suppose it was arranged for the umpire to do this to get me angry, seeing that Clay's brothers were cops and collaborating with the

Institution for the Less Fortunate. We only had idle chit-chat, as it seemed at the time that she was too good to be associated with me, but now I know what she was really up to all these years. I wonder what they got out of all this, the bloody mental abusers? Who likes to abuse little kids in the worst possible way? Now the cops included are all trying to make themselves look like they help kids (Cops for Childhood Cancer and the like), it makes me sick; they should all be locked up for this kind of thing. After baseball season, I enrolled my daughter in karate because there was a club in the church hall right across the street from the apartment, and when I told her about it, she was quite interested. She quickly lost interest, though, and only got as far as a yellow belt when she decided she didn't like it anymore. She didn't like the idea of having bare feet, and she said it was too hard for her. I wonder now what the guy was doing to my daughter while she was in his class.

By this time, I had gone to see my psychiatrist, Dr. Bore, regularly once a month, and I told him I thought I suffered from Post Traumatic Stress Disorder. This was just after Father's Day, when I went up to the house out in Metchosin, and John tried to steer his own daughter and me off the road and over a cliff, and I saw the bitch Kathy in the nude. Dr. Bore never spent more than five minutes with me, so he really didn't know anything about me, so I thought. I had been going to the library at Eric Martin because a girl, Sandy, who I worked with in the dish room, told me they had all kinds of videos in there, which would help me. She mentioned John Bradshaw, and so I got some of his trashy tapes and viewed them, and at the time, I took it all in. All they were about was the immediate family members and the cycle of abuse. However, it was hard for me to believe I had become so psychologically sick and was searching for answers. That is when I first started to write "My Book of Poems" "Depression Obsession." While I was there, I started to look in various books, and I came across a diagnosis of "Post Traumatic Stress Disorder" and read all about it, and I thought, This is what I have. I told my shrink I think I have Post Traumatic Stress Disorder, and he said, "No, you don't." Well, I said you don't really know anything about me, and you aren't doing anything for me; therefore, I fire you. Before this, I had asked Bore if I could get some counselling, and he told me, "No, I don't think that would do you any good." One time, just after the lady tried to run my daughter and me off the road and gave me the finger when we were returning to the Second Stage program for Battered Women after swimming, I went to see the evil demon shrink, Bore. I told him straight out, "You can tell your people to stop trying to run me off the road." I just knew somehow he had something to do with it, even though at the time I thought I needed a psychiatrist because I was collecting long-term disability. I was back to work now, and I saw no use in having a shrink anymore. In my eyes, they are useless, and from having many years of experience with them, I know that's a fact. I stopped taking the no-mind drugs that weren't doing anything for me. Shortly after, I started to get my memory back. I was still working in the dish room after I fired Bore, and I saw him come from the supervisor's office in the main kitchen of Eric Martin. I had a poem I had just written and was going to give it to Bore if I saw him up on the floors when I was delivering the hot wagons. I signalled him to come over when I saw him leave the main kitchen and gave him the poem then. It was about who the real sinners were, and the poem was entitled "Don't you ever treat me that way." I gave one to the Col-wood RCMP because I had requested copies of the police reports, which I thought they had made out on my ex-husband, and all I got was a bunch of garbage, lies about me, and it pissed me right off. One of the lies was that I had been speeding and they couldn't catch me. I even requested them to do an investigation into the female RCMP officer who told me to leave my kids with an abusive man that night and go to my mother's, but after all was said and done, they didn't do anything to her. Actions were justified according to the report I got afterwards. The evil demon John literally got away with murder or attempted murder anyway, because it is by the grace of God I am still here today, and my kids are still alive too. I was told through my computer that John was trying to kill me and the kids all the time he was married to me. The cops at the Colwood RCMP station thought the poem I wrote was bizarre, which just goes to show you where their heart is. They don't have one.

Well, just after I gave the poem to the shrink, I was out for a break with my fellow employees, and we were all coming back to work, and the morning cook commented, "They burnt them off," and everyone started laughing." My supervisor, Kathy, was there, and so was Sandy, the girl I worked with in the dish room, and I was so embarrassed because I knew they were talking about me. I had made some lengthy police reports out at the Victoria City Police Station in July of 1994, just after Father's Day, when my memory started to really come back to me. I reported the evil demon Dr Turd for mental abuse for what he had done to me, and that phrase was in the police report. I also reported various other people for sexual and mental abuse. The evil demon, Shrink Bore, got the information and spread some of it to my fellow employees. I found out it was one of the so-called counsellors at the "Women's Sexual Assault Center" who gave him a copy of the reports. I told my supervisor, Kathy, I had been going there for counselling, and when I told her, she looked surprised. One day, as I was having a break with some of my fellow workers, I mentioned I would like to line my abusers up and shoot them all, which was just a figure of speech, and I didn't think anything about it. Since that time, I have had to watch what I say or do, and sometimes that is hard when you are constantly being stalked, harassed, and mentally abused.

Then the Dietitian got her fat stalker, Anne, to introduce me to a guy named Damn. Anne came over from Vancouver, and she and her husband had just bought motorbikes. She wanted to give me a ride on her bike. She only had one helmet, she said, she knew a guy at a downtown motorbike shop who could lend her another. She and Russ were staying at my place that weekend, and she convinced me to have a barbecue and invite this guy Damn, whose helmet she borrowed as a thank-you to him. I agreed, and that day at the barbecue, the phone rings, and it is the emergency health squad from the Institution for the Less Fortunate. They wanted to know if I needed any help, and I said, "What are you phoning me now for?" "Where were you when I needed you?" Just as I said that, they disconnected the line. I suppose so, I wouldn't say anymore, but I was referring to the time I took all those sleeping pills at the Second Stage program for Battered Women, and I called them, and they never came. Well, Damn came over to my suite after the barbecue and asked me if I wanted to go to Western Speedway with him, and his parents would be going too. He said he knew I had left an ugly marriage, but wondered if we could be friends. He mentioned at the barbecue that he had just left his wife, and I thought he was quite nice, wanting to help cook the meat and bringing over salad. He had made friends with my daughter that night, helping her with tasks like tying her shoelaces and showing her how to line dance. Anyway, I agreed to go to Western Speedway, and I had a good time. He wanted to take me out again, so I agreed. Shortly after I met Damn, the Dietitian told me she didn't want me to come to work because she got a notification that I didn't have a doctor anymore, and she sent me home. Meanwhile, I had been working for ten months already with no problem. I told the Dietitian who my family doctor was now, a doctor named Harry, but that didn't cut it. I was never without a general practitioner at that time. I found him right after I moved into Tillicum Terrace and started seeing him regularly, because, of course, I wanted a doctor who wouldn't throw me into EMP like Turd did. I wanted someone closer to where I lived, and he was in the Tillicum Mall right down the road from my home, so that's why I got him. But it didn't matter to the Dietitian who had set up the relationship with Damn in the first place, using fat Anne to stalk me until she finally matched me up. But Doctor Harry was no better than the other doctors. I had gone to him right after I met Damn and told him that I was starting a relationship, and I wanted to make sure I didn't have any sexually transmitted diseases. I also got a book from the Tillicum Mall, "Women and Doctors," published in the States, which told me all about what I needed to know. I had started to remember having the bladder cauterization for Carcinoma in situ, and I thought for a while I could be dying, and no one was telling me. When I got the book, it told me there was a ninety-nine percent chance of the cancer being cured by this procedure. Things were starting to come together for me then. When I asked for the results of the tests, doctor Harry said you don't have any sexually transmitted diseases, and old, gullible, me, I believed him. I believed the prick. I hadn't remembered what I saw once on my ex-husband just before I got ill and admitted myself to the Institution for the Less Fortunate. I suppose that was what they were all afraid was going to happen. There were some other incidents that had happened before I met Damn that also contributed to my having a relationship with him, which lasted about five months.

I had met my new neighbours beside me, who moved into Sandra's old apartment. Bob had a teenage daughter, Lynn, whom he had custody of and was living with him. I used to go over for coffee at his place every morning, and I would listen to him and his problems, and he would listen to me and some of mine. He had an aneurysm and had a gaping hole in his head from the operations he had, and I felt sorry for him. One night at about one o'clock in the morning, I heard some tires squealing outside my apartment on Tillicum Road. John's East Indian friend lived only a couple of streets away on Kerr Street, and I thought maybe it was John. I reported the incident to the cops just after it happened because the squealing of the tires went on for a while, and I was scared. It probably was the cops knowing already I was afraid of John and wanting to make me look crazy to cover up all their evil tracks. I talked to Bob about what I heard, and he heard it too. Once, my daughter and I came home from somewhere, and there was a poster at my front door of the apartment with all sorts of scary things on it, and right away, I thought the only person who would do such a sick thing would be John. I knocked on Bob's door, but no one was home. I wanted to see if he noticed anyone put it there. It freaked me out so much I took the poster to the police station and told the female officer I spoke to that I thought it was my ex-husband, John, who put the poster at my door. She took down his name and phone number, saying she would find out if it was him, and then I left. Well, just to spite me, she told the Norrises not to be home, but I didn't know this at the time, so when I got back home and noticed Bob and Lynn weren't there, I just went into my apartment waiting for them to arrive, and when they did arrive home, I went over there and told them about it. That's when I found out it was Lynn who put the poster at my door as a joke, she said. I had to phone up the cop shop and tell them I found out who put the poster at my door. I also told Lynn, "That wasn't a very funny joke." They both knew how abusive my ex-husband had been to me and my children. When Lynn graduated, I was told she went on to take a legal secretary course at the College, and I wonder now if that was her payment for having the shit scared out of me.

Damn, was over at my place shortly after we started going out when Social Services came over to my house, along with a member of the emergency health squad, and said, "There was a report you are hearing things and seeing things and could be a danger to your child." I told these people I suffered from Post Traumatic Stress Disorder, but to my surprise, they didn't even know what that was. I figured they were talking about the squealing of the tires, and I told them about that, and they could go to my next-door neighbour and ask him about it, because he heard it too, and I knew being a danger to my child must have come from where I worked. That was when I mentioned I would like to line my abusers up and shoot them because there was never anything else I said or did to make them think that. Just before Social Services came to my house and before I met Damn, my daughter was attending Kerr Park for their summer program, and Social Services came there without my permission, questioning her about me. My daughter had just taken the babysitting program at the Pearks Arena, so they didn't have anything on me, which is what I thought at the time, but it still annoyed me. My daughter told me she showed her card, which she got for completing the babysitting program. She was only eleven, but she wasn't getting along with Robin and wanted to be at home watching TV until I got home from work at around six-thirty. This was only an hour and a half. Anyway, that day, Damn was over when Social Services made me go to the Health Center out in Royal Oak to see a shrink by the name of Seagull, or they were going to take my daughter away from me if I didn't go. When I saw him, I told him the basics of my life, like the sexual assault by my first husband, and some of the things he did to me, and the sexual abuse by Robin. I also told Seagull how my ex-husband John had been terrorizing me recently and had terrorized my family in the past, and he agreed with my diagnosis. I did suffer from Post Traumatic Stress Disorder. This was at the beginning of August 1994, and I filled out some new disability forms, which this shrink signed, indicating Post Traumatic Stress Disorder. Later, however, I went back to my employer to get a copy of it, and it mysteriously went missing. This shrink Seagull wanted me to go back on an anti psychotic drug, but I refused, telling him I was not psychotic. But I agreed to go back on the antidepressant Zoloft because with everything that was going on, I thought maybe it would help me cope. If this system didn't put me through Hell, I wouldn't need any of it. Seagull assigned a health nurse named Sharon to come to my home and be involved in my care, and although I didn't feel it was necessary, it seemed I didn't have much of a choice if I wanted to keep my daughter. Sharon ended up being the instigator in my life, nosying into my business so they could all set up harassment wherever I went. The evil demons. It was she who told Social Services my daughter was attending the summer program at Kerr park. Damn, and I didn't go out socializing much. We went to a couple of dirt bike races up Island and Western Speedway a few times with his parents. Anne, the fat salad girl, from Eric Martin, stocked me for five years in total. She came over to visit. The so-called gentleman would open the car door for me all the time. At one point, the ass told me he wanted to marry me and spend the rest of his life with me. But I knew that wasn't going to happen. I was going to the Metchosin Elementary school every week so I could see my son, because at this point, I didn't want to have anything to do with the evil demon I was once married to. I looked at the boy's school work once and noticed he could barely write his own name, and he was in grade six or seven, and I got pretty upset with that and demanded to talk to the principal of the school. I found out he was not getting any learning assistance, and because John had custody, he wouldn't make the time, nor did he care to. He didn't want to take the time to go through the procedure needed, so there was nothing I could do about it. It had to be John because he had custody. Damn came up to the house once with me to get my son, and John said to the boy right in front of Damn, "If she does anything crazy, phone me and I'll come and get you." We took my son for a haircut that day because he mentioned he wanted one, and he looked so scraggly. That was the last time I ever went up to the house, because, of course, I was terrified of John by this time.

I got Lynn to babysit one night, and Damn and I went to the nightclub in the In-Graham Hotel on Douglas Street. It was a popular rock and roll club, and the place was packed. We were sitting at our table, and a couple who Damn knew came and sat with us. They were cops from Vancouver, trying to get in on the action. It was quite loud in the nightclub, so Damn talked in my ear and asked me if I wanted to go out and smoke some dope with these two cops. Of course, I said "No." I had quit smoking dope shortly after I admitted myself into Eric Martin in December of 1992, and I wouldn't even allow it in my place.

One night after Damn and I had split up, I went to the nightclub with John's best friend Angus's old girlfriend, Sue. I met her while I was shopping one day, and she invited me to go out with her sometime, giving me her phone number. I took her up on her offer. I went over to the house she was renting once, and it was a pigsty, with dirty floors, dishes, and clothes stacked a mile high everywhere. And she was a nurse. We were at our table, and I noticed there were all kinds of cops walking around in the place, and it frightened me. Nice, hay, afraid of cops. But really, they were the kids of police officers dressed in their uniforms, apparently. Sue was talking to me about how I should go after Angus, that he was a nice guy and good in bed, but he wanted children, and she didn't want any more, and that was why they split up. I told her I would never do such a thing. I considered him a friend, and that was it. That night, Sue took me outside, and I had one toke with her and some guys. They were the cops' kids who had been dressed in these uniforms and were being their informants for them, and whatever other intentions they had. She ended up inviting these guys over to my place for a drink. Sue went home with one of them, and the other one, well, I got rid of that drunken bum. Later on, I found out from Angus,when I bumped into him, Sue got a job nursing in a hospital up North, where her son was working, so maybe that was her payment for getting me to toke up and then trying to hook me up with a fucking cop's kid, all unknown to me at the time. I never took another toke after that. I saw Margaret in the bathroom that night, the girl who killed the father of her child. She asked me how I was doing, and I told her I had left my husband. She was asked by my ex-husband's good friend's Dad to ask me about my kids and if I saw them or not. I didn't know at the time that Angus was a cop's kid. All along, I thought his Dad was a teacher. No wonder I had custody of my daughter, and my ex-husband had custody of my son, and I didn't see my son that often because my ex-husband's best friend's Dad, the fucking good-for-nothing pig, had something to do with it. She told me I was lucky, at least I got to see him, because she didn't get to see her daughter at all.

I went to Dr. Harry, and he filled out some forms for Federal Disability because it was required by my long-term disability from my benefits at work. The Dietitian wouldn't allow me to return to work. She wanted me to see the hospital psychologist first, and she said they would pay me until after I saw her and got the permission to come back to work, so I didn't pursue my disability claim. I took my holiday pay and some holidays because, at this time, I received a check from Family Maintenance Enforcement in the amount of $5,000 for back payment of child support. After all, John hadn't given me a dime since the check he wrote out in anger, Food for kids. John was back in England, and they had raided his bank account, so I arranged a bus trip to take my daughter to Disneyland. I thought if I didn't go now, I would never be able to afford to go again. Social Services found out I was going on holiday, and they phoned up my screwed-up ex-husband and told him about it to create a little more shit for me. As if he wasn't mad enough already, he got a woman to sit away in front of me on the bus trip. I didn't know this at the time, but I did notice her turning around and looking at me from time to time, which I thought was odd. But thinking back now, I suppose it was Kathy, his blushing bride, and some other criminal wanting to kick us off somehow while we were on this trip. I had made up my mind that I was going to educate myself, so on the bus trip, I read the whole dictionary. While in San Francisco, my daughter and I were walking back to the hotel after shopping when, all of a sudden, we heard a voice over a loudspeaker say, "Sniper on the loose; Sniper on the loose." My daughter and I ran to the hotel, which luckily wasn't too far away by this time. I wonder now if that was just a prank to scare the hell out of us.

Well, when I came back from my holidays, I went to see a woman who they said was a psychologist but wasn't. But of course, I didn't know that at the time. Her name was Marsha, and she worked in the emergency room. I suppose she was going to school to be a psychologist because she got me to do a couple of psychological tests in pencil. I only saw her three times, and she made this degrading report about me, how I relied on men to be in my life, and I played the victim, and one time someone must have replaced her report with another one, because in this one, she said that I was in Purgatory. This woman must have really wanted to be somebody to do something like that. Damn was over then, and I showed it to him because I couldn't believe my eyes when I read it. But it disappeared almost immediately. Good old Angus's Dad took it. Little did Marsha know I was already living in Hell. Damn took me to his parents' townhouse once, and they showed me around. When they showed me the bedroom, I saw Jesus on the cross and other religious memorabilia all over the place. Damn also told me he was brought up Catholic. One day in October, fat Anne and her fat husband Russ were over, and so was dear old Damn. The doorbell rang, and it was a courier delivering some court documents to my place. When I read the material, I couldn't make heads or tails out of most of it, other than I was under no "legal disability" and this document was all X-ed out, along with other parts like the division of assets. Anne, Russ, and Damn didn't know what to make of it either, but they didn't comment about it. It went missing, I didn't realize how corrupted this system really was and how everyone in it was after me to keep my mouth shut about all this. I called the bastards at the cop station again and reported it missing, and they were the ones who took it, compliments of Damn, telling them about it. I knew someone had been in my house because some of the words to my poems had been changed, and I made the mistake of telling the cops about that, too. My Dad told me to put a matchstick on the top of the front door before I left. That way, when I came home and found it on the ground I would know someone was coming in. But I always forgot to check it when I arrived home. It wouldn't have mattered anyway, seeing as it was cops who were coming in all the time, terrorizing me.

The Dietitian had me cut off my income right at Christmas time and left me with no money. I suppose word got out to her that I was going to get everything, or she obtained the court document as well, and also didn't like the fact that it stated I was under no legal disability. I had to go on unemployment disability benefits after getting letters from both of my doctors to collect it. In the meantime, I pursued my Federal Dsability claim, which I had to wait for two months to get because the Dietitian still wouldn't allow me to come to work until I got yet more counselling. Meanwhile, I had no income. I had already produced a letter that said I had received counselling from the Sexual Assault Center, which was a total waste of time. I gave them one hundred dollars for about six sessions, only to get so-called information about how I was being sexually and mentally abused, some of it compliments of the Sexual Assault Center. I met with a Crisis Intervention counsellor by the name of Susan, and I showed her the police reports I had written out, and she took a copy of them as she said she needed to for their records, and the bitch advertised them. Good Crisis Intervention.

By this time, I had written a book of poems, and I showed the counsellor I had Margaret, who was also a psych nurse, my book, and she kept it for a few days and showed the women in the assault center it without my permission. I gave it to her when she wanted to show me the family tree, and I think it pissed her off because she was showing me something I already knew about. I told her about the relationship I was having with Damn, and I told her I didn't like the idea that he spanked his kids when he wanted to discipline them. At this point, I was considering breaking it off with Damn because of that, and I was starting to clue into what was really going on. Damn had a girl, a year younger than my daughter, and a boy about four years younger. He was involved with Beavers and Cubs, and he talked me into enrolling my daughter in Cubs because his girl was going, so I did. We did a bottle drive for the organization, and after we broke up, I saw him serving hot dogs and drinks in his Cub uniform, and I wondered how he was still able to work for an organization that deals with children when he had been reported for abuse to them. I could see he needed help, so before this, I gave him my STEP parenting book for him to read, which I never got back. However, it didn't seem to help him. I wanted him to use a different approach. I was trying to help him with that. The so-called counsellor at the Sexual Assault Center must have phoned Social Services, playing the righteous counsellor, and reported his abuse to his children, because no sooner did I tell this counsellor than Social Services went to Damn's house to so-called investigate to cover all their tracks yet again. Another thing I didn't like about Damn was that while he was with me, he'd go over to his wife's house to babysit all the time, and the kids were getting hopes about their parents' relationship. He thought I was jealous, but that wasn't it at all. I ended up breaking up with him on Christmas Day, and by this time, I had figured out, with the help of the bitch Marsha, the so-called counsellor at the Sexual Assault Center, that Damn was a setup paid for by my extended health benefits I had at the hospital. In the union book, I noticed it said the hospital could provide care for those on disability. I never let on how pissed off I was about it for fear of what would happen to me, but it happened anyway. My care was the sexual and mental abuse provided by good old Damn, so he could cover his dirty ass, which at the time I didn't know he was doing. I told him about my past, and he said he didn't care, and now I know why that was. He needed someone to blame. He had also told me he had his house in his children's name, who were underage to have made such a purchase. After this, my employer took that provision out of the union book. The fucking bitch of a counsellor, Marsha, was the one who told me I was a "Victim of the system," and I told dear old Damn what Marsha said about me being a "Victim of the system." He, being the instigator, informed me that the government can do anything it wants to you. They can even make you disappear, and now I realize just how right he was. Big time. After I had told Marsha all the personal details of my life, in which she then got hold of the police report, she had the nerve to ask me if "I had learned my lesson yet?" further spreading the news around about me. After this, I got this terrible feeling of being ashamed of myself, and when I was in the bath one day, I got the nail scrubber and tried to wash the filth off my body, and I was beside myself, crying. I never went back to see her after that. And quite frankly, I hope she rots in Hell. Wherever they all think that is. I myself think it is right here on this earth. I know I live in it. Well, Tammy, my daughter's old babysitter, told me not to go out with Damn, and I should have listened to her, but I had good reasons, as far as I was concerned then; they were going to take my daughter away from me. I thought if there was someone around who could witness my parenting, they wouldn't take her away from me. I was terrified of this. They already took my son. I wanted to keep a friendship with Damn for the kids' sake, but he said that he was so upset with me, he didn't want anything to do with me. One time, I took Tammy to Social Services, who were all a bunch of piss tanks, emergency workers themselves, to confront them with their accusations, thinking we were friends. She wouldn't stick up for me, and I should have known better after the wallet incident, but who would have put this all together? I told my parents about what Social Services said to me: they were going to take my daughter away from me if I didn't see a shrink, and my Dad marched right over there to confront them about it. Dad said to them, "I fought in two wars, and I deserve to live the rest of my life in peace." "You should be going up to the mountain and dealing with the real lunatic." Dad was so angry. After that, they left me alone regarding my daughter. I felt so bad for my Dad because he was going in and out of the hospital all the time and was having a hard time breathing. Both my parents had been through so much already, and I was trying to keep them out of things. He said to me once, "This isn't a life, this is torture; I have to fight for every breath I take. I may not know what he was going through, but I know just where he was coming from.

Well, I couldn't afford to pay for counselling, so I had to wait for a while before getting my Unemployment Insurance medical benefits. In the meantime, I found a place where you could get ten sessions a year of free counselling —the Gorge Community Resource Center on Gorge Road, not too far from my apartment. I saw a lady who pretended she was consoling me, but all she talked about was how she put herself through university to be a counsellor, and she was on welfare and had no money for a long time, so she knew what it was like to go without. She didn't seem to care about what was going on for me. As a matter of fact, she was a real shit disturber. She phoned the squad for the less fortunate once on me when I told her that Damn was a setup, and they came and tried to have me thrown into EMI. At the time that happened, I didn't know she had called them. I didn't even go to see her for six sessions because she was a useless, self-absorbed, heartless, human being. Anyway, they allowed me to go back to work after that in April of 1995, but it only lasted for three days because the dish machine just about took my head off when the dishes got jammed up at the end of the machine, and I tried to fix it. I was sent home because I had made Sandy, who was visibly upset over the incident, a nervous wreck, and she had a heart problem. They didn't even consider how the incident affected me and how I could have been killed. It was just what they were trying to do to me again, unknown to me at the time, but that's why. Outrageous. My X-co-worker Lorraine told me they were having problems with the machine before I came back to work, and so I know it was just another one of their plots. She also told me they had a meeting at the hospital and brought counsellors in after the incident with the dish machine, and good old Damn attended that meeting.

Apparently, a lot of people were taking time off due to stress in the workplace, and apparently, the Dietitian thought the employees would benefit from some counselling, but I don't think anything will help those people. A fellow employee always kept in touch with me, and we talked about how screwed up the hospital was. She had decided then she was going to get the Hell out of there. She wanted to take the Early Childhood Education program and quit the hospital because she felt she was educated enough. I decided I wanted to get the Hell out of the hospital, too, somehow, maybe go to school and become a counsellor myself. As far as I am concerned, there is a need for someone with some compassion who can understand abuse because all the authority figures I met don't know their ass from a hole in the ground and are not what I consider to be professionals. Maybe professional criminals. While living at Tillicum Terrace, I called over to Vancouver about a counselling program they offered at the Counselling Training Institution, now owned by someone else. I didn't take the program then because they didn't have a college here in Victoria at the time. But some of the people whom I had never met before, I eventually took the program with in Victoria when it first opened up a college over here. Apparently, they broke into my home, all pissed up with guns, and were trying to kill me and my daughter, unknown to me at the time. This is what I was told, but it was probably by the terrorist who is on my computer constantly. Terrorists have also been coming into my homes on a regular basis, causing mental abuse to me. Unbelievable!

CHAPTER THIRTEEN

I was pissed off that the lawyer I had at the time wasn't even able to get me what I said I wanted, which was rightfully mine, so I canned him. He should have known most of the people he said he represented in the Intuition for the Less Fortunate were abused. I told him my ex-husband was abusive. I feel he should have requested a police officer to escort me so I could get my personal belongings. But then again, I suppose there wasn't any willingness to go. John kept everything of any value. He went through my jewelry and took everything of any value, which wasn't much. He also kept a black wool jacket, which was my mother's. It had pearls and rhinestones on the collar and on the pockets, with a silver, satin lining. I didn't receive any of my leather shoes or boots, which I bought when I was working at Mansfield's Shoes in England, or any photo albums of the kids. I suppose the slut he was with wanted all of it. I suppose she can't wear any of it now, seeing the loony snuffed her off, apparently. Well, I told legal aid I wanted yet another different lawyer because the ones I had I thought were just abusing the system, taking matters to court one thing at a time, and I felt like they all had abused me and my family enough. One day, just after I moved into Tillicum Terrace, I got a phone call from another lawyer, and I agreed to meet with him. At his house, where his office was, the first thing I said to him was that I wanted to get my son back. It was he who got the second court advocate, Sharon, for me in January of 1994. He didn't think I would be able to get my son back now because too much time had passed, but what he really meant was our system of law is so corrupt that there is no way you will be able to get him back, seeing who you are on top of the whole matter. I also told him I wanted to sue my evil demon of an ex-husband for mental abuse, and he shook his head no. He knew all along the government had set up our relationship.

But somehow, I knew this guy would help me, so when I started to get harassed at work, I documented it and gave it all to him. One day, I had an appointment with him, and I was crying. He asked me, "What are you crying about?" and I said, "I don't know." I really didn't. I was actually sobbing. All I could say was "grief," and when I looked at him, he had tears in his eyes, and I have never forgotten that. Never. That is what keeps me going to this day. He is the only person who has ever shown any kind of compassion for me, besides my doctor, who I was lucky enough to have. Now that she is retired, she has become my best friend. It was he who recommended me to her. Another time, I was waiting to see him outside his office, and this guy came in and he asked me if this lawyer was representing me, and I said "yes," and he told me to keep him because he is the best. He said he was a human rights lawyer, but at the time, I didn't know what he meant by that, as I didn't need a human rights lawyer; that's what I thought. Not for what I was going through, boy, was I wrong, big time.

Human Rights were about as effective as a donkey's ass when I finally did go to them one day. I was at work, and it was five o'clock, and the supper cook was getting off work. I saw him take a big container of food out the door, and it was clear he was taking it with him. All my fellow employees were taking food home in bags and were trying to get me to do the same, but I was a single mother who needed a job. I was scared to take anything home with me. Once, I was throwing the food out because that was part of my job as a porter, and I decided to taste this vegetarian dish. The supervisor who was on duty that day caught me and asked, "What do you have in your mouth?" and I said, "Nothing." By this time, I had swallowed it. I never tried anything again after that. Some of the workers used to feed the commissionaire so he wouldn't bust them for taking the food home. I caught onto this scam of theirs, so I decided to report the cook who took a big container of food home to Employee Relations at work, and they did an investigation. They told me he lost his job because of it, but I found out when I talked to him over the phone one day that they transferred him to another hospital. I think by this time, I got the feeling the whole hospital was against me, and I was right in assuming that, but not in the way I thought at the time. That is why I started giving my documentation of the hospital harassment to my lawyer. The hospital was trying to get me to steal so they could make out that I was the criminal, among other things, and get rid of me. They were going to get rid of me anyway, while on their way to persecute me or kill me.

I started to go to college to upgrade, and I found some information about a course called the Better Education and Skills Training. There was a similar course to this, which only allowed women, but I took this one because it offered help with preparing for the English and Math assessment tests, whereas the other one didn't. I suppose they were trying to make it look like I "relied on men," and that is why I took it. I was also getting help from my neighbour, Lynn, who was in grade twelve at the time. I then found out I didn't need Math to go into counselling, which was a good thing because Math for me was always hard. I had to take English writing, and then I could take the Provincial course after that, which I did. I had saved up some money to buy a computer for going back to school, and in the (BEST) program, which was what I was taking, they taught you the basics of the computer, and Lynn's friend Rod, who was a whiz at computers, came over and helped me figure the basics out, too. He also installed some games on it, which, at the time, I didn't know were illegal. I also did a number of different psychological tests in this program to find out what I would be good at. When the results of my tests came back, I found out I should go into counselling, which is what I wanted to get into before I took this course. Some people had a couple of pages of different areas they could go into, but I only had eight different areas, and they were all counselling. There were different sexes participating in the BEST program, and another program for women was offering lectures. One time, a police officer came into the women's program, and we were allowed to attend. He showed a film and talked about women's abuse issues. I had to leave the room. I left the room because the cops never did anything for me, and this guy was portraying that they did. I suppose they wanted to piss me off, and that is why we were allowed to attend. We also did a CPR course and a women's defence program, which was part of the other program, too, and we were allowed to go to that as well. Just to cover their tracks. It was a six-week full-time course, and in June, I got a certificate and a letter of reference for taking this course. We had a barbecue at Beaver Lake and everyone brought something to eat. While I was taking the program, I felt like the odd person out, even though I tried to mingle. I still would like to know what the rumour is about me to make people act the way they all do towards me. I can only imagine. When I started upgrading my English, and I wrote a book report, I would ask Lynn to read it, and she would give me her opinion on what I had written. And even though she did what she did to me, I valued her opinion. It took four months to get my Provincial English, and in the meantime, Lynn and I did a first aid course together at my place at night, then I took How to parent your teens, at the Gorge Community Resource Center, which was about six weeks long, once a week at night. I always wanted to know how I could be a better parent, and I also thought that if I took this course, it would look better for me if Social Services were going to try to get on my case again. I also applied for a Big Sister through "Big Brothers and Big Sisters" for my daughter, and I was matched with someone who was only interested in pursuing her goal of becoming a child and youth counsellor. I had to go and watch a film on sexual abuse before I could qualify to have a big sister for my daughter. I thought it should be the other way around. I wonder what their trip was trying to get me to feel bad for all the sexual and mental abuse inflicted on me in my life? Mental fucking abusers who like to hire people to abuse kids. Kathy was the name of her big sister, and she always ignored both my daughter and me every time the organization put on a function. Everyone would be sitting with their big brother or big sister, and Kathy would be off sitting with someone else. She treated us like a piece of shit in public. When she finally dumped my daughter, there was a ski trip to Mount Washington, my daughter was looking forward to going to, and I was so ill I didn't want to let the girl down more than she already was, so I took her. I sat in the chalet the whole time, my head down on the table, sleeping. I tried skiing with her, but I was just too sick to. I suppose that was all planned. Just before Kathy dumped my daughter, she came over with some pictures she had taken of her in dangerous places. So, I decided right then that it was a good thing she left. However, at the same time, I was also angry at the way she left. Wow, what an EVIL system.

 I was starting to feel that when I went to Fairways in the strip mall beside the apartment I was living in, I was being stared at. Maybe because of my unpublished book, I had copyrights to at the time "My Book Of Poem" "Depression Obsession" was now in circulation. I had written out a copy and given it to dear old Dman as a goodbye gift to him, but it was around the issue of the "cycle of abuse," which is all a bunch of bull shit if you ask me—another cover-up. The prick who put on that he had respect for my family, and I was nothing but a good-for-nothing criminal. Had I known that he was going to circulate it, I would never have given a copy to him because it wasn't finished yet. I was still trying to figure this all out. Once, I was in the meat department trying to decide what to buy, and this old lady was a few feet away from me and just kept standing there staring at me the entire time. The manager, Tina, and Tom didn't stop harassing me either. One time, my daughter was riding her bike, and some little kids from the complex were following her. Tom told her, "If one of those kids were to get hit by a car, you would be held responsible for them getting hurt." My daughter was upset about what Tom had said to her, so I went out and said to Tom, "If you have a problem with my daughter, you should come to me about it, and I will deal with it; that's my job." Well, he started yelling at me at the top of his lungs, about how I had big problems, etc., and after that, Tina told me that Tom had been sexually abused. I thought to myself, he should get some sort of help then, because it was obvious that he needed some. Besides, I believe if he treated a woman with respect, like all women should be, because we carry the future generation of this world, maybe he wouldn't have been sexually abused, the nut case.

In the meantime, my daughter was missing her friend Laura Utah's and Don's little girl, who she would play with at the Contact for Kids group in East Sooke's No Man's Land. I started phoning Utah to get the two of them together. I was invited to a summer pool party at their house, and that is when I learned that Utah and Don were splitting up. At the party, Don told me that he had just had an operation for Crohn's disease. He stopped at my apartment on his way home from work once, and I thought it was for a visit, but I wonder now if that was to blame me for his Crohn's Disease, which would have been a lie. Well, the harassers, the Seiloops, were there and a bunch of other non-entities. Jan didn't show up, though, maybe because she knew I was going to be there, and she had sided with John, because after all, he had a machine now, and they had one hundred acres which needed to be worked on. I brought my camera and took some pictures of the kids and some pictures of all the piss tanks who were there, all making a fool of themselves. My daughter told me she felt left out at the party because Laura was playing with Dorothy's daughter, Tess, all the time and ignoring her. Dot told me she had left her husband, Larry, and that was just after the pipe bomb incident, where Larry had shown his boy and Pat's boy, whom I didn't know very well, how to make them, and Pat's kid got seriously hurt. I thought Dorothy had come to her senses, but I still didn't want anything to do with her because of her addictions. One day, I went to Utah's so the kids could play together, and Dorothy had been living in their suite, which they had made above their garage, growing closer to each other. Dorothy was moving out to a half-duplex she bought, and I got sucked into taking some of her belongings to her home. She had custody of the girl, and Larry had custody of the boy, and I asked her, "Don't you miss your boy?" and she did, but she said she didn't have room for him; the duplex was only a two-bedroom. She commented that he was older now and could basically look after himself. I thought to myself, I am doing everything in my power to get my boy away from a lunatic like her husband, and I couldn't understand how he got him in the first place after what had happened with the pipe bombs. Now I know because our system is so corrupt, and no one gives a damn about the future generation of kids. They must promote this kind of violence. Utah wanted me to move into the suite above their garage because, at the time, I had told her I was looking for another place to live. Then John could come out there and snuff me off. Because of everything that had gone on at Tillicum Terrace, I wanted to get the Hell out of there, but no way did I want to live way out in East Sooke again. I wanted to be close to my work. When Don stopped at my apartment that day, it was the last time I saw any of them for a while. I tried calling Utah, and it seemed like she was never there and would not answer any of my calls or messages, but I suppose she really was there, and their excuses were all a big scam. Don was living part-time in the house, apparently. They were sharing the house during their separation, one week on and one week off. Because they said, "We don't want to disrupt the kids." Utah would stay with her parents, who lived down the road, and Don would stay in their house. I got the idea that Utah didn't want anything more to do with us, and I couldn't understand why at first, but I sure as Hell do now. By this time, my daughter had made new friends where we were living, and she soon stopped talking about Laura. Which is all a good thing, the fucking no mind, drug addicted and big-time criminals.

When I got told to go home after three days back to work in the dish room in April, I knew for sure I had Post Traumatic Stress Disorder. I had exhausted all the low-cost, so-called help available in the community, and the shrinks were useless, so I thought if I went to school and kept myself busy, I would be able to cope. However, I had visited Dr. Harry to discuss how I was having trouble walking due to severe back pain, and he advised me to consult a chiropractor. So, there was one guy covering all their tracks in the strip mall beside the apartment, and I went to see him. Brent was his name, and I saw him for twelve sessions before I could walk without pain again. He told me I was sixty percent disabled in my back due to stress, but what was really wrong with me was that I was suffering from Pelvic Inflammatory Disease or Crohn's disease, but at the time, I didn't know that. After I got sent home in April, I pursued the Federal Government disability and long-term disability from work. During this time, I had Dr. Harry in the Tillicum Mall. No sooner did I get this all done than he went on a trip to England for his payment to keep his mouth shut. A few years later, I found this bogus letter of reference for the shoe company I used to work for over in England, among some papers, and wondered if he had something to do with that, and no doubt he did. My original letter of reference was gone, so I suppose they were all trying to get rid of my evidence of being over there in England. Then they realized they couldn't do that because I had a copy of my passport registered with the courts. So they gave my references back, and theirs disappeared. And those two jobs were all set up for me when I came over, so they could suck me dry before having me kicked off. Oh, "God save the Queen." No wonder Prince Harry isn't going to fight in the war with this story coming out on the shelf. Well, just before doctor Harry was about to dump me, I had been lining my cupboards in the townhouse, and the shelving paper cut my eye, and it hurt like Hell. I went to the clinic, and who was there but doctor Harry, probably waiting for me to come in, seeing my home has cameras in it. Trying to make himself look good. And that day, out of the blue, he told me he could no longer help me, and I needed to find another doctor. I just thought he had too many patients at the time. He suggested I see a woman named Doctor Lemon, and what an evil demon she turned out to be. I only went once to see her at the beginning of Sept 1995, as she was right across the street from Tillicum Terrace in a dump made up just for me. At the time, I thought it was really handy, but looks can be deceiving, and she was probably a good doctor. Besides, doctors who would take you on were hard to find. Three weeks after I saw her, I became very ill. I thought at first it was the flu or something I ate, and when I started to get severe stabbing pain in my stomach, I thought I should go to the Victoria General Hospital to get checked out. I noticed my eyesight was blurry too, which I thought was weird. I had been reading the book Women and Doctors just before I went to the hospital, and I wondered if I had contracted a sexually transmitted disease from dear old Damn. Even though I went for physical check-ups, I began to not trust doctors. They all knew things were coming together for me. They all knew I had this book with me, "Women and Doctors." When I got to the hospital, I told them I thought I could have some kind of sexually transmitted disease and asked them to check for it. The book also mentioned Chlamydia, and it mentioned something about it affecting your eyesight, and I wanted to make sure they checked for everything. The doctor in the emergency room checked me over and gave me some blood tests and a urinalysis test. I waited for hours for the results of the tests, and finally, I was so sick, literally, of waiting, I decided to go home, and I told the nurses in the emergency department to get them to call me about the results of the tests. I went home, waited until the end of the day, and then decided to call the lab myself to see if I could get the results. When I called the lab, the lady I talked to told me I should never have left the hospital, that my white blood cells were really high, and I should be admitted immediately. I went back to the hospital and informed them of what the lab technician had told me. When I was finally seen again, the doctor tried to assure me there was nothing to worry about, but I still wondered why the lady at the lab would say such a thing; she should know her job. The next thing you know, there was a hospital security guard by my hospital bed wearing surgical gloves, holding his hands up in the air, and I wondered what the Hell? The woman doctor who saw me said we are going to admit you to Eric Martin. I wanted a reason why, but they wouldn't give me one, and she threatened, "If you don't sign this voluntary committal form, we will commit you anyway." I ended up signing it, but I put down that it was against my will, and she gave me a dirty look when I did that. I was so sick, and I was crying because I couldn't believe what was happening to me again. They transferred me to the Jubilee Hospital and then to the Institution for the Unfortunate, where they put me in the Psychiatric Intensive Care Unit or PIC Step-Down. The next thing you know, they are holding me down, poking my ass with a needle. Right after they did that, I got on the phone and called my lawyer and told him what they had done to me, and he wrote it all down. His comment was "that's very degrading, isn't it?" I wanted him to get me out of the Institution for the Less Fortunate. I asked for a review panel hearing and for my lawyer and my X-co-worker to be there, but after they shot me up, I didn't realize it was going on because I was drugged out of my mind, and they didn't tell me either. Whatever they gave me knocked me out, but good. While I was basically incoherent, this scary woman wearing glasses, whom I thought I had never seen before, came by my bedside, and when I opened my eyes, she looked at me, twirled her finger around her head, and told me I was crazy. Shortly after that, when I was up and about, the evil demon doctor Lemon, whom I had only seen once at this time, also told me I was crazy. Now I think it was she who came to my bedside, twirling her finger around her head. She pulled the statement out of thin air for no reason at all; I didn't even say anything to her. She is the nut case. One of the nurses who was attending to me was trying to tell me how I should wipe my ass after I go to the bathroom to prevent getting a bladder infection, because that was what they said I had when really I had a lot more physically wrong with me than that. As if I didn't already know the fucking dirty mouth bitch. They were all continually degrading me. A little while after, I got thrown in PIC, and they asked me if I wanted to go out onto the ward, but because I knew almost everyone on the floors, I told them I didn't want to. There was a patient in the PIC Step-Down who befriended me, and he was asking me questions about my life. I told him about how abusive my ex-husband was and how he wouldn't give me my son, but I wasn't going to stop trying to get him. I told him I was sick of going to court all the time, fighting for things and getting nowhere, and I threw some of the court documentation out because I had so much of it. I also told him about getting lying, degrading write-ups about me from the RCMP, and that they never took any reports on all my ex-husband had done to me, and I ended up throwing those reports out, too. I mentioned to him that when I asked for reports on my physical condition, all I got was crap from the shrinks, which I also threw out. He told me not to throw any of it out, so I kept it all, from that time on. Even though documentation was disappearing, I listened to him. A couple of us went outside the hospital grounds and collected leaves. I then got a big piece of paper and drew and painted a huge tree. Then we pasted all the leaves on and hung it on the wall to try and give the place a better meaning. I was in PIC for three weeks, and they made me start taking the anti psychotic drug again, which allows people to walk all over you, and it affects your memory too, Loxipine. You don't remember anything; you become a walking zombie. The only thing it is good for is weight gain, and that causes problems along with the other health risks that are involved in taking such a drug. It was so kind of the doctor to treat my bladder infection when I should have had emergency surgery, the fucking bitch. Before the evil demon shrink Seagull, who I had discharged me, he badgered me by asking me, "Do you still think that you have cancer?" because in the emergency room I told them I thought I could have that too. When the demon asked me about it, I said, "It's a possibility," which is exactly what they wanted to happen again, and it could have. However, God was on my side. I didn't get rid of doctor Lemon because I thought that once she got to know me, she would see I am not crazy. Besides, finding a doctor who would take me wasn't easy. I eventually forgot what she had said to me in the hospital, "You're crazy," because they had me doped up on that shit, Loxipine. I continued to see her almost every month for around four years. I was always rushed in and out of her gungy, run-down office in less than five minutes. Every time I had a complaint, she had an excuse for it. I told her about my back aching, and she sent me for an X-ray, and then she told me I have the start of "osteoporosis," which she never did anything for. Being medically uneducated and doped up, I didn't think there was anything for it, but there is. Plus, I trusted this healthcare system like millions of other people do, and I shouldn't have. I took my daughter to see her because she was having trouble breathing when she played sports, and Lemon said she has "sports-induced asthma," all part of this god awful disease, and she gave her a prescription only to make herself look good, but my daughter wouldn't use it. My daughter still complained about her back being sore, and I was so wired on the shit they give you at the Nut House, I never took her in again for it. Besides, she didn't want to go. She kept saying it was her mattress, just as Lemon had told her in front of me. So I got her yet another mattress, thinking the last one was just another dud. "I believed everything this nutball told me. Little did I know this doctor was a greedy, evil demon, one of the worst kinds out there. Sharon, my so-called health nurse, stayed out of my way for a while. Then she started coming to my home again nosing into my business once more, and one day I mentioned I wanted to stop taking the anti-psychotic, and she said, "If you stop taking it, I will inject it into you." She looked just like the Devil when she said it. I was beginning to feel like a mistreated prisoner. There was nowhere to run to, and nowhere to hide. Never in a million years did I ever think something like this could happen to me.

 In December 1995, a divorce was granted to me by another lawyer, and I didn't find out about it until the trial, which took place in February 1996. There was a discovery before that, and John didn't get a lawyer; he went to it alone. I couldn't believe how brazen he was to show his bitterness and abusiveness in a process I thought would be used in a court of law. He lied through his teeth about everything, and he said cruel and thoughtless things about me. He said, "She should be kept locked up," and when my lawyer mentioned I did the books, John said, "Like Hell she did." "Do you think I'd have a mental patient taking care of my books?" After he said that, I received a letter from the accountant, Eva Banks, verifying that I had done them. As a matter of fact, I have excellent letters of references that say I am a clean and tidy person and get along well with everyone from all the organizations and almost everyone I have ever had any kind of contact with over the last twenty-five years and still counting. All the assets we had purchased while we were together were worthless, according to him. He had around twenty-five thousand dollars' worth of assets besides the house, and he said the assets were only worth four thousand. There was also around ten thousand dollars in a joint bank account, which I never touched, that he got to keep. He told me and my parents that once I was taking a thousand dollars a month out of this account to pay for a drug habit, which he said I had, that he was really trying to hide. My parents never believed him for a minute. John asked at the discovery, "What am I supposed to pay for her drug and alcohol problem?" He said the

Dodge Charger was smashed up when I left, which was a lie, and that all his vehicles were valued according to the blue books, without considering the work and money he had put into them. When he was confronted with all the harassment he had inflicted on me and my family, he played ignorant, saying, "I never did anything." "A bunch of lies." "Pack of lies.' "That's totally false." John had the nerve to say, "Oh yeah, you haven't seen half of the bizarre stuff she comes out with." "If anyone is bizarre, it's her." He accused me of threatening to kill his girlfriend, which was an absolute lie. I guess he meant to say his wife; he only married so she could do his dirty work. He accused my Dad of being an alcoholic, and he said, "He's got half his guts out to prove it." He had the gall to say my parents brainwashed my daughter; she didn't have to be brainwashed, she saw for herself how much of a lunatic her father was. Any question my lawyer asked John was always answered condescendingly, like "So what about it?" "What are you trying to get at?" or "I haven't a clue." What, yeah, so or Ha. When confronted with my son's difficulties in school, John's reply was, "If you say so." Besides the check he wrote out in anger, which said "Food for Kids," he also wrote on a check, mental Case #___, and my lawyer asked him, "How do people know about you?" and John answered, "I'm that good." "'Cause I'm good at it." But he claimed he wasn't getting any work. No, not as far as he was concerned; he made sure of that because he was trying to get away with not paying maintenance for his daughter. When he was walking, he made out he was too good to be associated with you; he'd flip his long hair back every so often and then stick his nose up in the air, the arrogant son of a bitch. I don't know why we even had a discovery because it wasn't even brought up at the trial. At the trial, John was allowed to bring a tape recorder into the courthouse and play it, which is supposed to be against the law. It said it was prohibited right at the front door. The evil demon had dubbed out some incriminating evidence of himself. In a conversation, I was talking to my son, and he had admitted his Dad was trying to run his nanny and papa off the road. All you could hear was my voice, and I swore once, which I never did before, in front of the kids, and so the judge laid into me for that. My parents came to testify, and my mother was so nervous; the judge had the audacity to abuse my mother when she was up on the stand. He said, "I've heard enough," and my mother had only just begun. My Dad had an oxygen tank, and he testified too, and got abused by the judge in the process, and what either of my parents had to say didn't seem to matter to this judge. My parents felt intimidated, and during a recess, my Dad approached my lawyer and told him he would pay to sue John, and he had enough money to do that. I recall my lawyer looking at my Dad with sympathy and tears in his eyes. I wasn't aware of this at the time, but it was because of my Dad's condition that he was in, and he knew then the poor man had been robbed of a life because of it. I just thought he looked at him this way because our justice system is so corrupt that this would be an impossibility, which is a fact, too. John didn't produce any financial statements to my lawyer, and he got away with that, too. This loony represented himself at the two-day trial. The whole time, my lawyer sat in silence, and when it was all over, I was so upset with lawyers, judges, and the court system in general, along with our system of law. I wanted to puke, and I didn't even know the half of it. Not a clue. When it came time to pay me my half of what the house was worth he got a lawyer or a "mouth piece" as he once called them, to take it back to court, May first when the money was due because he owed ten thousand dollars in back payment for child support and wouldn't pay me until the judge dismissed what was owing. The evil demon got away with it. I was left with no order for child support. Was I ever mad at my lawyer then? I thought he was just like all the rest of them. I paid for the trial out of my own money, and once again, the government abused me and my family and ripped me off big time, causing a whole shit load of emotional pain. And that's just how my Dad died with a whole shit load of emotional and physical pain. Years later, I found out I was really being represented, but at the time, hands were tied and mouths were shut because a gag order was in place. But I am still mad because I have been working at justice all these years and haven't seen any, so I am writing books to try and get some. But it really isn't what I call justice for my family and me. There is no amount of money or justice that will make up for all of this, but someone better damn well pay up. Knowing payday was May 1st, I started looking around to buy a place to live. I didn't want to pay much for it as I knew my income couldn't provide for much, and with all the layoffs and bumping going on, and with all they were doing to me, I didn't know if I would even have a job left. When I finally found a place I could afford, I promised my daughter I would get her a dog because she didn't want to move and leave all her friends she had made. Also, she had a hamster that died right in her hands, and she was upset about it. However, her friend Reanne came right over when she found out about it and wanted to have a funeral for the hamster. She was dressed in all black with a black veil over her face, asking for a Bible so they could have a service. We set up chairs outside and put the hamster in a plastic plant pot, which my daughter held during the service. She read excerpts out of the Bible, and often my daughter would blow her nose in a hankie. I couldn't help but laugh at them then. They kind of made a joke out of it, but really, they were just covering their sadness up in more ways than one because she did care for her hamster. We had our dog for a short time in Tillicum Terrace, and we used to put him in a cotton carry bag to hide him when we took him out because you weren't allowed dogs there. His adorable little head would peek out, and we would have to stuff it back in the bag. It was a new breed, and he cost me $300.00, but he was worth every penny of it. My daughter named him Tye because she had a fish that she called Bow, and she said, "Bow Tye," and we thought that was kind of funny. I bought a masked townhouse on the "First Nations' property and we moved in on June 15th, 1996. It was called Pacific

Village One on Admirals Road. She continued attending Tillicum Elementary, and since my daughter was starting grade seven, her last year of Elementary school, attending the same school was less disruptive for her. I drove her back and forth.

I only lived at Tillicum Terrorist for three years, and before leaving, I scrubbed all the walls, which were hard to get clean because I was a smoker then, and I got the rugs shampooed. I made sure the oven and the fridge were spotless, along with the bathroom windows, sills, cupboards, and floors. "Do you think they gave me my damage deposit back?" Not in your life, the cheap bastards who helped make my life a living Hell, and the managers were bonded; good one, hay. Well, I thought I was moving to a respectable place, but after a short time living there, I found out it was just as bad as Tillicum Terrorist, if not worse. The property management was Diversified Properties, and they got themselves involved in harassing me right from the start, but I was so doped up on the anti-psychotic that I never realized it at first. As usual, I just let everyone walk all over me.

Once again, I got ripped off buying the masked townhouse. The lady from Remax, Jane, had arranged for me to buy it and had advertised it in the Times Colonist, the city newspaper. She said it had been freshly painted with pastel colours. With a stove that had a rusty bottom drawer, some of the stove elements didn't work, and the oven didn't work because the connection was not safe; the fridge didn't work at all. I had to live out of a cooler for three weeks until a new one arrived from Sears. Then, the fan on it went while it was still under warranty, and I had to pay over thirty dollars to get it fixed, despite their free service advertisement. My Mom and Dad bought me a new fridge and stove because the crooks took all of my money for the pigsty I moved into. The carpet, which they said was only eight months old, was put over the dirty old one. There were just a few baseboards in the house, which were dark brown, and eventually I replaced them. The cupboards were filthy; I had to scrub them and take a knife to scrape all the shit off, and then I put new paper down before I could use them. There was no cupboard space; the shelving in the master bedroom had completely fallen and couldn't be fixed. Dad put together a shelving unit for me, and he put tile around my countertop. Dad had to stop for air because he couldn't breathe. My Dad came and installed a screen door that I had bought from Sears for five hundred dollars. However, I was taken advantage of because other people had the same door and paid half the price for it. Sears had installed it for them, which they claimed they didn't do. When you tried to clean the walls, the paint would come off because it was painted with cheap paint. You could see the old dark blue paint through the one coat of pastel blue paint they put on in the kitchen. I had to give it three more coats of paint before it was covered. I called a guy from the paper to paint the halls, which cost me four hundred dollars, but he used cheap paint too, which came off when you tried to clean the walls, so I ended up painting the whole house by myself with semi-gloss paint. All the doors only had one coat of white paint on them, and you could see the brown through the white paint, so I had to take all the doors off and give them three coats of paint. Eventually, I painted the cupboards in the kitchen with three coats of paint, too. The linoleum in the kitchen, dining room, and downstairs bathroom was just hosed, individual squares which were bought from Sears, but you couldn't get them anymore, and they were all lifting. I eventually replaced the linoleum with laminate flooring from "End of the Roll." All their workers did was mentally abuse me, thanks to the Owner's Council, who insisted on knowing who your contractors were. Tom, one of the workers, wanted to put plywood down on the floor, but I told him it wasn't necessary. They put pieces of vapour barrier underneath the flooring. They threw the old stuff that was on the floor into the big garbage bins outside the complex. The manager at the time, Derek, was going to fine me five hundred dollars for that until I phoned the company and told them to get their ass over here and get it. Their minds suddenly changed, and the stuff could stay in the bin. They were initially going to slide the flooring underneath the fridge, claiming they couldn't move it, but I insisted they move it. The carpet needed cleaning, so I called the Bay, and a guy named Tom, who worked for them, came and didn't clean it properly. I paid fifty dollars just for the pissy ass living room, and he didn't even move anything. The countertop was rotting, so I had to replace it. I chose Colonial Countertops, who did a good job. They even replaced the water valves underneath both sinks downstairs, as they were corroding and needed to be replaced. My mother bought me a new kitchen sink and some taps because they needed replacing, too. The toilet seal in the downstairs bathroom needed to be replaced, and Home Depot gave me the wrong ones, compliments of the manager, Derek, who told me to go there. I called a guy who redid tubs and sinks, and the materials he used to redo my upstairs bathroom sink had a really bad smell. I paid him ninety dollars, and the stuff just peeled off. I phoned him back to tell him about it, but he was no longer in business. I had to replace the sink after that. My outside patio needed to be replaced and painted, so I got the other manager, Steve, to replace it, and then I painted it, including the upstairs bedroom balcony; otherwise, it might have started to rot. I had to spend a lot of money just to get the place livable, and it took me a few years to do it all. And during all this time, I was being harassed to no end.

When I first moved in, the neighbours, who rented the unit across from me, were a couple of hoodlums. The guy was in the Navy, and he was married to a First Nations woman. He came over to my house in his boxer shorts a few times at six o'clock in the morning, banging on my door because our eight-week-old puppy wanted to come off the patio. I was trying to potty train the pup, so I was keeping him outside at night as it was summer time. One morning, as I was taking Tye out to do his business, this native fellow, who wasn't the woman's navy husband, came staggering out of their house with his pants down to his knees, pulling them up. He knew I was coming out and was harassing me, but I didn't know this at the time. I was deeply disgusted to see this, and I certainly didn't want my daughter to know the kind of people who were like this in the complex. They would also leave their garbage spewing all over the place and wouldn't pick it up. I wrote a letter of complaint to the manager, Steve, about these people and what they were doing, and I was beginning to think moving to Pacific Village One was a big mistake. He told me there was nothing they could do about them. They eventually moved, and another couple, Kathy and Darrel, rented this unit across from me. At this time, they had a teenage boy just finishing high school, living at home still, and a daughter who was a young, single mother living on her own. Darrel was the gardener at the complex, and his wife, Kathy, didn't work then because, apparently, she had stomach cancer. For a couple of years, I thought we were friends. I even got Kathy to take care of my place when my mother, my daughter, and I went on holiday down the Oregon coast, but I found out later it was a huge mistake to trust her.

After I got settled into my home at Pacific Village One, I started to think about going back to work, but I didn't want to work at Eric Martin anymore because I was too embarrassed by all that went on when I was working there, and also because I had been a patient there. I was sure everyone who knew me was aware of my business, including the housekeeping department, building services, and all the nurses. I told my shrink about my concerns, and he wrote a letter to the effect saying it would be in my best interest if I didn't work at Eric Martin, and I gave it to employee relations. They sent me a bump list in the mail, and because I was not working at Eric Martin, it limited my availability; I found there were only part-time positions doing shit ass jobs I could bump into.

I couldn't survive on a part-time job, and without limitations, I could have had a full-time job. I told the union rep at the time, whose name was Red, about all of this and that I was beyond washing pots for a living. I was actually a short-order cook by trade, and because I got harassed out of Eric Martin, I wanted to be retrained in another position, as there were no suitable jobs in the foods department. The Health Benefit Trust agreed to pay for me to be retrained, and I decided to get into clerical work. I guess they were all just waiting for the day I wanted to come back to work in a different area so they could have their fun harassing me some more, and that would really make me look like some diagnosis from the one screwed up book, the DSM-4 Diagnostic and Statistical Manual of Mental Disorders, fourth adition. Once, after receiving some medical files, they stated something to the effect that I didn't get along with anyone. I went to Memorial Pavilion and got letters of reference from my fellow co-workers. When I went to Eric Martin, the bitch of a Dietitian banned me from there, saying I was a "disruption at the workplace," so I couldn't get any more letters of reference, but I know I could have gotten many more. I thought maybe I could work in the records department in the hospital, so I looked into what I would have to take to qualify for a position in that department. The college was offering a Records Management course, which was only about six months long, so I enrolled in that. I knew I would have to learn typing too, so I bought a Mavis Beacon program for my computer and started to learn how to type right away. After I finished Records Management, I enrolled in a beginner's typing course at the same college, Camosun, and by the time I finished the course, I was typing at almost fifty words a minute. While I was taking Records Management, I met a First Nations woman named Gail, and we became friends during the course. She lived in the trailer park on Cooper Road, which was land owned by the First Nation, just a block away from where I was living, so it was convenient for us to study together. She had Microsoft Works for her computer, and although I told her I was going to buy one, she insisted on putting hers on my computer. She didn't finish the program because she fell sick with depression. Then my Mavis Beacon went missing, and in its place was an empty box for Microsoft Works; all the instructions at my house were thrown away. Funny hay?? **NOT.** Later on, Gail mysteriously disappeared to Vancouver. She and her family went to Disneyland, then sold their trailer so her drunken husband could go back to school and take Engineering or something to that effect. I suppose that was her payment for illegally putting Microsoft Works on my computer. Once I got her husband to replace my hot water tank because it blew on me, and it was a weekend, and all her husband wanted was a couple of cases of beer. Well, I finished Records Management and got a certificate in September of 1997. I finished the typing program in November, and all of a sudden, a job became available to me, which I believe they created just for me at the Victoria General Hospital site in January of 1998, and if I passed the typing test, it would be mine. I had to go for an interview with the coordinator of the health records department, Sandy. She wanted to know why I was off work, and I told her in part because of depression. Then she wanted to view my medical information, and at the time, I didn't think there would be any incriminating information about me in my files. I had a different shrink now who had agreed to my diagnosis of Post Traumatic Stress Disorder, so I allowed her and only her to look at them. This was a big mistake. I think they were just trying to cover the fact that they had already released confidential information about me, and this way, they could say I gave them permission. I had many chances at the hospital typing test, and I must have been the laughing stock of the personnel department because of it. You were only supposed to have three tries, and I don't recall how many I had, but I know it was more than three. Finally, I got forty-nine words per minute, one under the required fifty words per minute needed for the job in the health records department. Sandy thought she was making herself look so kind to let me have the job, but I knew something was fishy. I was so desperate to have some kind of a life, so I didn't care. I started working right after New Year's, and I worked damn hard at the job. I thought it was weird I didn't have a desk and everyone else did, and I thought then, too, that this job isn't going to last. Every time I made a mistake, there was someone photocopying it. Like they photocopied a wrong date I had stamped on a file, which is easily done if whoever was using the stamp last at the end of the day didn't change the date. They didn't have anyone to train me, so the others were all trying to do their own job and help me with mine at the same time. One day, I heard one of the girls complaining about how she didn't have the time to train me and was cutting me down to another co-worker. I confronted her with what I heard, and I apologized to her if she thought I wasn't pulling my weight. I told her, "I am doing the best I can." I made sure I was always a good twenty minutes early for work every day, and quite often I would leave late. They had me doing so much work that I didn't have time to take a coffee break. One time, I was filing some records, and I knew I filed them correctly. After I had finished, I walked by the room and saw my supervisor taking files out, which were in the right place, and putting them in the wrong place. I walked in there to see if there was a problem because I knew they were watching my every move, and she immediately took the file she had misplaced and put it back where it was, and told me I filed it incorrectly. I said, "That's funny, I could have sworn I saw you take that file out of the right place," and I walked away. Did she ever look guilty after that? I think she told the coordinator, Sandy, the uneducated fool who can't even write a letter of apology correctly, that she didn't want anything more to do with framing me for a poor job because of my not filing the files correctly, which was never brought up again. I even asked for a meeting to talk about what I thought was happening, and at the end of the meeting, they put it down to a misunderstanding. You bet it was.

My Dad died on February 8th, 1998, and they gave me the allotted time off work, which was three days. My Dad died on a Sunday, and I even came into work on Monday and told them I would stay until they found a replacement for me, but my supervisor told me it was all right, I could go home. I was devastated by my Dad's death. His bowels burst, and he died of septicemia due to years of trauma caused by Crohn's disease, which is all totally preventable, but I didn't know this at the time. I still think about him every day, and how much I miss him, and how much he suffered in his life, and it's been almost thirty years. And it has gotten harder to accept as the years go by. not easier like they say. Not for me anyway. I was only back to work for a few days when they called a meeting, and I had to scramble around to find a union rep to be there with me because I had a feeling they were going to tell me I wasn't working out. They had people from the employee relations department attend this meeting. One of them was Brian, the guy who you would hear yakking and yakking up a storm on the radio for the organization he volunteered for, how the Hell they help women and children. Yeah, right, help make their life a living nightmare. At this meeting, the union rep, Randy, said, "Some of the girls are afraid of you." I said, "What?" "Well, you are a lot bigger than them, you know," was his reply. I couldn't believe what I was hearing. I said to him, "You're supposed to be representing me." His comment was, "I also represent your fellow workers, too." The whole works of them had me so upset, I was sobbing, and with my Dad just dying, it didn't help matters. The ignorant bastards. So much for our brotherly union. Now, some of the hospital is privatized (food services included), and you all wonder why. Now you know. I knew then there was something incriminating said to everyone about me. After that, I swore to myself I would never go back to work for the hospital again, and I never did.

Running From the Demons

CHAPTER FOURTEEN

I was completely beside myself at the reality of everything that was happening to me, and with my Dad dying, it made everything much worse. The day Dad died, he laid some carpet in the basement for Mom. It was a Sunday, and I went over to my parents' place for some reason, and Mom and I took off somewhere. In the last year before my father's death, I wouldn't let him drive anymore because at this point, the man was taking morphine for all the pain he was in all the time, and I didn't think it was safe. He would ask Mom for it often, and my mother would tell Dad, "You just took some not too long ago." She would have to monitor it for him, and I wonder now if Doctor Turd only prescribed him a small amount because he wanted to make sure he suffered yet some more. When we came home that day, we rang the doorbell a few times before Dad finally let us in. I could tell something was not right with him; he seemed incoherent and disoriented. I went home, and shortly after that, my \Mom called me, telling me she had to phone the ambulance to take Dad to the hospital again. He had been in the hospital the year before nine times, so I should have seen it coming, but I suppose no one is ever really ready for something like this. One time when Dad was in the hospital, a nurse gave him the wrong pills, and if it wasn't for my mother noticing it, I don't know what would have happened to Dad. I went to the nurses' station and told them about this, and I asked them, "How could you be so careless?" Another time, a female doctor took Mom and me into a private room and told Mom, "I don't know how long your husband is going to live, and you should be prepared for the worst." We called my brother up from the hospital, and he came right away. Dad ended up coming home with us then, and we were all upset over this female doctor telling us that. Mom and I lived at the hospital that year, and we made sure he was getting the care he deserved. Mom had to help him have a shower sometimes because the nurses didn't have time to, and Mom knew he couldn't do it himself. Mom would have to help him at home, too, because he couldn't breathe very well anymore. One time, the doctor who looked after Dad's COPD came up to me while I was making Dad some tea and told me he thought my Dad was a nice man. I said to him, "He is the best," which is an understatement.

When Dad was in the Emergency Room of the Victoria General Hospital, he was left there by himself for a while before we were able to be with him. We were standing in the Emergency Room, and we heard Dad asking if he could go to the bathroom. All the nurses were laughing at him, and I thought, "How heartless could you be?" I had the feeling that I would never see my Dad again. I phoned my brother Brian from the emergency department soon afterwards. Dad was put in the treatment room on the fourth floor of the hospital, and I didn't want to leave his side. He kept wanting to get out of bed, and I knew he was suffering, so I would go to the nurse's desk and tell them I thought he should have something more for the pain. Then they would come in and fix his interventions. Brian came when Dad was put in the treatment room, and he sat on the other side of him, telling him, "Hang in there." I had to leave once because I knew it was the last time. A nurse came to console me when I broke down. After I got myself together, I went back into the treatment room. Some doctors came and told us his bowels burst, and they could operate on him, but he would probably die because his system was so weak. Not only did he have COPD, but he also had a form of leukemia. After that, I sat by my Dad's bed in shock and cried and prayed. I prayed that Dad would not suffer anymore. I prayed to take him to heaven because it is where he belonged. Mom sat in a chair in the corner of the room, the whole time her mind and body paralyzed with shock. Someone came and asked us if we wanted a minister to come, but we said "No" because we knew Dad would not want that. He didn't want a funeral or service. We talked once shortly before he died, and I asked, "Don't you believe in God, Dad?" He said then he did. He knew in his heart he didn't have too much longer to live and was holding onto faith that there was a better place to go to. I am glad I had the opportunity to tell him that "There is a God and you will go to heaven." The Christmas just before he died, he wanted a big Christmas tree because he said, "I don't know how many Christmases I will have left." Before that, he would say, "Only the good die young, and I will live a long time."

It was supper time, and my brother Brian convinced Mom, my daughter, and me to go home, have something to eat, and he would stay with Dad. We should not have left because just as we all finished dinner, we got a phone call from my brother telling us that Dad had passed away. Mom answered the phone, and she started crying, and then I broke down sobbing uncontrollably, and my daughter broke down too. My daughter was sitting on the couch, sobbing her eyes out because my Dad always made her feel so special. He would save all his change up for her and put it in a jar, aMom and Dad were looking after her while I was in the hospital for those months, Dad was the only one able to get her up in the morning to go to school. My mother would call her, but she wouldn't move. I think she waited purposely for her papa to call her in his loving voice. He always hugged and kissed her, too. Both my parents gave her the kind of love she deserved, which every child deserves.

We told the hospital that Mom wanted Dad to go to the Crematorium in Royal Oak. We left for Mom's then. My mother called up my half-brother Lenny in Ontario and told him what had happened, and my Mom said he shouldn't be mad at her for not telling him sooner, that Dad was going to pass on. It happened all so fast. I suppose he wanted to have time to go to a lawyer and blame it all on my mother, so he could clean up. No doubt that is just what he did. When it was happening, we wanted to believe he would make it through this, like he always did. We arranged for a viewing just for Lenny because he wanted to see his Dad when he came over, being the sick Catholic he is. Lenny made me go into the room with him, and Dad was dressed in his green army blazer, and he didn't look at all like himself; he looked like a mannequin. I suppose because he was embalmed. To this day, I wish I had never gone into that room with Lenny. Mom gave Lenny Dad's leather coat, his shoes, and Dad's ring. Brian said he didn't want them. He told Mom to give it to Lenny. When I think back now, when Mom gave Lenny these things, it looked like he was disappointed it was all he was getting. Dad was on his last legs, so to speak. I saw it in all the pictures of him with his Dad. Dad was so skinny. Mom offered him some of Dad's clothes, but he didn't want any of them, so we eventually gave them to the Salvation Army. Dad said when he was in the war, they were the only ones who helped them out with things like warm blankets. They must have wanted to make themselves look like they contributed to the war, but in actual fact, they were all a bunch of cowards hiding behind the Catholic Religion.

Shortly after Dad died, Mom started having problems with Dad's car, and by this time, the car was only a few years old. I started to notice that whenever you turned the heater on, you could smell a burning smell. I took it to the corner service station, and the attendant there said there was nothing to worry about, but he didn't provide an explanation for what was causing the smell. Then the radio just stopped working, and Mom and Dad hadn't even used the CD player yet. I phoned up the dealership to see if there was some kind of warranty on the unit, but there wasn't, so Mom went out and bought another one, which wasn't as good. After that, the battery was dead every time we went somewhere in it, and that was Angus's Dad, a cop, apparently. Can you believe that? The loony ex-husband of mine had gotten my son to come over to see who got the car. And I was told by this woman lawyer, whom the nutball had at this time, that John could clean me out of my mother's Will even though we were divorced. So Mom and I went to her lawyer to see if that was true. **NOT**. Great laws in Canada, everyone fighting over money, clogging the courts up while all the loony's run free. The first time the battery went dead, we didn't know what the Hell was going on. This must have happened five or six times, and each time we had to call the British Columbia Automobile Association and have them come out to charge the battery for us. We got a new battery, and it still was happening, so we went to the dealership to see if they could find out what was causing this problem. They checked everything out and said they didn't know what the problem was. All this was freaking my mother out, but of course, I was already freaking because of everything I had been through and was going through. Finally, the BCAA guy told us of a reputable service station on the corner of Richmond and Hillside, and we took it there. He kept it for a while, but it didn't do anything while he had it, and he said the only thing he could think of, which may be causing this, is that the seat belt was getting caught in the door. So for a while, every time Mom and I got out of the car, we made sure the seat belt was inside. I bet that fucked up cop, Angus's Dad, was trying to keep all his land. Fucking loser. But soon we stopped checking for it. After that, it stopped happening, and at the same time, the seat belt problem went away, and so did the burning smell. Mom and I always thought someone was sabotaging the car because we never had any problem with it when Dad was alive.

The year before Dad died, they started to have problems with the neighbour who lived in North's old house. A female Elementary teacher bought the house from the Norths, and my parents got along just fine with her, but then she had this man move in with her, and later they had a couple of kids. That's when the trouble started. He put dirt on their front lawn to raise it, and while they were doing this, they diverted the water from the drain pipe onto my parents' property, and it stayed like that for a couple of years. Good old Dale, the cop across the street, gave them the idea. Then they planted a row of huge evergreen trees and large laurel bushes between the two properties. First, they made a rock retaining wall on their land. Mom and Dad were concerned as to what they were doing, so I went out there, and that is when I found out he worked for the Capital Regional District Parks, and they both assured me this was all they were going to do. However, the next thing you know, this guy parked his boat beside my Dad's bedroom and would constantly start it up, and all the fumes would come into the bedroom and into the house. Another suggestion from my Dad's so-called friend, the cop. Dale, how he sucked on the beer my Dad bought just for him. My Dad's friend Dale can rot in Hell, too. Of all things, I called Dale up, telling him that I forgave him for what he did to me, but I am going to leave the forgiving up to God now. My mother got angry one day, so I asked him not to do this because Dad had breathing problems, but this didn't stop him. Every summer, even after Dad passed away, he would do the same thing. Mom also had problems with the bitch who lived on the other side of her. After junior, her Dad, shoved his father into a home, he allowed his daughter to move into it. She was a single mother who had different men coming in and out of her house all the time, and she started to create trouble for my mother. Her dog was always barking at all hours of the night, and Mom told her about her dog keeping them awake at night. Furthermore, she never let her dog out, so we think she was allowing her dog to do his business in the basement. She had these bird feeders out on her deck, and all the cats of the neighbourhood would come and sit waiting for the birds to come to feed off them. They were sitting on my Dad's car too, and scratching it up every time we came home from somewhere. All purposely done. Because the engine was hot, the cats liked the heat from the engine. She also piled all of her garden refuge beside the fence Dad had built dividing the properties. Mom was afraid this was going to cause the fence to rot, so I wrote her a letter explaining all of this, and she got all worked up about it. She wrote us a nasty letter back, threatening to sue us for harassment and had a cop sign it. Man, did that disappear fast, Angus's Dad again. Nothing was done about the pile of grass, so we called the CRD and reported it to them, and they came out and asked her to remove it. Not only would it rot the fence, but it would also attract rats. I suppose they were trying to tell me something then, but I was still doped up out of my mind and wasn't aware of bugger all. After that, she bought three more bird feeders, one a standing one, and placed them on her lawn and in the tree beside the fence, and left the bird seed to rot in them. The birds were being poisoned by the rotting birdseed. We saw a couple of dead ones on her lawn. Mom calls her "Cow Face" because she is as homely as a cow's ass. Dad used to say all the men she had coming in and out must have had to put a bag over their heads.

It was hard for us all to cope without Dad; he always took care of everything right until the day he died. My mother had to learn how to manage their finances because my Dad always took care of that. She even had to be shown how to write a check, as my dad handled all that, too. I did a lot of work for my mother after my Dad died. I painted all the outside trim, back doors, and cement work around her house. I suppose I thought if I kept busy, I wouldn't think about the pain of losing Dad so much.

Mom hired Derek from the townhouse complex where I was living to come and paint the kitchen and Dad's bedroom, and I painted the trim in both rooms. In the summer of the year Dad died, Mom paid for us to go to Hawaii. She had to get away from it all. It was a nice trip, but the reality of my ignorant neighbours and my Mom's ignorant neighbours was still there when we got back.

This guy who lived behind me at the townhouses took this bag of dog due and threw it on my patio. I had told the manager about this idiot not picking up his dog's shit. When I saw this dog shit on my balcony, I picked up the bag and put it at his front door. This guy was a lunatic because after I did that, I stood on my patio and waited for him to come, and he swore his head off at me using the foulest words you could imagine. He then took the bag of dog shit and threw it on my car and said to me I'm going to smear it all over your car. I got the manager and showed him the dog shit on my car and demanded he do something about this madman. To cover my ass, I took a picture of it on my car. Shortly after this, I got this letter in my mail box from Kathy, my neighbour, telling me her life story and how she, too, had nothing when she left her first husband. She said something to the effect that I had brought on all my problems myself. Well, I gave her an educated letter back to her, and on the other side of it, I wrote "No, we do this to each other," and I put it in her mailbox. However, since this time, I have come to realize all these evil demons have done this to themselves. Well, no sooner did I do that than the nun, Kathy's friend, came banging at my door, and when I answered it, my daughter was standing beside me, and she said she didn't want me coming over to her friend's house, Kathy, anymore, and then she stormed away. Afterwards, I started to get stocked everywhere I went, it seemed. Once, while my mother and I were in Sears, I met up with a few of my X-fellow employees, and this one lady kept following me everywhere I went in the clothing department. I talked to another lady I had worked with, who was at Sears, and she said she was getting ready to go on a trip somewhere. That same day, I saw Jan, who I thought was my friend when I was living out in "NO Man's Land." She was in Sears too, and I called her, and she saw me, but she just kept going, and she had this real evil look on her face. Then I thought it was all so weird. I had finished working on the Government Affidavit, the story of my life, and had it printed up at a place in town because my printer went on me. After that, I went to track down the lawyer I had been looking for, because I had somehow figured out he was involved in all of this. However, when I finally found him, he told me that he was doing something else. He then instructed me to go to Legal Aid, so I went there, filled out a form, and just left. By this time, I was fully aware of being stalked everywhere I went.

While I was at legal aid, there was a woman staring at me and peering at what I was writing on the application. I was so freaked out about all of this, I just put stocking on the form, but what I really meant to put down under what this case was about is Mental Abuse too. I had viewed the government affidavit, all 125 or more pages of it, when I first got it printed, but never looked at it again till the following year. I put my copies of it underneath my bed in a small black suitcase. My daughter was getting harassed at school. One day, she came home and told me a girl was saying nasty things to her, like "You like to lick ass." I had gone to this school before, about remarks which were being made to my daughter by kids, and wanted a report about it sent to me, but I never got one. When this happened, I went a second time and requested a report on the incident, but again I never got one. One of my daughter's friends almost got into a fight one day at school because of things that were being said about her, but this friend was a very smart kid and knew better than that. Even the teachers got in on the harassment. Apparently, one of the teachers there told my daughter that vitamin C wasn't good for you and that she had cancer once. Another one told her whole class of students that they could die from Sexually Transmitted Diseases (STDs), and this was in her physical education class. Another teacher was giving out C+'s to the same distance runners and was giving the other ones who chose a different route a higher grade. Then I attended a seminar with a couple of women, and one of them stole the information I had collected and had left on the table when I went to get some coffee. Even my daughter's friends' parents were in on things. This one lady, who was sitting with us and was at the table the whole time, said she didn't know anything about it going missing. The other woman pretended she was busy writing when I came back, and she made it obvious to me that she took it because she didn't say anything when I asked about it. This woman had the nerve to tell her daughter when she asked her what was wrong with me, I see things and hear things. I could see the poor kid was worried about what her mother had told her, so I explained to her about depression and how the brain is lacking certain chemicals, but they are replaced with antidepressants for the time being until you deal with your problems. It's just like diabetics needing insulin. I also told her about how, when you are young and you have many traumatic events in your life, and you don't know how to deal with them, sometimes they get filed away like a computer does. Then you don't remember them, but one day they will all come back to you, and then you will find it hard to cope because you never learned how to deal with them at the time it was all happening. That's why it is important to tell someone if you are having problems. The girl then went up to my daughter's bedroom, and a little while later, she came downstairs and gave me a big hug and said, "Thank you, I love you,"and I could see I had eased her worried mind. I had a doctor from the States, and he had taken extensive notes on my history, and I decided to make an appointment for him to see my daughter. At this point, I had realized (PID) Pelvic Inflammatory Disease and Crohn's Disease were basically the same thing, so I said I wanted tests done on my daughter to see if she had it too. I told the doctor from the States, who I had at the time, that I was going to tell my daughter she had to take some tests to see if she had Crohn's Disease, and he thought it was a good idea, so that's what I did. I brought my daughter in with me, and I was in the office with her when he started asking her a bunch of questions like "Do you smoke?, do you do drugs?" My daughter told him she didn't, and then this doctor from the

States asked her, "Would you tell your mother if you did?" My daughter said, "No."

Afterwards, I asked her about that, and she said, "You would be able to tell anyway." There was an intern present too at this visit, and for some reason, I mentioned the incident when I was little, of getting the end of a New Year's Eve blower stuck in my throat and having to wait for six hours, coughing up blood, before they did an operation on me. When I told them about this, the intern's eyes just about popped out of his head, and I could see he had a lot to learn about this fucked up medical system we have in this godforsaken country we live in. At this appointment, the doctor from the States didn't write anything down about what my daughter was telling him, such as the fact that she had stomach pains and back pain in the past. We left the office with no request form of any kind for my daughter to get tested, and I was pissed off at him for that. The only thing he did for her was write a prescription out for a puffer. I was so disappointed. I thought I really had a doctor this time who was going to do something for us. Shortly after this, I had an appointment to see this doctor again, and he was going to give me some information regarding laser treatment for that nasty wart fungus I was still carrying around. I was just fooling around when I said this because he was a kidder too, one time pretending he was a bit slow and making me laugh, but I said, "When they do the operation, make sure they pull the plug." The next thing you know, he called the cops and the Squad for the Less Fortunate, and they hauled my ass off to Eric Martin. When I asked about what section I was going under, they told me section 28, so later I looked it up, and it was referring to the fact that I was a danger to the community and/or to myself. It was at this appointment, while I was waiting to see the doctor from the States, a lady came in and sat beside me, and just out of nowhere started telling me she knew this woman who had a teenage daughter, and they threw her daughter in the Institution for the Less Fortunate. Anywhere and everywhere I went, I was being stalked. Well, like all the other times, they threw me in the locked room. The officer who took me there said she would stay with me, but didn't, and I wanted a lawyer like I always asked for, but never got. Soon afterward, this really scary dude, a shrink, comes into my room. I didn't say a word to him, but the first thing he said to me was "You like to hear yourself yap, don't you?" as he was writing and writing and writing like a madman, about me? I have no idea, because the only thing I said to him was "This abuse has got to stop." I was too scared to say anything more to him. He was one of the scariest men I have ever met. He looked possessed, another evil demon, doctor. I saw him again after I assumed he had committed me, and when the elevators weren't working. A bunch of us girls wanted to use the stairs because it was dinner time, and they only give you about half an hour to eat. We asked this nut case if we could go up the stairs with him because you need a key to the door to the stairwell, and only personnel have one, and he had this disgusting look on his face like he was too good for us and told us, "I don't think it would be a very good idea." I got the feeling the nut case was trying to let us know, in a smug sort of way, that he didn't want to be in danger, but I think he is one of the ones you should look out for. While I was there, they assigned me the evil demon shrink Seagull, and I had to have him again. At least I got the opportunity then to say to the bastard he was a murderer when he was at the nursing station one morning. I didn't care who heard what I said to him. That is because of the drug Respridol that he gave me, which I shouldn't have had because of my physical condition. I could have died from that shit, the pamphlet said. I am sure all the nurses know what goes on in that place. That's why some of them don't last very long, I found out, because I see them once, never to be seen again. The regulars get themselves involved in mentally abusing you in there, along with some government informants who stock the place. I remember, while I was in the hospital this time, I went all over the place with letters of complaints to various organizations. Some informant came with me, and she left her wallet in my car when she came to drop off some of these letters. I guess to see if I would return it to her or not, which of course I did. I had written a letter complaining about the kind of treatment I had been receiving, and I personally delivered it to them. They did so many no mind things in there to try and play with my mind, but I knew just what they were up to, because now I was educated. There were instances of them putting me in a room which faced a Catholic school, and they would put me in the bed closest to the window, and I would see all the children playing in the playground. One time, they got a baby from somewhere to come into the Nut House crying, "Nut," now meaning almost every professional who continues to work in that place. I suppose they were trying to make me feel guilty. What for is beyond me. Little did I know at the time how violent this world really is. Isn't that what the Catholics do? God forgives no matter what? Just ask for forgiveness. What I have to say to you Catholics is, "Why don't you listen to all the little children crying in pain, suffering from Crohn's Disease because of a dirty Catholic?" I was only in there a week before the doctor from the States changed his mind and let me out. I had started working on some court material to take this Health Care System to court for all the stuff they did to me. Unbelievable! I decided I was going to call up legal aid and see if I could get a lawyer for this, and I talked to a guy there. I met with him, and I remember showing him the picture I had taken of the mucky big bruise on my arm and various other documentation I had, and he was going to get back on this with me, but he never did. I was so traumatized, and I figured this guy could see the pain I was in. I was still physically sick, too. Because of the doctor from the States' actions of throwing me in the Institution for the Less Fortunate and his uncaring attitude, I decided I was going to look for yet another practitioner. I went to a new building, which I knew was taking on patients and saw a doctor who wanted my medical records, so I decided to allow him to have them. He seemed so eager to help me, but I knew he, too, was going to reject me once he saw all the lying shrink and doctor reports on me. The first time I saw him, I told him about me having PID, and he was all gung-ho, wanting to make arrangements for me to have an operation for it, but he, too, turned me down. I even brought a picture of myself when I was little. When I showed it to him, he said, "Please don't." and I thought, "No, you please don't." I was becoming sick again and was in pain, and he gave me a prescription for Tylenol three, but it was all he was willing to do for me. I told him about my daughter being born with this, and he referred me to the clinic that deals with children who have emotional problems, and I went there to tell them about this abuse of children. I still didn't have a doctor. I was in so much pain, I went to the hospital with the PID report, looking to get treated, and they did a urinalysis test and told me there was nothing wrong with me. You are delusional, the bastard said to me, who wanted to throw me in the Institution for the Less Fortunate, but my aging mother, who came with me, convinced him not to. I said, "See, this is what the Pope was talking about on TV about the pain and suffering of innocent women and children." I was crying my head off, and there was a young couple in there getting their little girl looked at, and they told my mother this guy was ignorant to them, too. I wish I had gotten this guy's name, but I was in so much distress, I just left crying with my mother and went straight to a clinic, and sure enough, I was sick again. A doctor at the clinic gave me a prescription for high doses of antibiotics after I showed him the PID report, which had been put in my townhouse by someone. My mother came with me, and when I came out with the prescription and showed it to her, she couldn't believe it. She never understood why. I have told her things about my life and what Crohn's Disease really is, but she was in complete denial. Even when I got sick, she sometimes acted as if I should get on with my life despite the agony of it all, both emotionally and physically, which was hard to hide from her.

A little while later, I started to get harassed by the manager of the complex. I had phoned the cops on this day too, about some guy behind me smoking pot, and I thought they came out to talk to me about it, but in actual fact, they had come because the manager had called them about me. They had all had enough, is what the manager told me when I freaked out about their intention to fine me five hundred dollars for these no-mind contractors putting the remnants from my floor in the garbage bin. I told this officer some of the problems I was having with my neighbours, like the break-in when Kathy and her nun friend put animal hair all over my floors and stole my pen, cigarettes and lighter, and she said she was going to go talk to them. She even came in and talked to my daughter about it, and my daughter told this officer just what she saw. The officer disappeared and never came back to talk to me like she said she would. I got on the phone to find out when she was coming to talk to me about what the neighbours had to say for themselves, and she said tomorrow. The next day, I had the cops and the Squad for the Less Fortunate knocking at my door. They started asking me all of these screwed up questions like "Are you seeing things and hearing things?" Then they asked me, "Do you have any knives?" I should have said to them No, I rip my meat up with my bare hands but I didn't. Instead, I asked them, "What kind of no mind diagnosis do they have me under now?" One of the Squad members said Psycho Effective Disorder. I then commented, "Oh, the cop out diagnosis for the shrinks." Then the cop opened my screen door and grabbed my arm, bare feet and all, and she said that they were going to take me to the Institution for the Less Fortunate. Then I said, "Well, at least let me get my purse and shoes." By this time, the other police officer who attended with her had me by the other arm, and they were both dragging me towards their cruiser. The BITCH of a cop took out her pepper spray and sprayed me right in the eyes with it at close range. It hurt like a son of a bitch. They threw me in their cop car and literally sped out of the complex as if in a quick getaway, ignoring the "5 kilometres

Children Playing" sign. And they took me to that Nut House again, where these Nuts claim to be helping you. Before that, they threw my gardening shoes in their car, which were outside by the front door. I was in so much pain with what they had done to me, and I was calling for my Dad. I just wanted to be with him. I knew if he were alive and found out what all they had done to me, he would have gone ballistic. Absolutely ballistic!

I had yet another evil demon shrink, a third one, Doctor Dirty and I was finally taken out of the locked room where some other scary-looking nut cases came in and committed me. This Doctor Dirty took me into a room to be off the cameras they had now installed throughout the place, so he could badger me further. A young female nurse who turned out to be really nice came in with us, and I had told her on the way to this room that I had a headache and wanted something for it. Doctor Dirty said to me, "If you try to run away, do you know what will happen to you?" I said, "I can only imagine." "I haven't done anything yet and have been abused." He also said to me, "If you don't do some psychological tests," which they never did make me do, "have an ECG and a CAT scan along with medication," he was going to prescribe to me. "He would have me put in PIC." He started me on an anti psychotic again, but he eventually changed it to something else used as an anti psychotic and for stress by injection. I guess he didn't want to be busted for trying to kill me because I should never have been on that either, because of my physical condition. I was crying because I mentioned the pepper spray, and I was still in shock at what had happened to me. I said, "Why didn't you just phone me up and tell me this, and I would have come in right away?" I wanted to know why they insisted on my coming to the Institution for the Less Fortunate again, and then Doctor Dirty told me what the doctors who committed me wrote in their report. Apparently, in their report on me, they mentioned the break-in and how someone had broken my downstairs taps, and I knew right away it had to come from the complex because I hadn't told these doctors about that. As a matter of fact, I never said a Hell of a lot to them because I was always so traumatized by their actions when I was forced there. When the badgering was over, the nurse got the doctor to okay some Tylenol for my headache. While I was there, I was supposed to be fasting for some blood tests, which I didn't know about, and a no mind gave me orange juice and coffee with two sugars in it that morning. Probably deliberately done. I went for the lazier removal of the nasty wart fungus, or excuse me virus, while I was in there, and my mother came there to be with me. I was crying, and she told me it was going to be all right. I was scared they were going to do me in right on the operating table or torture me like they did before. A lady there told me lazier treatment was only two years old, the big liar. Another guy in the operating room started singing "Make the whole world go away" and was laughing. The mental abusers! Even they must have known what was going on. The next day, I had the ECG and the CT scan in another part of the hospital. The mad man shrink, read the results and said I don't have Schizophrenia. Apparently, there were some dead brain cells, I guess from all the pot they had shoved down my throat over the years. The bastard evil demon shrink Doctor Dirty wasn't even going to give me passes. However, after my brother came and dropped off some clothes for me, his attitude changed, and he let me out so I could get my mother to be with me for the operation. If my brother hadn't come, who knows what they would have done to me there.

I had revised one of my poems from "My Book of Poems" called Victimizing in this Screwed up World, because I was so pissed off with some of the management and Owner's Council members for getting themselves involved in harassing me. Well, when I gave that poem to the perpetrators of the complex, they all knew then I was onto them, and the terrorists all decided to devise another plan to have me thrown in the Loonie Bin again. One of them was out on his patio, staring at me with this smirk on his face as I came back from the last stop with my dog in the Uplands. I asked him if he had a problem, and he didn't say anything, so I said, "Well, spit it out." The nun heard this and she came over abruptly, putting her hand up to her head like in a salute, screaming, "You're insane!" "You're insane!" I said, "It looks like you're the one who is insane. "Then I moved a couple of steps, and when I did, the nun put her hand up like she had a stop sign and informed me not to come any closer. Then I said to her, "If you want the name of a good shrink, I can give you one," and then she stormed off like a madwoman.

I was in the Institution for the Less Fortunate still and was out on a pass when I came to the realization the EVIL DEMON family doctor was actually guilty of murdering my father and the attempted murder of me and my children so I decided I was going to make a police report out on him for that and on two EVIL DEMON shrinks for attempted murder of me and another Evil Demon Quack for attempted murder of me. I also made one out on the EVIL DEMON EX-HUSBAND for the attempted murder of me and his own two children! On my way there, I noticed there was an undercover police officer following me, and then when I got to the door of the police station, there were dignitaries all standing around the front door. The realization of it all traumatized me, and I was so distraught after I scribbled the reports out that I was sobbing. An officer directed me to "Victim Services," and the two women there nosed into my business, asking all sorts of questions. I told them about the police reports I had just made out. I believe they called the Institution of the Less Fortunate and told them that I was d-compensating, whatever they meant by saying that. Boy, all these people sure are desperate to hide their crimes. I felt uncomfortable telling them my horror story and said to them, "I have to get back to Eric Martin because I was just out on a pass." A lot of help they were. A couple of uncompassionate human beings who have no idea how to console someone. I remember thinking they looked like a couple of vultures. Another disgrace to our justice system. By the time I was released from that god awful place, Eric Martin, I was so doped up I soon forgot all about beginning procedures to take the fucking Health Care System to court. Just what they wanted to succeed in doing because by this time some terrorists had come into my house, stolen the government affidavit, filed a revised copy of it and put a copy of it under my bed. They had been doing this sort of thing all along. Every time I got something, they would take it and replace it with something else. A year later, when I took it out to review it again, I discovered that it had all been filed by my last lawyer, who had become my representative. At least that is what I thought. However, I am not sure it is him because to this day, he still denies it, even though I have a Motion with his name on it. Maybe it was just another sick trick by the terrorists. I even had security locks put on all of my doors, but they were somehow able to get in, even when I locked the doors. Whenever I was drugged up, once in a while, I would forget to use the locks, and they would be right there ready to harass the shit out of me some more and steal whatever I had of any value to them.

CHAPTER FIFTEEN

I had to go to the clinic to get drug injections every two weeks after I got out of the Hell Hole of the Earth, Eric Martin. When I was discharged after three weeks in that place, I saw the doctor from the States for a follow-up appointment. I had decided, however, that I was going to try and find yet another doctor, someone who wouldn't throw me in the Nut House because I was so sick and tired of being abused in that place. No sooner was I home than my screwed up neighbours, Kathy and Daryl, were moving out of the unit they were in into a unit in the uplands of the complex, and apparently, it was totally remodelled just for them. They were all so pleased with themselves for having me put into the Nut House that my old neighbour decided they were going to continue harassing the Hell out of me to see how much they could all get away with, I suppose. While moving out, this neighbour pretended he was going to run me over with the moving dolly, running towards me with it as I stood on the sidewalk looking at my garden. When he did this, I told him, "Maybe the cops will come and take you away this time." Anyway, I guess he was excited about the prank they had all devised against me for the next day. It was known I was having problems finding a doctor, and I guess they thought if they had an emergency response set up that would send me over the cliff, so to speak, but I just thought it was all so pathetic. There were two ambulances, two cop cars and even the Fire Department attending. A mother of a friend of my daughter's took the kids out shopping that day; I guess so they wouldn't be exposed to this abuse. My old neighbour was running around like in a panic before they all came, and the manager and his family, including their kids and another family with their kids, were all standing waiting for them to arrive, and every time an emergency vehicle arrived, they would wave them in the direction

of this so-called emergency. Other kids came running out of
nowhere to see what was happening. After about 10 minutes of
everyone from these emergency vehicles running around
pretending they didn't know where to go, they came out with a lady
on the stretcher, moaning like a ninny. By this time, I was standing
outside my home, and two little girls came up to me and asked me
what was going on. And I said, "Oh, they are just practicing so
they can get better at their work." One girl commented, "How did
you know it's a... trick?" And she hesitated when she said a trick. I
said, "I can tell." After they took this woman off in the ambulance,
a cop was going to get into his cruiser, and I stopped him in the
parking lot by asking him, "What's going on?" He shrugged his
shoulders as if to say he didn't know, so I replied, "How pathetic,"
and walked away. I could see how this affected all the kids
standing in the parking lot watching all of this, so as a councilor, I
felt obligated to report this to the police because this is a form of
abuse to children, mental abuse, which I did. The next day, my
daughter's friend's father decides to get in on the action again,
using one of my daughter's friends and his son to try to deceive my
daughter.

My daughter's friend came over to our house, and he was in a hell
of a hurry to meet the girls. So much so, his nose started to bleed.
They had talked about going to the lake; however, the gang had
changed their plans to this particular day instead of going on the
day all their other friends were going. I found out, while my
daughter and her friend were there waiting for the other friend, the
cop's step-son, that two hot guys approached them and started
hustling them. My daughter's girlfriend kept looking up the hill and
asking if the other kid was coming yet. I figure this kid was scared
because she knew it was a setup.

My daughter had a ball game one day, and I felt she was being
mentally abused by all her coaches. The typical things parents

usually complain about are coaches, but it went beyond that. They were literally mean to my daughter, yelling at her all the time to get the ball, telling her things like she should run backwards to get it. Only playing her outfield, sitting her on the bench most of the time, putting her at the bottom of the batting list. That kind of bull shit. Over the years, I made several complaints, but the same coaches coached every year. One time, one of the coaches said to me something I thought was way out of line about my daughter's friend. "She really has developed," and he wasn't talking about the ball. I reported this and told them this guy had better stay out of the dugout, and I will be watching him closely. Another time, the parents in the stands started in on me about the score because I was keeping the score. Their team had won by an outrageous amount, at least ten runs or more. The coach of this team, who won, I believe, has huge problems; he was utterly out of hand, loudly arguing about this. I just gave him the score sheet and said to him, "You do it next time, then." They even had the kids from his team in on it all, giving me dirty looks and telling me off. Then they left a ten-dollar bill on the ground once for me to find, hoping I would take it, but I turned it in. This woman was standing close by when I told her I had found ten dollars. She said it was hers, but I told her she would have to go to the concession to claim it. There is more, but it is all too pathetic to even write about. Well, this particular day, I had a meeting with the bigwig of the park to discuss how my daughter was being treated, and this guy didn't like what I had to say. I had suggested these so-called superiors should receive some counselling before they take on the responsibility of other people's children, and never mind their own. I said, "If this abuse to these children continues, I told my lawyers to go after everything they could, and I wouldn't want them to go after the ball field because it is for the kids." That was the last thing I said to him as I left, and he jumped up and grabbed me by the arm as I was going out the door to his office, and told me, "You should go back on the medications." How he knew about that is beyond me, but I would imagine by this time, the whole of Victoria must have been informed of false and discriminatory information about me. I decided to report this abuse to the children, so I made some lengthy police reports and took them to the cop shop. They took me to a room in the police station, and instead of asking me about the reports I made out, they had a so-called officer badger me about my well-being, asking questions like "What medications are you on?" "How much of it are you on?" When I left the police station, I went to the desk which is supposed to deal with abuse of children and told them I had just made a report on abuse of children and that they should look into it. On my way home, a white ghost car sped up behind me and then passed me, cut in front of me, then slowed down. Just after that interrogation, when I went home, I started to get flashbacks of being in a room like that. My daughter's girlfriend came over in the afternoon and wouldn't come into the house, which was unusual. Well, if they didn't decide to come and get me after that, because after I dropped the reports off on these incidents, the Squad of the Institution for the Less Fortunate were banging at my door again at midnight, waking my daughter and I up and they took me off to the Hell Hole of the Earth, to be abused some more. I had just gotten out of that place. They never did tell me why, but I would imagine it was because I was assaulted and because of the police report I made out. Three officers came to the door that night. Pepper sprayer and the cop who was with her last time, and another officer. One of the members from the squad who came that night badgered my daughter, trying to get her to go to her girlfriends, but she said, "No." I think my daughter had come to realize what a bitch her friend's mother was. My poor daughter has been so traumatized because of all this. What a fucking system we have going on here in this god forsaken country. Unbelievably disgraceful. The next morning, my mother called the emergency department of the hospital when I didn't show up at her house to take her out, and they told her I wasn't there. The bitches in the emergency room wouldn't let me use the phone to call her. Mom said the next evening, she was contacted by a worker there who pretended to be helpful, but really, she was fishing for information.

They really doped me up again. I only remember seeing one doctor this time in the locked room, and to my knowledge, two doctors are supposed to see you before they are able to commit you. He asked me if my doctor was the doctor from the States, and I told him it wasn't, and it was the only thing I said to this guy who came in with what I believe was a full report on me already. They put a wristband on me anyway, indicating my doctor was this doctor from the States. They threw me in the Psychiatric Intensive Care Unit (PIC), and I asked to use the phone, and they decided to let me. I called up my brother to come and pick me up, and I said to him, "You can do that," because apparently, they had told my family before that they couldn't. Out of nowhere, this male nurse snatched the phone from me and took me off to my room, where a wicked woman shot me in the rear on my swollen side and locked me in there. I later said to her, "The government is onto you," and she gave me a dirty look. The evil demon shrink they had assigned to me, Doctor Dirty, put me on a different anti- psychotic, or what is sometimes used as a stress-reducing drug, until I guess he decided he should put me on the injections again, so he too doesn't get charged with attempted murder. When I came to and used the bathroom, there was shit on the toilet paper, and they made me use the bathroom with no lock on the door. This stalker walked in on me.

Another guy from PIC was stocking me all the time there, too. I was in PIC for days without a smoke or my own clothes to wear. When I finally got to go to Step-Down and was awarded my clothes and smoking privileges, I made a card for my daughter, and I put, have a happy life on this card, and someone stole it. I guess they wanted to make it look like I was suicidal or something. I wanted to go out on the floor, but the shrink told me there weren't any rooms. But as soon as I talked to one of my relatives, a room became available. Finally, when I got onto the floors, the harassment didn't stop there. I told this nurse about the harassment I had been receiving at the complex, and she told me to close my blinds and ignore them, but I had lived in darkness all my life! I wanted to call my daughter, but they wouldn't let me use the phone. Some of the nurses were playing mind games with me when I wanted change for parking after I had caught the bus home to get my car, which my ex-husband had stolen. They even had the commissionaire downstairs involved in the matter, along with the security guard who was standing there with him when I went to ask them for change and about parking. There is no parking for patients because the government has fucked all of their lives so badly that no one can afford cars, so why have parking for them? Then there was this young guy who followed me everywhere, harassing me. He said he was sexually abused as a child by other children, and he told his parents, and his parents said to him, "You probably liked it." Yeah, well, I never told anyone, and I didn't like it, punk. He said his shrink was the madman, and he likes to take lots of urine samples from people. I knew he was a sicko when I first met the demented bastard. This kid also informed me that you can make acid out of cigarette filters. I get it, so I'm a drug addict from the drugs the government supplied me. Well, their little plan just didn't pan out. I mean, this is the kind of crock I had to take constantly from everyone I'd meet all of my life. It didn't matter where the Hell I was. Only I am privy to it all now. The dink of a shrink, Doctor Dirty, finally let me out of there. I still had no representative, though. He let me out on what you call a Committal Certificate, get that hay? Once they get a hold of you, there is no getting away. I mean, no way. Until they decide to take you off of it, then, you're in fear, some no mind will decide to use Section 28 to have you thrown in there again for just sticking up for yourself or with me, it seemed like there didn't even have to be a reason, just for seeking medical attention. He also assigned a health nurse who would at first come to my home every so often to check up on me until I mentioned all the harassment I was receiving again, and she decided to stay the Hell out of it.

When I finally got home, it seemed like all the dogs were still shitting in front of my place, and people were letting their children run around barefoot because it was summer. I was afraid a kid was going to step in it. I was at my kitchen window one morning, and I saw my new next-door neighbour let his dog out, and he didn't pick up after him, so I decided to write a note to "Please pick up your dog due because a kid is going to step in it if you don't." Shortly afterwards, I saw the woman go over to the manager's place with the note in her hand, and a little while later, I was outside tending to my garden, and she came out ranting and raving how she wanted me to take the plants I had put in their garden out. I had previously offered to take these plants out of their garden when they first moved in. I did what they asked me to do and planted them in the community garden. I took the hose then to give them some water, and when I came back with the hose, I put it on the ground and was going to turn the tap off and it accidentally sprayed their closed front door. I apologized to them, but the woman ran over to the manager like a hot head, and right away I said to the manager, "It was an accident." But it didn't matter. Her husband made up some lie about me, saying to his wife, the cops were going to come and take her away, and they fined me fifty dollars for spraying their closed front door. I said that to the old neighbour once when he was trying to run me over with the moving dolly, but I sure didn't say it to her. These neighbours soon took off in a hurry. I guess they're running away from their lies. Then they fined me again, this time $100.00, because I wanted an explanation as to why I couldn't put a ventilation system into my home. A bunch of them were in the parking lot digging dirt for the gardens. My old neighbour was harassing me because I also wanted edging done around the flower bed adjacent to my unit, and I thought this would be a good time to show them what edging was, seeing they told me they didn't know what I wanted done. Then my old neighbour stated, "You are not responsible enough," when I asked why I couldn't put a ventilation system into my home. I said to him, " I know more about building houses than you ever will. I called him a long-haired pissy ass creep as I went to leave because I was getting fed up with being mentally abused by all of them. They said I swore in front of kids, but that too was a lie. When I told my mother, she was kind enough to make a check out for me, and for me to pay these fines because I told her I wasn't going to. She said they will keep bugging you if you don't, and insisted I take the money because she knew herself they had no reason to fine me. On the check, I put charity in the memo, and it made me feel better about giving those assholes money. My daughter came with me when I delivered it to one of the council members, and I said, "You have some nerve finning me. I am a single mother now, get off my back." I also said, "Your gardens can all go to Hell." I had been keeping the gardens up for years by this time. Eventually, she took the Hell off. I just wanted to move away from everything, but I soon realized there was nowhere else to go where I could afford to live, so I felt stuck there. I wasn't about to give my townhouse away after all the work I had done to it. I also realized the trouble would just follow me wherever I went. That was my realization due to experience. I asked this woman why she was leaving, and she told me it was too political. I finally got a piss poor explanation why they wouldn't do the edging. I think it was because the roots of the trees would be in the way. Who did they think they were kidding? Then this other woman and her family, who were also involved in harassing me with the lady I gave my fine to take off somewhere. Soon after, another guy who was always involved in church meetings took off with his tail between his legs. When he saw me crying, once, he told me mental abuse wasn't painful. What the Hell does he know except what he might have read from a book? I once told this guy I was going to be left to die, and I wanted to know if he knew of a minister I could talk to, and he said, "We are all going to die sometime." He said he would try to find me someone, but of course, it never happened because he, too, was most likely out on a mission.

Once, I was given some poppy seeds to plant in the community garden by another one of my neighbours, named Donna. When the poppies came out that year, she was looking at them and said the ones on the property they had were red, so I showed her a red one, and I said," The soil must be different here." She looked worried about something. Then some little girls came to my door, holding the poppies, telling me someone was picking them. I told them I don't own the property here, and I am not the manager, and they should tell their mother about this. But thanks for telling me. Shortly after, the drunk who helped out around the place sometimes said, If you pick the poppies and have them in your house, the cops will come and take your house away. He then started to explain to me how you can make opium out of them. I got upset with all of this, so I went into the garden and pulled every last one of them out, then threw them in the garbage, and when I did that, I noticed an undercover police officer on his cell phone watching me. In the late summer, the management at the complex had me thinking there were termites in my place, and they had a guy come in and take a look. A few months afterwards, I got yelled at by the nun for my dog scratching after he had done his business. She yelled, "he is ripping up the grass". As always, I didn't say anything to her. I just kept on my way because by this time I was composed on the shit they dish out at the Nut House, "Nut" meaning the shrinks.

Meanwhile, the bitch next door to my mother's house was harassing my Mom again. Mom had this large board up against the fence to stop the leaves from her rose bush that she never looked after from coming onto her driveway. This woman had been seeing a different man, once again, who would come over to Mom's property and take the board down all the time. When he came over to tell her to move the board, Mom told him why she had it up there, and she wasn't going to move it, but he went straight over there and took it down anyway. Mom then got furious with this guy and told him to stay off her property, but he never did. Mom would put the board up, and he would come and push it down again. We eventually took the board down, made some slats, painted them, put some netting on them and nailed them to the fence, and it stopped him from coming over. The guy on the other side, the bald-headed creep, still continued to fire up his boat, which was beside my Dad's old bedroom window. His kids were always playing ball on the road in front of Mom's house. One day, the kids were playing with a ball, and it kept coming over and hitting my mother's plants. And she had told them that if the ball kept coming over to her property and hitting her plants, she was going to take it away from them. They didn't listen to her, so she took the ball, which she was going to give back after a while, and the next thing you know, the bald-headed creep came over to my mother's house, ringing her doorbell like a madman, for it seemed like five minutes, Mom said. He even tried opening the door. When he did that, Mom finally opened the door, and all he went on about was how she had three feet of their property. My mother commented, "Oh, what does that have to do with anything?" and slammed the door on him. Meanwhile, my parents had been living in their house for forty years. Long before they ever came on the scene. I eventually took my mother to the cop shop. They must have notified them about this because my mother said she wanted them to. She didn't have any more trouble with them afterwards.

I was even more aware of my environment because I knew anyone could call up the Squad for the Less Fortunate, and have you thrown in the Nut House under section 28. Just phone them up, tell them someone you know is acting strange, and they'll come and get you. There doesn't even have to be a valid reason for them to take you away. I was still a volunteer at a Victoria Youth Custody Center, and when I went to see the demon shrink Doctor Dirty after I got out of the Hell Hole of the Earth, I don't know why I told him this, because I said to myself I wasn't going to tell these no minds I was going to the kids center, but I did. The Monday after, I went to volunteer at the kids' center, and the co-coordinator and two employees came into the room where I was helping out. I figured the asshole shrink had said something to them because these people never come in here. I stopped going there shortly after because I got the feeling even the kids didn't want me there. They started to shy away from me. I started out once again on my search for a doctor who wouldn't throw me in the Institution for the Less Fortunate and one who would treat me and my children for this so-called PID or so-called Crohn's Disease. I had talked to legal aid over the phone, and they told me I had to find a lawyer who would take Legal Aid, so I phoned around looking for someone because I was so doped up by this time, it didn't occur to me I had a representative. I thought the government was sponsoring my lawyer to look after the case involving my ex-husband, which included the Government of Canada, because they brought him over here, and I needed to find another lawyer for the Health Care System case, too. I thought I would go to legal aid personally, and when I went I was so physically sick I couldn't wait in the waiting room to be seen, so I just left. In the meantime, I even talked to some lawyers about what was going on with me. I just wanted to get away from the evil demons at the Institution for the Less Fortunate. Later on, the guy at the information desk at the courthouse told me my last lawyer wasn't practicing anymore, and that's when I found out, after asking some questions, that a counsellor can represent you in court. They are also called representatives. At this point, I wasn't even sure if I was being represented anymore and if the government wasn't just going to take my story for their own profit and screw me, which I was told they were doing. But I wasn't going to give up. What did I have to lose but a whole lot of money, filing all of this shit and time educating myself to be my own lawyer. Besides that, it didn't take me long to figure out that if I didn't take it to court, I'd most likely be dead. My representative doesn't talk to me and is limited to what they are allowed to tell me, I suppose. They are not allowed to trigger my memory at all, I would imagine. I wanted to know who I would send the court procedures to if I were to take the Health Care System to court, and so I made an appointment to see a lawyer in town who would take Legal Aid, and she didn't even know who that would be. She said she would have to look at the doctor's reports on me. After I told her about all the lying reports, she said, I would have to get doctors on my side. Another lawyer told me the same thing over the phone; I would have to find a doctor who won't allow me to be admitted to the Institution for the Less Fortunate, and suggested a good person to see. Another lawyer, when I told him some of what was going on with me, the mental abuser didn't believe me. I was crying after I talked to him. He had this small shack by the court house with the windows boarded up, and I thought they should lock him in his kiddie shack for a few days and have him abused. Maybe he should have to fight for his life along with it. With all this, I got discouraged, and by this time, the medication was really kicking in. Not only that, I found out I needed a lot of work done on my teeth. I had the process of finding another shrink going, but it wasn't until over three months later that I was able to see him. And this guy was supposed to be so respectable.

I finally found a doctor who was in the same little mall as my new dentist, and I thought this would be handy. She referred me to a vitamin doctor, but she said, "I don't know if he would be able to help you or not." By this time, I had seen the specialist for a follow-up for the removal of the nasty wart virus and had given him a copy of the PID report, and when I asked him about it, he told me I didn't have PID anymore. I was well on my way for people to step all over me again, so I didn't pursue that with him. Besides, I don't like mental abusers. I had shown my new doctor the PID report and provided her with some additional medical information about my daughter and my physical condition. I was thinking that maybe she would be the doctor who could help us, but I was skeptical after what she said about the vitamin doctor. She was short-lived. I only had that one visit with her because when I went in there once, after a dental appointment, to talk to her about seeing another specialist, she had disappeared with her tail between her legs to another part of town. No one else was taking any more patients in that clinic, so I was left without a doctor again. I wanted a practitioner close by because I was having work done on my teeth all the time and didn't want to be flying all over town to get treated for everything. My mother was going to a new doctor because the evil family doctor, Turd, had given up his practice or was forced to quit. Mom started going to a replacement, but one time she went to have her annual examination, and he wouldn't leave the room for Mom to take off her clothes, and this made her feel very uncomfortable, so she found someone else. Because her new doctor knew my mother by this time and was treating her fine, I believed he would do the same for me. That was a big mistake. Huge! Another evil demon. Another nightmare had begun, but this time, not only was I ill with Pelvic Inflammatory Disease, but I was also having a Hell of a time with all my teeth. The tooth was abscessed. I eventually had a root canal done on it. I decided I wanted a bridge on my front teeth because there were three of them that were just screwed now. I said the tooth they were looking at had been done about ten years ago, but I was told it needed to be redone before they put the bridge on. I had a feeling this tooth was going to break, and sure enough it soon did. For over a year, I had one dental appointment after another to try to fix the mess made by all my other dentists I had in the past. I got someone else who pulled half of a tooth out and left the other part in. When I went in there one day to get the other part of the tooth out, I saw someone who had an identification tag on his coat waiting in the office, and I wondered if he was there to see this butcher and why he did this to me. I refused this guy's treatment afterwards because I was off the no mind drugs then. I was so doped up on the anti psychotic I was on at the time he did this, I didn't realize what this asshole had done. I thought a wisdom tooth was coming in where he had pulled the tooth out. Who would think someone would do such a thing? Once when my daughter had an appointment, I told this dentist I wanted plastic coatings on her back teeth because she had this done on one when it first came in by the dentist we had before, and the asshole told me they didn't do this anymore, and I believed him because I was so doped up on shit. Well, when his replacement did this, it never dawned on me that whenever I went for a dental check-up every six months, he, for some reason, would never be there to look at my teeth. The hygienist who cleaned my teeth eventually had me coming in every four months because I guess she knew I was going to have problems with them soon. Meanwhile, all my teeth were rotting out of my head. I was good business for everyone to take advantage of.

I was reading the local paper, and I came across an ad for someone to volunteer at the desk for a resource center. There, they provide various programs and twelve counselling sessions per year for low-income parents. I felt it was ruined for me at the Victoria Youth Custody Center, although they never let me go, so I decided I would go down and see about this ad. You had to take a course beforehand, and I thought it would be a good experience working at the desk as a receptionist since I had never done anything like that before. The person who interviewed me convinced me to take another course, a Volunteer Program instead. I suppose she thought I wasn't good enough to work at the front desk. Anyway, I got an interview and I started the program. I phoned up the Victoria Youth Custody Center and told them I wouldn't be coming in for ten months because I was taking this Volunteer Program, and I left it like that. The program was free, and it taught you communication skills, assertiveness training skills, self-esteem, anger management and self-care. It was a good refresher to enhance my counselling skills, I thought, and it also provided speakers to come in from various places who were looking for volunteers for their organizations. Sometimes the students would come in and be having a rough time in their lives, and she would listen to us. We always had a check-in at the beginning of the class to see how we were all doing. At Christmas time, volunteers went around canvassing for donations of gifts to give to families who couldn't really afford Christmas. When the donations all started coming in, our group helped wrap them, and we labelled who the gift would be suited for. Such as a woman or a girl aged five, etc.. I also donated my time selling Christmas trees in town, which were donated to the Resource Center. All the proceeds were going to the less fortunate at Christmas time. One time after, the medication was reduced and I was getting my emotions back and some of my memory back, I broke down because of the way the Institution for the Less Fortunate had been treating me. I believe this was around the anniversary; they threw me in the locked room and put that big bruise on my arm. Linda, our teacher, commented, Our Health Care System is septic, and I think that is a good word for it. Sometimes we watched a film and had a discussion afterwards. At the end of the program, you got a certificate of completion, and it was through this program that I got information pertaining to volunteering for a safe house, which interested me, and I eventually took the program you needed to do to work on the phone lines before I started volunteering my services. I eventually had to stop working there because I was coming down off the medications again and was getting triggered while answering calls. At the same time I started taking this Volunteer program I joined a fitness center because I was starting to feel very unhealthy as I was now about one hundred pounds overweight thanks to the drugs they dish out at the Nut House. The first day I went I saw a girl who I had seen in the Institution for the Less Fortunate when I was in there last and felt I was even being followed at the fitness center so I stopped going there shortly after I joined up and lost out on a couple hundred dollars. Not only that, but I soon became nothing but a useless walking Zombie because they had me so doped up again.

The vitamin shrink started to reduce the drug I was on, and then I started to have problems with my feet. I eventually had to have special inserts made up for my shoes that cost me almost three hundred dollars and did absolutely nothing for me. One of these inserts went missing eventually, and I believe it was a terrorist who took it. Then I had to take 20 milligrams of this shit. I couldn't wait to get off of these no mind drugs and give the shrinks at the Nut House "Nut" meaning most everyone that worked in that God awful place, the heave ho. When I finally did see the vitamin doctor, he said he could probably help me and started to reduce the drug I was on even more. When I told evil demon shrink Doctor Dirty about going to see the vitamin doctor, he told me if I wanted to come back to him, he would take me back, and I thought to myself, I hope to hell I see the end of your big mouth, PRICK.

But that never happened, and I think then he knew I would be back. At my first visit, I started taking vitamins right away, and he gave me a prescription for the drug I was on to take orally at a reduced level and instructed me on how to go about lowering it. He will see me in another three months. By that time, I would be off the drug I was on completely. He wanted my files from the Institution for the Less Fortunate, and I told him they were all full of lies, saying things like I was schizophrenic and psychotic. He told me he used to work in the Institution for the Less Fortunate, and he asked me what was wrong with being schizophrenic. They are talented people. I said, "Nothing is wrong with schizophrenics;

I'm just not one of them." But I permitted him, anyway, to get the files because I had high hopes this guy was going to be different.

I bought a new computer for Christmas that year because I had been told my computer needed to be updated before the new printer I had bought would work properly. So instead of updating it, I got a new computer. This was a bad move. I didn't inform my representative about this because when I was wired on all that shit, I would never communicate with them, it would fuck you up too much. I remember when I brought it home, the manager saw me take it into my house. I guess from that point on, they all got together and derived yet another plan to have the fucking life scared right out of me. Everyone knew I would soon get my memory back; therefore, I would continue to pursue the Health Care System lawsuit, which by now everyone knew about. I continued to go to the Volunteer program, and I took a couple of courses during this time, one of them was a Food Safe course and a Life Savers program at St. John's Ambulance. If I was not at the Volunteer program, I would have spent the day at my Mom's because I just hated living where I was living, and I didn't want to get into any more altercations with the harassers of the complex. I was starting to get flashbacks of all of the traumatic events which had happened to me in the previous year around this time. Because I was coming off of the no mind drugs, I was in fear of the reality of not being treated again for my physical condition.

I had a doctor's appointment to see my mother's doctor, and I gave him a report from the doctor who was assigned to me while I was in the hospital and asked him about seeing a specialist for PID, but he too told me I didn't have PID anymore. A few days later, when my mother had an appointment to see her doctor, I decided I was going to drop off some information for him and made another appointment to see him because now I was starting to get sick with PID or this so-called Crohn's Disease again. I left it with the receptionist. I thought he would get me treated, but it backfired on me. A few days later, I went to the vitamin doctor's office and dropped off some information for him because I thought when I saw him next, I would tell him about me having Post Traumatic Stress Disorder. I was starting to get really sick with Pelvic Inflammatory Disease, and memories were beginning to surface of the Squad and the pepper sprayer taking me off to the loonie bin again. I left it with his receptionist. I thought for some reason this information would help him make that diagnosis, and he could see for himself what they were all trying to do to me. Besides, he had told me he used to work in the Institution for the Less Fortunate, and I thought he must know what goes on in that place, which was why he got the Hell out of there. After all, a lawyer did refer me to him, so I thought I could trust him. It was around this time that a write-up showed in my living room that someone had taken off the internet about PID, and in it, they related it to AIDS, and I only read the first few lines of it, and then it went missing. I was really freaked out about what I had read. I was still going to the dentist to try and get the mess which was made of all my teeth fixed at this time too. Then my car started to break down. I had to get a new muffler and then right after that a new clutch, which cost me a pretty penny. I had started to write up the affidavits to take the Health Care System to court. I guess it didn't help matters, bringing up all of the terror of the last ten years of being bounced in and out of the "Hell Hole of the Earth" trying to stay alive, realizing all of these so-called professional people were out to try and kill me. Well, I went to see my mother's doctor and told him about my back being really sore and pain in my gut, and he said there was nothing wrong with me, so go back on the injections. He then ordered an urn test, which I did at the lab, but the asshole never got back to me. I knew I was sick again, so after I saw the bastard, I went straight to the clinic to get looked at. They prescribed 250 milligrams of an antibiotic to take twice a day for a week. Still, after a couple of days, I knew this wasn't enough, so I went back there again and, after showing another doctor the PID report, he prescribed 500 milligrams of Cipro to take three times a day for ten days. I was so sick all my body wanted was water, and I drank it all day long, and I never really liked water. I was getting flashbacks of being thrown in the locked room again, and being abused, and I kept pacing, and I couldn't stop looking out of my window to see if they were coming to get me yet again. The terror of it all sent me running, and I had to get the HELL out of here, and it had to be right then and there, and I didn't care what it was going to cost me. I was right out of my mind with fear that this time I was going to die. It just felt like it. I phoned up my half-brother in Ontario, who, by this time, I had forgotten all about what his true intentions were, and told him I was coming out there. He seemed happy about it and wanted me to move there, and in my confusion, pain and fear, I made all the arrangements to do just that. I bought a plane ticket to fly the Hell out of here on the following weekend. I left the house with a large water bottle to carry with me, and every chance I got, I kept having to fill it up because I was still really dehydrated.

I was in no condition to travel, as sick as I was with Crohn's. I sat down to wait for the connecting flight, and this person from the military sat down beside me and asked me where I was going. I told her, and when she told me where she was going, I froze up with intense fear because I knew I was being STALKED again. But this time by the MILITARY. My Dad was stationed in the very same place she was going when he was in the army. When I got on the flight, I kept looking around for this person and sizing up all the people who were sitting around me. I suspected everyone of stalking me. My half-brother picked me up at the airport and took me straight to the hospital, and he left me there by myself to wait for five hours before I got seen. I suppose he knew I was going to be there for a while, and he had to get up early to go to work the next day, and he never gets home until late in the evening. I had the Pelvic Inflammatory Disease report with me, and when I finally saw the doctor in the emergency room, he did a pap and an urn test and came back telling me I didn't have any symptoms of PID. I said to him, "Well, what if it is in the tubes?" and he got this scared look on his face and said, "Well, we aren't going to do anything for you tonight," and then he went on to tell me how to go about getting help. He told me to go to the nearest clinic and see a doctor there, and then he will refer me to a specialist. I had no way of getting around, so a relative, my Dad's brother Bill, offered to take me to the clinic and to get my health problems straightened out, but this relative, too, was sick and having to go for therapy all the time. When I arrived at the clinic, a fifteen-minute drive from my half-brother's apartment, the doctor, after reviewing the PID report, referred me to a specialist and informed me that it would take around two weeks before I could be seen. I remember this doctor sending me to get some blood work done and a urine test too to see if the antibiotic that I was on was working, but I don't think he got the results back because I was starting to come around right after I got there, and thought, **WHAT THE HELL DID I JUST DO?** I thought the specialist would want to see my health records before they do an operation on me, because apparently, there were a lot of lawsuits going on there with doctors. All I had was a list of all the doctors I had been to, and I realized my records were all botched up, and I wasn't going to get anywhere. Most importantly, I decided if I was going to die, I wanted to be with my family, so I decided to phone up my divorce lawyer, and I told him where I was and if I came home, could he find a doctor for me, and he said he could. I also told him that if I were going to die, I wanted to be with my daughter. I was so distraught over everything that was happening to me, what I really meant to say was I wanted to be with my family if I was going to die. After I talked to this lawyer, I started to make all the arrangements for me to go home. I went back to the clinic and told the doctor there I was going to go back home, and could he prescribe some more antibiotics for me to take because I didn't want to get sick on the plane, and all of mine were gone now, and I was still really ill. He couldn't understand why I left, being so sick. I didn't want to tell him because I thought I was going to be left to die, so I told him because all the arrangements were already made before I got sick, and I didn't have cancellation insurance, so I had to go or lose out on a bunch of money, which was half true.

After the arrangements were all made for me to go back home, I asked my half-brother if he ever sees his mother and sister? He told me he did see them quite regularly, so I gave him the History Summary to read, and after he skimmed through it, he asked me if I had a lawyer, and I said, "Yes, and I phoned him up, and he said he could find a doctor for me, so I am going to go back home." That night, he took me to a place just outside of where he was living, and I bought a ticket for a shuttle bus which picked me up right at his apartment and took me to the Airport. I started getting my appetite back just before I left. While I was waiting for my flight home at the Airport, I got a chicken burger. When I got to the Airport and made it to the terminal where my flight was leaving for home, I thought I saw my new neighbour, who was now living across from me in my ex-neighbour Kathy and Daryl's old townhouse. He was standing talking to another guy, and I wasn't sure if it was him or not, so I didn't approach him then. Besides, we were all going to load onto the plane soon. He was on the same flight coming home as I was, and he was sitting in the opposite row behind me. And I got this creepy feeling he was looking at me, so once in a while, I would turn around to look at him to try to make out whether it was him or not. When I got to the airport, I saw him standing where you wait for your luggage, and I went up to him and asked him if he lived in the same complex as I did, and he said he did. I asked him where he had been, and he said he had been to the same place as I had, only he'd been at a business meeting for a few days. He left the same day, only a little earlier. I thought it was all too ironic and knew then I was still being STOCKED.

Deborah Anne Kimberley

CHAPTER SIXTEEN

I got the name of two doctors, and I went to one who was in a clinic in a mall because it was the closest one to my home, but they weren't taking any more patients. I thought, what the Hell and was freaked out about the other doctor whose name he gave me, saying the same thing, because by this time there wasn't any left around my place. I had exhausted them all. But I managed to make an appointment over the phone. Before my first appointment, I dropped off a bunch of information to view beforehand. In the meantime, I had scheduled dental appointments to attend to. When I went to my dentist to get some bridge work done on my front teeth, I was tortured. It was so painful. The preparation for the bridge work was finally done. I still had a temporary plate until my bridge was finished being made.

I went to see the vitamin doctor and he gave me more vitamins to take, one of them "Niacin" which, when you first start taking them, makes you go beet-red, you get really itchy, and you feel hot like you have a temperature. That is, if you get the non-flush kind, like I did, because it is cheaper. It is used to lower your blood pressure and cholesterol. At this appointment, I told this vitamin doctor I had just come back from a trip, and I was sick with PID again, and I was afraid the Squad for the less fortunate was going to come and throw me in the Nut House and abuse me like they did before. He told me they don't abuse you in there, and if you don't do anything, they won't throw you in there. I told him I didn't do anything, and they threw me in there anyway. I left, assured by him that he would not let them throw me in there.

A little while later, Legal Aid called me, instructing me to bring copies of the Health Care System's court materials. He would have a look at them, so I took them to him and on the cover of the folder, it was all in. I wrote that if I didn't hear from him by Friday, I would be taking it to court on the following Monday, which was the twenty-third of April.

I wanted court accompaniment but couldn't find anyone to go with me. I had also called the hospital and told them about what I was doing. I had written them a letter the previous year about the harassment I had been receiving, and no one ever called me about it, or no letter was ever sent, and now I was going to take legal action. This woman, who replied to me, made a pathetic excuse that their computers had crashed, and that was why they didn't get back to me. I would now be receiving a response to that letter. I also talked to the director about what was going on for me. When I filed the documents, there was a short, fat guy watching me. I finally found out who I had to give the court materials to, so I got a courier company to come and pick them up and take them there. In the meantime, I was writing out more Affidavits for the court case, and the Exhibits were going missing while I was busy on my computer. The terrorists were leaving harassing notes on my computer desk every time I left it, and I can't remember what all they wrote on these notes because I was so frightened someone was in my house playing tricks on me right under my nose. I believed they knew my daughter's password to the internet and made a pun out of that.

I went to my mother's house, and the cops were sitting just down the street by my mother's, STOCKING me. How they knew I was going there is beyond me, but I guess the government can find out anything they want about you and do anything they want to you and get away with it. That's because they put cameras in your home, tap your phone and release false information to stalkers about you everywhere you go. That afternoon, well, the BITCH of a dentist put the bridge on with this cement, which hurt so much I couldn't believe the pain I was in, and it never stopped hurting for a long, long time. I was literally out of my mind, sobbing in her office. It was excruciating! I could hardly do anything after that. Then, when my mother and I went to Walmart, there was a guy just standing in the food aisle staring at me.. One time, my mother phoned me up to tell me some man was standing on the road right in front of her house staring in her direction. Another time, my mother noticed someone had opened her visa bill when she retrieved it from her mailbox. I suppose the Director released false information about me because suddenly he was no longer working as a Director.

By this time, I had seen another new doctor, some blood tests were ordered, and a urinalysis test for me to take, so I went around the corner to a Lab and had most of what was ordered done. I had to fast for one of the blood tests. I asked when the results of these tests would be back, and the reply was in a couple of days. I went to one of the only labs open on a Saturday morning. I went there and to my surprise, the person who was sitting there beside me pretending she didn't see me was my dentist. How ironic is that? Stocking was she? A few days after I had the blood work done, I started calling to find out the results of it, but I never got a call back for a while, and I was getting worried that maybe I didn't have a doctor again. I was panicking. When my doctor finally returned my call, my blood tests revealed I had to start taking vitamin B12. I told her I had a bad experience when I took a vitamin B12 shot once, so I wanted to take the vitamins orally, and she told me to get the 100 milligram tablets. I mentioned to her that my Dad had to take vitamin B12 when they first diagnosed him with Crohn's Disease. I also told her I wanted a laparoscopy done because I had read about this procedure, and I thought that way they would be able to see that this PID hadn't gone away like I was told it had. By this time, I was in so much pain with it. I had chronic pain in my lower back and in my legs, and I wasn't sleeping much because it seemed to hurt more when I was lying down. And that, too, I believe, is caused by this god awful disease. Either that or arthritis. She eventually got me in to see a specialist, and I knew from his attitude when he did a three-second physical check on me, he was not going to help me either. He said he would do a laparoscopy and that was all he was going to do. After I had it done, my whole stomach went black and blue, and then the incision he made in my belly button got infected, and it was a long time before it finally cleared up. He told me my tubes were stuck to my pelvis, but he fixed that for me, and there was no evidence of me having PID, the liar. It was in the fucking tubes, which I guess proves I was born with it. Anyway, on the day I had set for the Health Care court hearing, I had a dentist appointment. I was in so much pain by this time, not only with my teeth, but my guts had been acting up, too. And I was sick to my stomach. My daughter took me to my dental appointment, then I took a cab from the dentist's office to the courthouse to attend. I sat there in the courtroom with all these evil demons surrounding me, and I could feel it. One of them said as I walked in, "I got to see this." When it was finally my turn, they wanted me to make another court date, but I said I am in pain now and I need a doctor, even though I had one, I did not know how long it was going to last. I was so desperate and out of my mind with all that was going on. We ended up setting another date. I recall someone saying this isn't a criminal matter, and I said, "OH YES IT IS. BIG TIME!" And there were swarms of people in the area where you set a new court date, all listening in, and I was utterly overwhelmed with everything and very ill. If these criminals, these EVIL DEMONS, had left me the fuck alone, I would have figured out that I didn't need to go to the courthouse, but OH NO!!!! They did their damnedest to try and PUSH ME OVER THE EDGE! Needless to say, another date was set for about two weeks later, but I was thrown in the Institution for the Less Fortunate, so I could not go to it.

Right after that, I had to go to the dentist again because I had another abscessed tooth and was having a root canal done through my bridge work. I had been on an antibiotic for it, and the dentist had given me some pain pills, Tylenol two to take because of the pain of it all. But someone came into my house and replaced them with Tylenol three to go with the antidepressant the shrink ended up prescribing for me. Unreal, the pain! By this time, I was really panicking because I was beginning to think I didn't have a doctor anymore, so I made an emergency appointment to see the vitamin shrink because I was suffering from Post Traumatic Stress Disorder too. I wanted him to take the list of doctors I had already gone through and call up my new doctor, but he wouldn't take it. He told me it looks like you are depressed, and the fucking EVIL DEMON vitamin shrink wrote out a prescription for an antidepressant with an anxiety component, which I never took because the side effects looked really scary. It said something about not being on pain pills when you take this shit. I should never have trusted the old bastard because he just looks like an evil demon. In the meantime, I was writing up Health Care System Affidavits on my computer, and I could hardly do this because of all the pain I was in. Then I get this letter from the property management telling ME to abide by the rules. After that, all HELL broke loose, my daughter told me she couldn't get her messages off of ICQ. That day, she told me this: Mom and I went to Walmart again to pick up Mom's prescriptions, and another STOCKER was standing in the aisle just standing there for a really long time staring at me whenever I passed by him. Then, some outfit that looks for missing children came knocking at my door, asking me for money, and I told this guy I hadn't seen my son for a long time, could he help me locate him, and he was eighteen now. He said he would have to talk to his supervisor and get back to me, but he never did. Next thing you know, there is no internet. These terrorists were coming into my home, taking all my legal documents I had in a big suitcase. I even called the cops about this, but when this officer and another officer came, and I told them about it, I don't think they believed me, even after telling them a former friend in this complex had the key to my place. I have had trouble with her and some other neighbours. While I was waiting for the cops to come, they were slowly putting the documents back, again. They left notes on some of the documentation, which had lawyers' names and phone numbers on them, such as a criminal lawyer. I thought I was supposed to call him about the Health Care harassment, which I did, and I made an appointment to see him, not realizing he was a criminal lawyer. Then, on another note, it had the name of another lawyer, and I thought I was supposed to call this guy for harassment at the complex because it was on that documentation, and I did. But, I guess I was wrong, or was I? I was also told on a note to call this other big-time lawyer firm and report to them that my legal documentation went missing, which I remember doing. I didn't know whether I was coming or going. It was so freaky. They emptied my filing cabinet, and then they slowly started putting it back, and replaced all my letters of references with bogus ones with recommendations for jobs well done, which I never had. I found things all over the house, on top of my fridge, and in drawers. They put a prescription receipt in my daughter's name, which she never had, on top of the fridge with some other ones of mine which had been in my filing cabinet. I found a piece of paper where someone had written all that was wrong with me and how this specialist was going to do all these bizarre things to me when he did a laparoscopy. When I saw this, I was HORRIFIED. There are just not enough words to describe this HORROR. Then they started to put old, blue, pyjama rags down everywhere I went, and I would put them back under my downstairs bathroom sink, where they came from, only to find them again around the house, their favourite spot being beside the chair in the living room. I was going to do some laundry. They put the dirty laundry I had collected and put in the washer in the dryer. Then one of my neighbours came knocking at my door, telling me there was a rag in the exhaust pipe of my car, so I had to go out and remove it. I had been on my computer, and someone was talking to me on my computer, telling me I should go to the courthouse myself, and maybe they would put me in jail or into the Institution for the Less Fortunate. I thought I was talking to my representative, and they were abandoning me. I remember sometime while this was all going on, I wrote up a story of my life and filed it under "MY LIFE," but I never got to reread it because I got rid of it pretty quickly afterwards. I didn't want any memories of this totally horrifying experience. I was so freaked out that someone was in my house right under my nose, and I never even caught a glimpse of them. Real SLICK. I was literally losing it with all they were doing to me, and I was physically ill and in pain still. I suppose a good description of this experience would be something like a Nazi war victim would feel as they were being tortured. How someone could do this to another person is incomprehensible, "VERY VERY SICK." I even got a fax from them, which said, on it. "All I want is a doctor." I believe they were getting ready to snub me off. Either by me doing it myself, or by making me think they were going to do it.

At some point, I believe my representative got wind of what was going on. I started receiving all these faxes, which said to notify various hospitals and organizations, like all the safe houses, of the break-in and that legal documents were missing because of what they had been doing. These faxes were all over the place. I was writing this information on these faxes as one was done for me but, at the time, I was so fucked up from whatever they left me on my counter to take, I was putting the wrong date down, I was also so traumatized. and I thought they were vitamins I had put out there because these evil demons put some pills down on my kitchen counter, but they weren't. They were something else because after that, things went vague. I called up the cops and told them my daughter was missing because there was a note left on my coffee table about who my daughter was with, and I freaked out. Big mistake, calling the cops. The Squad for the Less Fortunate came knocking at my door with the cops, and they asked me the last time I saw a doctor. I couldn't remember off the top of my head, so I went to get my calendar because I always write everything down on my calendar, and it was gone, and another one was in its place. I knew they were coming for me to take me to the HELL HOLE OF THE EARTH, again. I had my bags packed by this time, and I packed some things for my daughter because I didn't want her in the house while I was gone, for fear of what they would do to her. I called up a health nurse who looks after Seniors to come and take care of my mother because I thought they were going to kill me in the Institution for the Less Fortunate, and I wanted to make sure Mom was well looked after. I even told Mom I wouldn't get out of there this time. Well, this idiot said, "We are going to take you to the hospital." Afterwards, he asked me what I did all day. I told him I do whatever needs to be done, and because I'm a writer, I go on my computer. Well, he got angry after I said I'm a writer, and when I said I didn't know the last time I saw my doctor, he threw his so-called authority around, and of course, I had no other choice but to go with these assholes. They took me to the Hospital Emergency Room lock-up, like they always do. I asked if I could call my lawyer, and this officer who took me there and befriended me wanted to know who my lawyer was, and when I told him, he laughed and took my stuff from me and said, he has an awfully long way to come to the NUT HOUSE, where the place was just swarming with STOCKERS.

In the locked room, they gave me my meal on a tray for the first time, but on the tray it had a big notice saying "NO CUTLERY" in huge letters, and I told them to take it off. They also gave me PJs to wear, which were way too small. Then, after they had me doped up some more, on god only knows what, they brought the no mind legal aid lawyer who sees everyone in there like it or not, to see me. I don't recall even seeing any doctors while I was in the locked room, which is supposed to be the procedure before they can commit you. All I wanted this no mind lawyer to do for me is to make sure my daughter stays at my mother's house because he is nothing but a mental abuser and as useless as two tits on a boar. I was frantic about my daughter being left by herself. I remember seeing a group of professionals while I was looking out of the window in there after they closed the door on me. They were all shaking each other's hands, and I felt they were doing that because they had me trapped where they wanted me once again and were congratulating each other for a job they thought was well done. That was all I remember of that solitary confinement. They left me there for the whole two days, which is all they are allowed to keep you in there for, and then they took me to PIC, where they were planning to harass the living daylights out of me some more. I was so distraught and scared about being in there again. I remember telling the first nurse I saw in PIC that I didn't want the door closed and locked on me. I was very concerned about that for fear of what they would do to me when they got me alone. I told him I don't like locked rooms. He promised me they wouldn't do that and took my things so they could all rummage through everything behind their closed doors, I would imagine, and left my door open. I brought the book Women and Doctors with me, my Bible and my green binder, which had a brochure of a Dispute Resolution Center to go to if you are having problems with Government Agencies. I guess the Terrorists put it in there in hopes I would call them up. I can't remember what all they did to me in PIC because with whatever they gave me on my kitchen counter and what all that they started giving me in there must have erased my short-term memory, but good. I recall PIC STEP DOWN, though, where I was assigned a different shrink, and he came into my room drilling me about whether I still thought someone came into my house and stole a suitcase full of legal documents. I said, "NO." I wasn't going to play their little game they had going with me. Then they had this practitioner come into my room, and he talked to me about my physical condition. A nurse was standing in my room with him the whole time I was talking to this guy and telling him some of my history and recent physical problems. I felt uncomfortable with her being there because she wasn't my nurse. I figured if this doctor really cared about me, he wouldn't have had me retaking the anti psychotic drug because of my physical condition. He ordered me to have a urinalysis test and some blood tests. When I was in Step-Down, and when I asked for something to wipe myself with during the mid-stream urine sample, they gave me a washcloth, and I thought that's not very sanitary. When the blood test came back, he said my electrolytes were down, but everything else was fine. I had read in the bogus government affidavit. I will go back on this anti psychotic. While I was there, they started me on it because I said to this shrink I would take it, but when I finally got some information on this shit, I realized I shouldn't be taking it with my physical condition, so I demanded to be taken off of it. That was another reality check that the evil government really wanted me dead. In the meantime, while I was in PIC Step-Down, a nurse brought in a cocktail on a little tray. She said what it was, and I told her I am not on that; and informed her what I was taking and then this BITCH pretended to look at her notes and said "OH, yes" and took the fucking stuff away. I was horrified she was humming and hawing about what it was I was on. I thought she was going to make me take it. There was a guy in Step-Down who said he played in a band, and he would draw pictures of dead people on the blackboard, and he put pictures on the wall. Someone had put a change of name application form in my green binder, and I had picked a surname for us Smith, and it was on some of the pictures. I guess someone was coming into my room and snooping in my stuff because I was beginning to document everything which was happening to me in there again, only I had the wrong date, and even when I saw a calendar with the date on it once I was out on the floors in the Nut House, I didn't believe it. I thought they were just playing another trick on me, and it wasn't until I got home that I asked my daughter what the date was. I realized I was wrong. Then, apparently, he had a pass for the weekend, which I thought they never gave out when you were in PIC Step-Down, and he never came back, so they went out looking for him. When they found him, they threw him in PIC for a few days as punishment, and he made certain he told me all about it. We all sat together at one big table in PIC Step-Down, and for some reason, he didn't want me sitting at this table during meal time either. When I got out of PIC Step-Down and onto the third floor, he was let out of PIC then too and one time I went for a smoke on the roof garden and he scared the Hell out of me by screaming at the top of his lungs, **"HOW DOES IT FEEL TO KNOW THAT YOU'RE GOING TO DIE?"** I was completely petrified! There was no one else there but this guy who was always watering the gardens, and he heard this too, and when this loony tune said this, the guy watering the gardens looked at me with this scared look on his face and left immediately. I didn't want to be left alone with this lunatic, so I took off right after he left. Sometimes, as I was leaving the roof garden, there would be some First Nations person singing an Indian chant somewhere close by, which made me feel uncomfortable too. There was graffiti all over the walls of the roof garden smoking area, and it made me feel intimidated. Something about the Holy Ghost. The guy with a pink shirt came into PIC Step-Down and wanted to visit with someone. They told him that the person had no visitors for six weeks.

When I got out of PIC, this guy, who, almost the entire time I was in there, wore a pink shirt, was in PIC Step Down. I think he was a stocker, not a patient, and he would follow me wherever I went. Sometimes, when I was out on the third floor, he would be alone in the dining area wearing sunglasses as if he was waiting for me to come out of my room, and he would have this foolish grin on his face as he watched where I was going. Well, just after this guy with the pink shirt came out of PIC and left Step-Down, my mother called wanting to speak with me, and I was still at the desk when she called. I got the feeling it was her, and when they hung up, I asked, "Who was that for?" But they said it wasn't for me. Shortly after that, they asked me if I wanted to call my mother, and I said "Yes," so they gave me the phone, and when I asked my mother if she had just called for me, she told me she did, but they wouldn't allow her to talk to me. Then the girl who was in PIC Step-Down and then the third floor and the fourth floor, every time I got transferred somewhere, she was there, too. She came out of my bathroom, and I went in there to do an urn sample just after she came out, and she had pissed all over the toilet seat. One time, I went to use the toilet after she had been in there again, and there was shit all over the toilet paper. She was gross. She was always bumming cigarettes off of me, telling me she would pay me back, but never did, and wherever I went, she went. If I sat down somewhere, she would be there beside me. When I went to the roof garden, she would go too, and she would try to talk to me, but I didn't want anything to do with her.

The no mind lawyer for us misfits in there came to see me in PIC Step-Down, and he had to tell me how sick I was when I first came in there, and that is why he hadn't been to see me since the locked room when I was first admitted. All I said to him then was, I wanted a Review Panel Hearing to get out of this place, and it was all he was worth talking to about. He left, saying he would set it up.

When I finally got out of Step-Down, they put me on the third floor, and when I was unloading my stuff, I noticed my wallet was missing, so I asked this nurse where it was. She apparently, went looking all over the place for it, and the end result was that I gave it to my husband when he came to visit me in PIC Step-Down. Well, I hadn't seen that maniac for years and years since he tried steering his own daughter, and I off the mountain. She tried telling me, "Well, some man came in to see you when you were in Step-Down, and you gave it to him." I said, "I don't see men and haven't for years". My daughter and my mother had come into Step-Down to see me, and I gave my wallet to my daughter so she could get my bank card out of it. She wanted to buy some groceries with it, but she gave it back to me, and I gave it to a nurse at the nursing desk. Then, finally, after hours of trying to track my wallet down, I decided to call my mother and tell her about it and what they had said to me. A man who they thought was my husband came into PIC Step-Down and took it. She said my daughter and she were going to come to see me and bring me some more clothes, and she would talk to them about it when they came and told me not to worry about it. I was really upset over this because I thought they were going to get rid of me in there in the first place, and then my wallet went missing, which freaked me right out. Well, I think they had the patient's phone tapped in there because no sooner did I get off the phone from talking to my mother than the nurse appeared with my wallet, telling me the security guards had it, and whoever that male was who came to see me must have returned it to the security desk downstairs in the lobby. The bunch of lying fucked up clowns.

They gave me the EVIL DEMON shrink Seagull, who tried to kill me while I was on the third floor, and I said I don't want him, and I didn't want the other shrink Doctor Dirty either. I wanted to see this woman shrink in there, which I had heard about and I filled out a request form to see her and my doctor but I was sick of waiting for this shrink to come and see me so eventually I said I would see the other EVIL DEMON shrink, Doctor Dirty after I had been stuck with the attempted murderer for a while. I had finally gotten information on this anti-psychotic drug from a male nurse after asking for it many times, and when he gave me the information, and I told him I had PID and shouldn't be taking this stuff, he had tears in his eyes because he could see how much pain I was in.

When I asked my nurse for something for pain, she questioned me about why I needed it, and I told her that I was in pain. She wanted to know where the pain was, and I felt like telling her right off, Just give me something. I then told the EVIL DEMON shrink Doctor Dirty, I didn't want to be on this anti- psychotic drug anymore, and he took me off of it and started me on the other drug by injection. I suppose by this time he wanted to make himself look good because it was the anti-psychotic drug that is also used for stress. I was also aware of this man in his late fifties, who I think was an Agent in there looking out for me. He was in PIC Step-Down when I was there and then on the third floor when I was moved there, and on the fourth for the brief time I was there. I had noticed he never saw a shrink because when I was in Step-Down he had this young practitioner coming in to talk to him all the time so I asked him" Is that your shrink" He said, "No that is my practitioner" so then I asked him if he thought his practitioner would see me and he told me he would ask him but he never got back to me on this. I wanted a doctor who had hospital privileges because the one I had didn't have any. Later, I assumed my representative put the message that was in my green binder telling me to request to see the doctor I had already, so I decided to keep her to see how she worked out. But while I was in Step-Down, I was beginning to wonder whether I should believe anything I saw in my green binder. I once approached this agent when I was on the third floor and said, "Did you know there is nowhere safe?" I had started to notice that when I signed the sign-out book to go and have a smoke, he would go and look at it, and I am sure he was looking at the people's names who signed out and in, at the same time as me, because there were so many people **STOCKING** me in there it was unbelievable.

I'm sure there were more STOCKERS in there than there were patients. Then, when I was assigned my room on the third floor, I think he went looking for it, but they never put my name on the door, so I got some spare masking tape from one of the name tags on the door and put my name on it and labelled my room with it so he would know where I was. I don't know whether it was a good move now or not. There was another incident which happened while on the third floor. Another guy who would follow me wherever I went was this fat guy with curly hair who was a total loser. My nurse at the time and a security guard were involved in this completely pathetic show they put on there.

Apparently, fat curly locks didn't want to take an urn sample, and the nursey was following him everywhere, telling him he would go to PIC if he didn't cooperate. So then he took off outside, and she brought this female security guard up to go and get him, who then got herself involved with this performance, and it went on and on, no word of a lie, for a couple of hours. This entire time, the nursey was carrying a bottle for the urine sample around with her. I mean, I was so afraid because of the way they were all acting, I didn't know what the Hell they had planned for me next. They kept moving his room, so I would get screwed up as to what room he was in because I guess everyone knew by this time I was documenting everything. The only person I felt safe with was a woman, I guess in her late fifties, early sixties, who had Alzheimer's Disease, and she would see me crying sometimes, and she would sit down beside me and hold my hand and tell me it would be all right. One time, while my wallet was missing, I was beside myself, lying on my bed, sobbing and this girl who was in the same room as me came into my cubicle and started to console me, rubbing my head and praying in Latin, which made matters even worse. She used to play the guitar for everyone in there at night, which used to make me relax a bit. I saw her afterwards on the roof garden, and she wanted my name and phone number, and I, being dumb me, gave it to her, not thinking she was just another EVIL CATHOLIC out to persecute me because she never did phone me to see how I was doing. The agent saw me give it to her, and I knew right away I shouldn't have because the look he had on his face was that of concern.

The dumb Institution lawyer finally came to see me about the Review Panel Hearing. I told him to request one for me, but apparently, he couldn't be there with me, so I decided to go in there alone. I just wanted out of this Nazi War Camp. When the dummy saw me that day, just a few days before the Review Panel Hearing, he told me about the procedure and who all would be there, and he drew a map of where they would all be sitting at this big conference table. I had found a piece of paper in the dining room with a sentence written on it that said "I think I can go home now because I am starting to do the things I like," so I knew when I went in there, I wasn't supposed to say too much. I was waiting in the hall outside the room of the first floor of the Institution for the Less Fortunate, where the Hearing was to take place, and this guy came and said to me, "You can call this off if you want to, you know." I noticed he had a tape recorder with him, and I guess he said that to intimidate me, knowing I could see he had a recorder with him, but I really wanted out of that Nut House, **BAD**, so I said, "No, it will be all right." The hospital spokesman, the killer Seagull, produced a bunch of lies about how he thought I was a danger to myself and how he was worried about my daughter. He had the nerve to say that after the MURDERER tried to kill me with one of his drugs he prescribed to me, "Well, your daughter is old enough to live on her own." Yeah, right, he's really worried about my daughter, who was still underage at the time he said this. He probably couldn't wait to get his evil hands on my children next, but over my dead body, you will EVIL SON OF A BITCH. I sat in silence, biting my tongue the whole time as this puke was yakking up a bunch of garbage, politely waiting my turn to speak. I spoke quietly and was never angry, like all those lying reports with their screwed up diagnosis of me said I was all of the time. I was very nervous, and I felt so alone, and even the lawyer who was supposed to be on my side gave me the feeling she really wasn't there for me because she didn't say a Hell of a lot during the whole Hearing. When it was my turn to speak, I first pointed out that I was not a danger to myself or anyone else, and I certainly would not do anything to harm my daughter. I told them I suffer from a physical condition, PID, and asked if they wanted me to show them the medical report on it because I had brought it with me, and they gave me this dirty look like they were all disgusted with the fact that I had PID and said, "No." Then I mentioned the fact that Doctor Seagull had diagnosed me with Post Traumatic Stress Disorder at one time when I first started seeing him. I just wanted to get out of the HELL HOLE OF THE EARTH so bad I thought if I went along with their little game, they would let me out, so I told them I had a brief psychotic episode. At the time, I was thinking only that I was disorganized, which would have explained to them the report they had on me, which said someone had stolen my legal documents from my suitcase. Right afterwards, I wished I had never quoted anything from that one screwed up book, the DSM-4, this government wants to hold onto so badly. Then I remembered the piece of paper I had found that had written on it "I think I am ready to go home now because I am starting to do the things I like", which was what I said to them then. I showed them some pictures I had colored while I was there. Just after that, a bozo asked if they had heard enough or said they had heard enough and called an end to this so-called Review Panel Hearing. When it was over, I knew what the result would be because of the stupid quote I had made, and sure enough, the EVIL DEMON shrink Seagull came up to give me his good news that I was going to stay committed. I had already been in the place for over three weeks by this time. That is when he asked me if I would see the other Evil Demon Dr Dirty, and then I said I would just so I could get away from that EVIL EVIL son of a bitch who tried to kill me. I got a cold chill just being in his presence.

They transferred me to the fourth floor, where the other EVIL DEMON Doctor Dirty was waiting for me, and I put my stuff in my closet to be locked up. The nurse who was with me told me not to keep anything out because things could go missing. I wanted to keep my documentation handy because I was still documenting everything precisely, right down to the time I went and had a cigarette, except that the date was wrong. I locked everything up but my documentation, which I put under the mattress of my bed, and I made sure no one saw me when I did this. I then went to sit in the sitting area and noticed the STOCKER, whom I had been told by a staff member before I left the third floor that she was being discharged on the weekend, and there she was. Why didn't they just leave her where she was if she was getting out soon? Then I saw the government agent and the guy who would water the plants on the roof garden, and I decided to go and document all of this, but my documentation went missing, so I ran to my nurse and told her this. No sooner was it out of my mouth than the Evil Demon Dirty asked me if I wanted to go home, and of course, I said I did. I packed my bag right away and sat down waiting for my health nurse, who was assigned to me again, to come up and take me home. The first words out of her mouth when she saw me were "You poor thing, you have been terrorized."

When I got home, I was so freaked out to be there that I didn't want the health nurse to leave, and she stayed with me to snoop around, looking at the vitamins and questioning me about the ones I had put back out on the counter. I had decided I should take them, and soon after that, she left. For days, I was freaked and was afraid to leave one room and go to the next. And I would look out of my windows to see if I could see anyone lurking around my place, and I was continually making sure the security locks were on all of my windows and doors. But the precautions soon petered out because once again, they had me doped up. A year later, the old evil demon gave it up at the clinic after he reduced the injection, perhaps by court order, to next to nothing, in which I finally got my mind half back. The harassers of the complex left me alone for a while because I spent all of my time being doped up at my mother's house for over a year. When I finally got my mind back they decided to get other fuck ups to harass me. Still, I made out some Affidavits so my representative could sue the shit out of those losers and if any money is granted for the all the pain and suffering they caused my daughter and myself because of their actions of having me thrown in the Nut House that money was to go to the Crohn's and Colitis Foundation Victoria Chapter so they can all start filing law suits against their doctors for causing them to needlessly suffer a prolonged agonizing death. All my so-called cop friends are now retired, and I hope they all run out of money in their old age for all they have done to me. I heard Pepper sprayer got transferred up North somewhere to terrorize innocent people up there. I sure hope her pepper spray freezes up on her, the BITCH, so much for our GREAT JUSTICE SYSTEM.

CHAPTER SEVENTEEN

Well, when I got home, I started to read the one screwed up DSM-4, and I looked up some of the diagnoses the shrinks had me under, and I wrote about them.

The following is what I wrote.

I have been reading the screwed up DSM-4, and I looked up Delusion Disorder, and I was going to ask the no minds what criteria I am under, but they were being so nice to me, it made me all so sick, so I thought, why bother. I wanted to find out if I fall under the Persecuting Type. What a definition. Do people really think they can diagnose someone with that and get away with it without any real proof? I have said next to nothing to them. What about Schizoaffective Disorder? A Major Depression, or a Mixed Episode, or Manic Depression. Make up your mind, which is it? All of these diagnoses? No No. And where do they get the information to come to such a complicated conclusion? A five-minute evaluation in their office once every three to six months, where they talk only about their lives and how wonderful it is. Just what I want to hear! They don't even ask you the time of day or let you get a word in edgewise. Maybe they get their information from evil Catholics and the release of false information about you that they spread everywhere. Anyways, the Major Depressive Episode must last one week. This is a sub-type; well, that is funny, I was told it would take two years to get over this. I guess I was supposed to be dead by that time. Oh yeah, what about Schizoaffective Disorder? Do they have someone hiding in your closet watching your every move, or do they have a camera set up in your house and watch everything you do because you'd have to, to come up with such a ridiculous outcome? Well, they did for sixty years and counting in my house, unknown to me, and they still lost out. Oh yeah, not to mention it could be a Mixed Episode they are having. Maybe it's because they are the ones who are really mixed up. But they wrote a book of poems, so they must be manic. This is called a Bipolar Sub-type. So they have a bit of talent. What a crime it is. Don't forget it must have a minimum duration of at least one month to apply, and the mood symptoms must be there for the greater portion of the time. Mood symptoms? What? Happy, sad, hostile or just plain stupid am I? Do you have knives in your house? No, I rip the turkey up with my bare hands. Barbaric, isn't it! Are you hearing things and seeing things? Yeah, a couple of stooges reciting a cop out diagnosis for the shrinks. I'm convinced they must have a camera in your home and/or a bunch of lying Catholics on their side. Remember, they must have a lack of interest or pleasure too. And that's because the evil government makes sure there is nothing out there for them by introducing fourteen-year-olds to drugs and crack shacks, or giving them drugs legally or illegally, doesn't matter, and they don't give up! If they get out of hand a little by just sticking up for themselves, traumatize them over and over again in whatever way possible. When they get older, why just throw them in a locked room for a couple of days and abuse them in there? That will teach them. Well, the delusions or hallucinations must last two weeks, but they may not be prominent. Well, make up your mind, is the Holy Ghost there or is it not? I saw it. But I wouldn't tell you because it is none of your bloody business! I'm convinced they must be able to step into your mind with a camera that can take pictures of all this happening. They say this can go on for three months if there is a Major Depressive Episode happening, but it must be at least two weeks. Wait a minute, it also said that all this could go on for a year or decades. But don't the feds think it is permanent? It doesn't say that in your stupid book, but it does insinuate it could just disappear. Make up your frig-gen mind! If it is the Bipolar Type, well, this must be present for at least one week. What precision! Well, this diagnosis is not caused by street drugs or a medical condition, so you can rule that out. So if it is not a brain disease, what the Hell is it? Explain that! And this book goes on and on about so much bull. How can logic become of all of this? Right, it can't! Because it was probably written to hide the crime that the screwed up, evil Catholics and the likes have caused. And that's who has all the money, so they are all the highly educated fools who get a kick out of their jobs of killing people off for no reason! Starting as children. Helpless little children! And I don't care if what I am saying doesn't make sense. I took this out of the nonsensical DSM-4 so you can see where it comes from. I get so pissed off when I read this screwed up book!! There are so many ifs, and's, and but's in the contents of this book, you would have to be half cut to believe it or high on some drug or just plain EVIL to see the justification this book lays out. How about Paranoid Personality Disorder? Well, doesn't this cover up harassment! Doesn't this allow the law to get away with all the setups and crime they help cause! Yeah, there is no proof, all right, because they don't document any for you! Then it says they appear to be cold and lack tender feelings. Maybe they are shocked and traumatized. Then again, if you didn't dope them up so much, they would be able to express their feelings. Here's a good one: they may be litigious and frequently become involved in legal disputes. Well, that just throws away any lawsuits against the Catholic Government and their International Underground Network for allowing this destruction! What do you say to yourself about the Health Care System being so messed up because of all the people who have Crohn's Disease because of the dirty, evil Catholics and the likes of them? I bet you won't find a Catholic with this because they cure all those! Just like my ex-sister in- law, who had something wrong with her blood and had to have a hysterectomy, apparently. Prove that away! And alcohol and substance abuse are likely to occur. What, you have to put this in somewhere because there is no denying this in some cases, is there now! But they say all these people are to blame but themselves, and that is another factor. Damn rights!! Someone has to take responsibility now! People just don't go downhill for no reason! There are influences around somewhere, isn't there? And listen to this. This is a good one, what a cover-up. This disorder may first be apparent in childhood or adolescence with poor peer relationships, social anxiety, underachievement in school, hypersensitivity, peculiar thoughts and language. These children attract teasing. What, protecting the poor little Catholic kids who haven't been taught to lie yet? Who may be afraid of God and who has done your dirty work for you! Can't convict them!! What a bunch of Shit!!! Don't forget other personality disorders can be confused with Paranoid Personality Disorder, so you can cover your ass if you're proven wrong in court! Let's get back to Delusional Disorder. You have to determine if their behaviour is bizarre or not to rule out Schizophrenia. But that nurse told me I had bizarre behaviour. I guess she was wrong! Well, they took X-rays of my brain, to prove what? And I don't have any brain disease, so BITCH what do you have to say for yourself now? Delusional Disorder is derived from real-life experiences, and they may appear unimpaired. Another cop out diagnosis. But in others, it may appear to be relatively substantial with impaired social functioning. Well, what do you expect when there is false information defaming their character smeared about everywhere they go? Don't forget there are subtypes to this disorder too, and if you fear you can't prove the Persecutory-Type, you can always resort to the Unspecified Type because this cannot clearly be determined. I guess that is what saves them all, so they can keep on killing and blaming it on suicides. So now I have a brand new shrink and I have to see him to fill out a form for my insurance, and seeing it will be my first and last visit for as long as I can, I suppose he will just have to figure out his own screwed up five-minute evaluation! They want to know if there are any legal procedures going on, but I left it blank because it is none of their business, and besides, I wouldn't want the new shrink to have something to go on now, would I?

To my general practitioner, Dr. Linda

I feel so blessed to have finally found a doctor who is kind and compassionate and takes time with you at every visit. Truly one of a kind. I love you, and you will always be my angel from heaven. This letter I wrote for one of my earlier visits.

I am writing this letter so that you will be able to read it in your own time. I want you to know that I am suffering every day with some kind of pain, either emotional or physical. There has to be a stop to this kind of suffering sometime, and I have hopes that the government will set an example for me to try and put some kind of reform to this destruction that has completely devastated me. You see, I have representatives and I have written my life story for them, and it is in the courts now. When I was little, I used to pray to God for me to do good in some way because I thought I was bad. Eventually, I lost my faith in God because my Dad told me that if there was a God, why would he allow all this destruction in the world? I worshiped the ground my Dad walked on. He was a good man and never deserved the suffering he went through in his life. I don't deserve this either. I believe in God now because I saw the "Holy Ghost" when I was dying. I also don't believe in Hell because I believe that Hell is here on this earth. I don't care what all those doctor reports say about me. And I don't believe in the DSM-4. I know that I was dying of cancer because I was told that my pap was in the third stage and that the next stage was cancer. After that, this doctor disappeared and another replaced him. When I went to see the new doctor about what I was told, he convinced me that my pap was fine. I never had the opportunity for an education because I kept skipping lines when I read, and I thought about two or three things at once because my life was so scary and confusing, so I believed the doctors. I had faith in them because, after all, they are supposed to save lives, right? Well, shortly after that, I had a mole on my rear that would bleed, and I had it removed. The doctor had told me that it wasn't cancerous, and again I believed him. Well, in 1992, my nightmare began. I was dying, unknown to me at the time, and no one would give me the medical attention I needed and deserved, so after going to the emergency room a few times in immense pain, a nurse finally took pity on me and told me to go to the Institution for the Less Fortunate. While I lay dying without any painkillers, they decided to give me electric shock therapy so they could secretly treat my cancer. I guess they thought that I would be dead before I would remember all this. Throughout these years, numerous attempts have been made. Many. After all, this affects your memory for at least ten years, and because I suffer from Post Traumatic Stress Disorder, I was used to throwing back traumatic events and not remembering them. I went to a specialist who did a bladder cauterization. When I asked him what it was, he told me it was Carcinoma In situ, and I knew that Carcinoma was cancer, I guess from working in the hospital. I found out about certain illnesses, etc.. Anyway, I feel that you should know this because I don't want to be in pain anymore. I have been through enough. I am tired of being bounced in and out of Eric Martin every time I go to the hospital with symptoms of PID. Do you have any idea what it is like to be thrown on the bed, administered a shot and bruised in the process? To top it all off, they threw me a rotten egg sandwich and water in forty-eight hours of being restrained and only let me go to the bathroom twice in all that time. That is just one episode, there are many more. I didn't know I had PID until 1999, when I requested my medical files. I didn't know what that was. I eventually got on the internet and found out all about it and how serious this disease is. I was able to figure out that Crohn's Disease and PID are the same thing, an untreated sexually transmitted disease that I was born with. You see, I believe there is a reason for everything. I was born with this, so I became the target for all the disgusting sexual cons out there because of a release of false information about me, starting at the tender age of eight. What saddens me the most is that children were involved in this vicious prosecution. How can our children ever be safe? I was told that you are a compassionate person, and I believe this because he is the only one who has ever shown any compassion for me. I don't think I can go on like this, and I now know why some people commit suicide because they are not getting the medical attention they need and deserve. I am counting on you to find me a specialist who will give me a hysterectomy and who will also treat my children for this, so they can live a life of promise, future and dignity.

("My Own Therapy")

There have been a few things that I myself temporarily found to be therapeutic during the years while all the Governments of Canada plotted to end my life, and which I BELIEVE STILL ARE. Of course, my children are who I live for. And my family. They shouldn't have to be a form of therapy for me, and had I BEEN ALLOWED TO BE IN MY RIGHT MIND, I would never have imposed that on them, nor would I or did I ever attempt to counsel anyone in my family. Shit, I was nuts anyway. I have to say that having my dog really was the only comfort to me. He knew when I was not well, and he put his little head down beside me sometimes as if to say, What can I do? He loved me unconditionally as I did him, and once in a while, when things were going rough for me, he temporarily put the joy right back into my life. Another form of therapy for me is gardening. When I garden, I don't think about anything, and afterwards I feel like I had gotten the cob webs out of my mind as doped up as I was from all the drugs they had pumped into me at that NUT HOUSE. I am so lucky to have my mother, who allowed me to come over and do her gardening for her. Although I am not a good artist, any form of art was helpful to me. I used to get lost in the moment of what I was doing, whether it be drawing, painting or doing crafts like ceramics, knitting or making things from nothing; for example, Christmas decorations and Hodge Podge. Music, to listen to, to sing to and to dance to took me to another place at times. Praying that one day I would regain my dignity somehow. Not ever relating to what was really going on. For many, many years, I never remembered my childhood. In 1994 when I was off the drugs for a short time that they insisted I needed at the Nut House. I suddenly found an ability to write poems and I compiled them into a book that I called "My Book of Poems" "Depression Obsession" and luckily I was given the opportunity to put the blame where it bloody well belonged. Eventually, I will get some psychological control of my mind and physical well-being. And I came to discover how and why I was mentally abused and what mental abuse really is. However, devastating that is to me now, and so, so, so painful. Now I will continue to live in a state of terror that I just have NO words to describe. Never mind not having your health on top of it all. And not knowing if you are going to have someone to look after you. Giving myself some credit, I knew all along, deep in my heart, my troubles went beyond this so-called family tree and cycle of abuse. All the EVIL DEMONS knew I did so they tried to keep my mouth shut so I was unable to think straight for over fourteen years while I almost died many, many times because of many, many EVIL DEMONS. I don't know if my immediate family and I will ever get out of here alive now. However, I was informed that it is good therapy to confront your abusers either face-to-face or in a letter. I confronted a few of my abusers face-to-face, and I found a little peace with that at the time. Reading the letters I wrote from time to time, I found it more helpful because then you don't have to listen to them lie about all they have done to you. It is helpful even if you don't send them for your own protection. Because this so-called system was not protecting me and I was being abused by all of them, I thought, what the HELL do I have to lose? I HAD NO ONE TO HELP ME, SO I'll HELP MYSELF! And I formed my own therapy. In a lot of situations where counselling is needed, the best form of therapy, so I was told, is Group Therapy, so that you are able to be around others who have experienced similar circumstances. However, I was not warranted that opportunity, and now I know why. I lived through all this in loneliness, despair and FEAR that you just can't imagine and still do. From the day that I first left that Nut House "NUT" meaning most everyone who works in that GOD AWFUL PLACE in 1992, I knew I was being stalked, but I had no idea why??? All the EVIL DEMONS tried making me look like a NUT CASE and degrading me in all their EVIL PLOTS to KILL me off. Like they have done to so many others who are all these EVIL DEMONS have the bloody nerve to call the DEVIL'S CHILD. Well, in Group Therapy, in time, they say you will be able to share your feelings and thoughts with each other and comfort each other through the difficult journey from your heart back to your head. I feel it is very important for one to keep holding out their hand and find someone compassionate to tell, and keep telling till someone listens to you. Don't give up. I know that because what I held onto and who I believed in was the only person who couldn't help but show some compassion towards me, as briefly as it was, and that was my lawyer, now my representative, I believe, but who denies that he is. I have also come to realize that there was a gag order on all this, and I basically was only allowed so much information, and that was through a computer in puzzle form, which I had to figure out. I then had difficulties because of all the International attention this all brought, as all this intensified, continually threatening everyone involuntarily. I struggled to be my own doctor, my own lawyer, my own counsellor and my own bloody friend because of how utterly EVIL and unbelievable this ALL IS. I might have gotten a sentence or two of my information out of a bloody book. I am going to write one poem from my book "My Book Of Poems," "Depression Obsession," that helped me to keep going. The following are some letters I wrote about only a fraction of the people who helped devastate me and helped this kind of destruction to continue in this world. For everyone's GREED.

(This is dedicated to all the real Sinners)

"Don't you ever treat me that way"
I am so tired from all the pain that I am in,
And I'm surrounded by nothing but sin.
My stomach is turning into knots,
Because I am so distraught.
It hurts, it hurts, it hurts so much,
I tremble to think of anyone's touch.
And you don't know me deep inside,
And you never will before I die.
But somehow I'll save the kids,
From all the destruction this world is in.
And before I die, I just want to say,
"Don't you ever treat me that way"

"DON'T YOU EVER TREAT ME THAT WAY!"
At the time I wrote this poem, I had no idea I had or my
children had PID or Crohn's Disease. Or how big this all
is. **HUGE.**

This letter is to a shrink I used to have when I finally started to stick up for myself.

I am writing to you regarding the appointment we had. I later
thought about it and decided I am not willing to be mentally
abused like that again, especially considering how physically sick
I was. I don't care if you were only doing your job and felt it
necessary to ask me all of those questions, as far as I'm
concerned, you got yourself into the wrong trade, and if you were
really as smart as you university students like to think you are,

you will go into counselling. You know more on the compassionate side of the scale instead of the persecutory end. I am willing to see you every three months, as this is a protocol according to you and my health nurse, but at our next appointment, I expect to be treated with respect, not disrespect. Quoting nonsense from the no mind DSM-4 is not acceptable, and at our next appointment, if I find you are doing that, I will simply walk out. Let's make our appointments as brief as possible because I have absolutely no use for shrinks, none. They don't have the time or know how to counsel me for as long as it would take to get over everything I have been through in my life. I will also take the stress injection, and I will be in every two weeks for that. You will hopefully get something from my doctor outlining my physical condition. I also notified my health nurse about this. My real advice to you would be to make sure I am not thrown into the Institution for the Less Fortunate again for simply seeking medical treatment for my physical condition because whoever doesn't treat me and treat me with respect I will get their names and they will be written up in the law suit which has been going on now for two and a half years. I am very aware of my environment, and I now know at all times what is going on.

This letter is to the same shrink.

This is in regard to the appointment we had. I never mentioned this, but my diagnosis of the Psychosis, adjective Psychotic, was so off base that I wanted to go home and think about it before I jumped to any conclusions. If I were you, I would be very careful about what you put down when asked again for a diagnosis, in my case. My so-called severe mental disorder, also referred to as psychopath, crackpot, crack brain, lunatic, madman, or insanity, must have some basis for you to form an opinion on, and I can't see where you could possibly have one. As I, too, have studied the one screwed up book, the DSM-4. The only possible diagnosis I can come up with at this time or any other time is "Post Traumatic Stress Disorder" due to over thirty-five years of stalking, harassing and mental abuse. My physical condition alone (PID or Crohn's Disease), given the fact that I probably won't get cured for it in this country, and neither will my kids, is reason enough to adhere to the diagnosis of "Post Traumatic Stress Disorder." I realize that you were only informed about my physical condition after the fact; therefore, I am not taking this personally. However, deep consideration is needed on your part the next time you make a diagnosis of my so-called mental health.

P.S. Next time, skip the gloves when you're doing an external check. I have a shower or bath before I see a doctor; my clothes are always clean, as is my house and my dog. (my soul mate.)

To Auntie Carol

I have been meaning to get in touch with you for some time now, but you know how life goes on. How is that piss tank husband of yours doing? Is he still having affairs on you? Whose shoulder do you cry on now? Did you ever get that secretary job you were always talking about getting, or did you continue recruiting models? Do you ever see that retired singing pig who befriends little kids only to persecute them for no reason later? Is he still collecting stolen items like black lights and posters and giving them away to kids? And does he still set up crimes from his hospital bed? Wow, so many questions! And what about your brats? How are they doing? Do they have kids yet, and are they breaking toys now, too? And how is that Saint of a sister of yours doing? Is that piss tank still alive, or did he get stung by a bee and croak? What does she do when D Day comes around? Celebrate? Make it a family celebration, do you? And her kid cop is he still stealing cars, or did he get thrown out of the ranks for that? Did that Saint give her grandkids a silver piggy bank? Oh yeah, they can't have any. What did she get treated? Not forgetting to mention your brother. Still, handing out stolen items is he scooping up money that doesn't belong to him, and running? Does he still have wine at every meal? The lying Catholic Prick! Well, I hope you're all running scared now! Never in a million years did you think this would all backfire on you, did you? I hope you all get what you deserve!

To my half-brother Lenny

I didn't want to believe that your intentions were really to become close to our family all along. I guess I always believed everyone had good intentions, just like my Dad did. I am sending you a picture of you and my Dad so you can see how happy he was when you came over, and I want you to take a good look at it. See how ill he looked, I don't want it cause it breaks my heart. It is too bad you never really got to know him because he was a good man, and he was faithful to his responsibilities as a parent to you and your sister. You were told this, and you both chose to ignore it. As I look back now at all the times in my life you came over, it was at a time of distress in our family. I suppose you got a phone call from some Catholic Prick or the likes telling you my Dad may be on his last legs, so you ran over to see if you could get in on his Will. Just like when I was at death's door and out of the blue you phoned Mom. What mental health was it that called you? All along, your dirty slut of a mother is partially to blame for all of this. Didn't you ever question Dad's custody of both of you? Anyway, God forgives right, but you see, you are going to have to answer to God, and he will decide if you will have life for eternity or not. Dad died for your mother's sin. To this day, it is hard to believe this kind of evil persecution exists in a country I thought was God's country, and you knew about it all along. How can you live with yourself knowing maybe you could have done something about this, but didn't? You see, I never thought I would amount to anything, but I have proven myself wrong. I wrote about my miserable life and figured out just what the Hell was going on. You told us at one time you never saw your mother or your sister, that was when Dad was alive, and you were stupid enough to tell me when I was over, you see them both quite regularly. You are an evil, selfish, lying Catholic, like so many I have met in my life and before I die, I will make sure you get FUCK ALL, not that there is much to get anyway, but you blew any chance of ever getting anything now. I hope to never hear from you again.

To my ex-mother-in-law

I am writing this letter so you can show this to your sick Catholic family, you have in your god forsaken country, you were always so proud of and still are, and who helped terrorize me when I was over there after your sick son had raped me on one of his trips around the country, to find out where he would like to live. I want you to know I have enough knowledge about your disgusting religion to say you are all Evil! Your sick criminal son over here in No Man's Land, is an actual Devil's Child! You see, I wrote my whole miserable life, and all it consisted of was how the Evil Demons of the Catholic religion were trying to kill me and my children. I want you to quit writing my daughter your stupid little notes and sending her your pathetic gifts. I don't want you or any of your Evil family to have anything to do with her, and you can stay away from my son, too. You have some nerve to do this, as you tried killing her once, remember, on the trip through the Rockies with your rich relative. What did you put her hand on the door handle so she would fall out? The only one I ever cared for was your husband, and you had him murdered, didn't you? You and your sick family would come over here and park your ass where it didn't belong and did bugger all for either me or the children. And your fucked up son never even thought enough about me or his own kids to leave that life insurance policy he had in Limy Land in my name, he left it in your name as he tried for years to kill me and my children off, knowing one day soon I would be dead too. Well, now you're all going to need more than just that insurance policy! Stop and think about what you and your sick family have done to me. You are an honest citizen. I don't think so. What about that lying Affidavit you wrote up about how you never did anything to provoke me spitting on you and swore to it before God? What a lie that was! Remember you called ME a tramp! You deserved to be spit on. But God forgives no matter what? I don't think it is that easy to go to Heaven. There is not enough room for everyone. And I believe that Hell is here on this earth, I know I live in it. Well, I want you to remember I didn't just pull that information out of thin air. I have representatives who have helped me figure this all out. In 1989, when your beloved died, your house was broken into, and all of his identification disappeared. Now, just who do you suppose that was? THE GOVERNMENT, that's who. I suppose the government, yours included, has come to realize how sick your religion really is, and is trying to do something about the destruction both countries are in because of it. There have been over twenty years of investigation into this case! My father died because of a filthy Catholic, and I'm probably going to die because of a filthy Catholic, but be damned if my children are going to die because of a filthy Catholic! You'd better get your New Testament out and start reading it because that is what the law is based on over here.

To DR. Turd

I want to send you a photograph of myself from around the time I started seeing you, so that you can picture all the little children's lives out there who are suffering just like I had to, because of people like you. You are one of the worst criminals out there, an Evil Son Of A Bitch.! (like a Nazi War Criminal), yet you had the nerve to phone my mother up after my Dad died to tell her how sorry you were. What do you do? Go to confession, say a few Hail Marys, and God will forgive your sins? Who made you God anyway? You see, I wrote my whole miserable life, and I figured out just what part you played in all of it and realized you are the main cause for my pain and suffering and my Dad's death; God rest his soul. You tried to make sure I wouldn't amount to anything, didn't you? I never got the opportunity for an education because I skipped lines, but you knew this. And I would think of two or three things at once because my life was so terrifying and confusing, but you knew this too. Mom would take me to see you because of all the pain I was experiencing, and all along, you knew just what was going on. Growing pains, you told her. Then, when I got older, it was arthritis. What a bunch of shit! You wanted me to keep my mouth shut, so you tortured me with the burning of the warts business! Didn't you set up a relationship I had with a sexual con? Didn't you have him stalk me after I left my husband, my first intimate relationship, you knew all about? And he pretended he was a respectable man. You did it with ease. A setup for the Catholic spread of sexually transmitted diseases. You made sure I would give in, didn't you? What kind of person would do this? It's sick! Not forgetting to mention what you did to my Dad! You knew about his two kids from his previous marriage, whom he got custody of because his wife would sleep around. Did you think you could say he was doing it when he was in the army fighting for the freedom you are enjoying today? He was a proud father and a good man, and you knew all this, and you murdered him anyway. A prolonged agonizing death, which was promoted by you. All the operations and procedures that were performed, and he had to endure and all the mistakes that were made on him. Mistakes, this was done on purpose! All this could have been prevented! He even came over to your house and built some cupboards for you for nothing. What did you decide you would allow him to live long enough so you too could suck him dry? But God forgives? One day you will find out if he does or not, but before you do, I hope you live in Hell like we did all our lives!! And before I die, I will make sure that this doesn't happen to my kids because I owe that to God!

To one of the sick quacks whom I had, doctor Lemon

I wanted to tell you all about the time I am having trying to stay alive, but I guess you already got your jollies out of that, didn't you? Your little incident with the vitamin B 12 shot didn't work because I'm still here, but you knew that because you were so surprised I was still alive, you had to phone me up and nosy into my business when I finally did find a doctor who cares. You tried to murder me, too, didn't you? You had me running all over Hell's half acre trying to get treated. What went out of business were you? You and one of the shrinks from the Nut House. And all the visits I made to your filthy dump of an office, and you did next to fuck all for me. You are one of the sickest people whom I have ever met, and you just have to be an evil, filthy Catholic, don't you? You had the nerve to tell me that I was crazy. The only reason I continued seeing you is because I was so doped up on all the shit the "Nut House" puts out, "Nut" meaning the shrinks, I didn't know my ass from a hole in the ground, but I sure do now. Well, there has to be an end to this Evil persecution sometime, and I feel the time is nearing, and I want you to know that before I die, I hope you too get what you deserve, and I'm there to see it. I really hope you have to live in Hell for the rest of your life, just like I have all of my life.

To one of the sick gynecologists whom I had

I am writing to you in the hope that you will remember seeing me. I have had many different doctors, all evil like you. I have finally found a doctor who cares about me, and I am wondering where you got your information from. I want to put you straight on your whole list of sexually transmitted diseases that you say I have had a history of. These diseases weren't mine to begin with. They belonged to your filthy Catholic pals twenty-three years ago now. I want you to know I am fully aware of this evil persecution which exists in this medical system, and one day you will find out it doesn't pay to make up reports about people you really don't know anything about. I was born with a sexually transmitted disease because of a filthy Catholic, and you, of all people, should have known that by the report indicating that I had Pelvic Inflammatory Disease, which I personally gave you a copy of. So I became the target of all the evil, lying, disgusting Catholics out there. What I want to know is who made you God anyway to decide who should live and who should suffer and die an agonizing death. I truly hope you will send another report to the hospital files and to my doctor, indicating the knowledge I have provided, which you would have had if you had shown the courtesy and decency to ask.

To the Research Review Committee

I am writing to you in regards to the letter I got inviting me to participate in a clinical research study you are doing for Type Two Diabetes. It appears the research that you are doing is for a good cause. Still, I am wondering why you are so concerned about my health when there have been many attempts to end my life with drugs that the Research Review and Ethics Approval Committee has allowed to be sold on the market. Maybe you should look for Catholics for your research, as they seem to be the ones who get proper medical treatment in this country. I can't help but wonder if this is another feeble attempt either to make yourselves look good or to destroy innocent people's lives. This Research Review and so-called Ethics Approval Committee should take a long and serious look at all the medications which are out there for these so-called mental health patients that help destroy people's lives who have already been through enough torment. I am a Professional Counsellor, and I believe the best way to treat the so-called mental health patients is through counselling, not by administering drugs which do absolutely nothing for them and turn them into nothing but useless, walking Zombies. I will assume you know that I have rejected your offer.

To my neighbour Kathy

I am writing this letter to tell you how sorry I am that the government won't pay you disability benefits for the stomach cancer you have because they say it is your fault. I see that you are working now to pay for all the thousands of dollars in prescriptions you said you had to buy because of your stomach cancer. How do you fit your Kemo therapy in? How is your eyesight? It must be hard to garden when you can't see what you are digging. You told me once your husband had to drive you everywhere because it was hard for you to see. Is that caused by your Crohn's Disease or your nasty wart fungus, or excuse me, virus you carried around for twenty-three years?. Do you still have those balloons I gave you that you said "I know I'm big, but I'm not that big?" Is your husband still trying to run people over with that moving dolly and ranting and raving? And what about your best friend? Is she still threatening people to stay away from you because you are so sick? Are the two of you still breaking into people's units and stealing things? Was that supposed to be some kind of sick hint? Does she still yell at people for getting their dog's hair cut? Is she still putting her hand up to her head in a salute, telling people they are insane? And is she still screaming at people to stop their dogs from scratching up the community lawn around your place? Do you all have those slippers that fit like a condom? Is your best friend's husband still mooning people? Wow, so many questions! Who's insane now? It's looking like you are!!

To a Royal Canadian Mounted Police Officer

I am writing to follow up on our conversation. I couldn't stop thinking about our discussion, and there were things I later thought about that I had wished I had informed you about. I truly hope you will find the time to read this. I should get on with my life, even though too many people think negatively of me? I want you to know that despite everything I have been through in my life, I am a very positive person. You want me to get on with my life? My life is just about over. I would like to know how I am supposed to, as you say, "get on with my life" with a record of being hauled off to the Nut House, "Nut" meaning the so-called Mental Health Professionals? Who is going to hire me? Besides that, I suffer from Crohn's Disease. I was born with it, and my daughter was born with it too, and we have been unable to get the treatment needed, which we so deserve for this agonizing condition, which is unnecessary to have to go through.

I have been stalked, harassed and mentally abused ever since I can remember and all because of environmental circumstances and a release of false information about me. If anyone knows that is criminal, I do. Not many people understand mental abuse, which is why most of the time the matter is called a civil suit, but this does not mean it is not a criminal matter. It is highly against the law. I would like to know what is considered harassment. You believe that your life has to be in danger for harassment charges to be laid? Who can unmistakably make that decision? I also want to inform you that I believe I helped pass the stocking law introduced in 1993, which became law, I believe, on June 23, 1995. I know that law like the back of my hand. I have been documenting everything that has happened to me for over thirty years, and my whole life has been in the courts now for over twenty-three years. Why don't I call the police to my home? The police have never protected me, so who am I to think they would help me now? They don't even protect our children. As a matter of fact, they have been one of the biggest parts of the problem.

I feel you felt my complaint was fictitious or frivolous. Do you know what it is like to be degraded and violated time and time again? No, I didn't think so. That's why I would be a good counsellor if given half the chance. I've been there, and I have the compassion needed. There isn't a place I haven't been at some time in my life, and I am not an alcoholic or a drug addict, which is a miracle in itself. I also know the DSM-4 like the back of my hand, and I say it is just a load of crock. An excuse to cover up all the crimes committed by the Catholics AND THE LIKES OF them in this god forsaken country we live in. It was also evident to me that perhaps mental health patients have some kind of stigma attached to their condition. Because I have been mistakenly involved with mental health, I know what they are all about. Drumming up business for themselves for the trauma they have helped cause in innocent people's lives. Do you think when you throw someone in the Institution for the Less Fortunate that you are helping them? No, you're wrong. You are helping destroy their life because in there, you are abused even more. Most of the time, people commit suicide because they are not getting the physical care they need and deserve. I know I was dying of bladder Carcinoma In situ, unknown to me at the time, and no one would treat me for it. I had to go to the Nut House to get secretly treated, and as I lay dying without any painkillers, they decided to give me ECT. Yes, they treated the cancer then, but they didn't cure the cause of the cancer, which I carried around for twenty-three years. It is by the grace of God that I am still alive. Since that time, they have had me labelled with every no mind diagnosis going. Yes, the Catholics of this country are trying to cover up a crime, and one day, if they don't kill me before that, I will have a little justice. But I tell you, no amount of money or justice will ever make up for what I have gone through.

I hope I haven't taken too much of your time, but sharing this information with you has been found to be very therapeutic.

www.ingramcontent.com/pod-product-compliance
Lightning Source LLC
Chambersburg PA
CBHW070907130626
46555CB00001B/31